Gentelligence

Gentelligence

The Revolutionary Approach to Leading an Intergenerational Workforce

MEGAN GERHARDT, PhD,
JOSEPHINE NACHEMSON-EKWALL,
AND BRANDON FOGEL

ROWMAN & LITTLEFIELD
Lanham • Boulder • New York • London

Published by Rowman & Littlefield
An imprint of The Rowman & Littlefield Publishing Group, Inc.
4501 Forbes Boulevard, Suite 200, Lanham, Maryland 20706
www.rowman.com

6 Tinworth Street, London SE11 5AL, United Kingdom

British Library Cataloguing in Publication Information Available

Library of Congress Cataloging-in-Publication Data

Names: Gerhardt, Megan W., author. | Nachemson-Ekwall, Josephine, 1995– author. | Fogel, Brandon, 1996– author.
Title: Gentelligence : the revolutionary approach to leading an intergenerational workforce / Megan Gerhardt, Josephine Nachemson-Ekwall, and Brandon Fogel.
Description: Lanham : Rowman & Littlefield, [2021] | Includes bibliographical references and index. | Summary: "No one needs another book about how to lead Millennials—what we need is a book about harnessing the untapped potential from the diversity of thought in a multigenerational workforce. 'Gentelligence' is that book. It presents a transformative way to end the generational wars once and for all"— Provided by publisher.
Identifiers: LCCN 2020046495 (print) | LCCN 2020046496 (ebook) | ISBN 9781538142141 (cloth) | ISBN 9781538142158 (epub)
Subjects: LCSH: Conflict of generations in the workplace. | Diversity in the workplace—Management. | Intergenerational relations. | Intergenerational communication. | Leadership.
Classification: LCC HF5549.5.C75 G475 2021 (print) | LCC HF5549.5.C75 (ebook) | DDC 658.30084—dc23
LC record available at https://lccn.loc.gov/2020046495
LC ebook record available at https://lccn.loc.gov/2020046496

∞™ The paper used in this publication meets the minimum requirements of American National Standard for Information Sciences—Permanence of Paper for Printed Library Materials, ANSI/NISO Z39.48-1992.

To Matt, AJ, Alison, Mom, and Dad . . .
and to love and learning across the generations. —MG

To Mom, Dad, Sarah, and Zach. —JNE

To Madeline, Mom, Dad, and Scott. —BF

Contents

Foreword

Paul Allen, Co-Founder of Ancestry.com and CEO of Soar.com

As the co-founder of Ancestry.com, I know firsthand the power of age diversity in a venture. I was twenty-nine years old when the idea of digitizing all the world's genealogy records and putting them on the internet first struck me. At the time, I knew little about genealogy—I was just a tech entrepreneur with an idea. However, I knew I needed help. I asked a seasoned university librarian, nearing retirement, about genealogy—who the reputable and well-known publishers were and where I could find the top five genealogy books of all time. She guided me to a Salt Lake City–based genealogy publisher named Ancestry. We first partnered with Ancestry and then later acquired its print business.

From the beginning, the company and our team intuitively recognized the importance of harnessing different knowledge and experience. The vision of young, tech-savvy entrepreneurs combined with the in-depth subject-matter expertise of people decades our senior is what brought Ancestry.com to life. Lou Szucs, one of our most senior executives, had been one of the most beloved figures in the genealogy industry for many years. She opened doors everywhere for us, and her wisdom and knowledge were of vital importance. Ancestry would never have become what it is today without her.

While I didn't realize it at the time, the founding of Ancestry.com was a real example of Gentelligence in action. We combined our complementary skills to generate creative solutions. We felt supported by our team members, which empowered us to produce innovative, original work. In an effort to help others discover, preserve, and share their family history, we learned how to unlock the potential of an intergenerational team and how connecting to the generations before us can give us perspective and wisdom. We saw that every generation has something to teach and to learn.

Connecting to our ancestors can be a powerful experience. It can affect your own identity and purpose in powerful ways. Through this venture, I have learned, as have millions of others, that connecting to those from other generations can make us better human beings ourselves.

* * *

I first met Megan Gerhardt, the lead author of this phenomenally important book, through our shared interest in the work done within the Gallup Organization. We were drawn to Gallup's mission to connect people by helping everyone see each other's strengths and talents. We discovered that we have identical top Gallup talent themes (a rare occurrence), and this connection allowed us to forge a unique bond. What this means is that our natural patterns of thinking, feeling, and behaving are very similar. We share a fascination with ideas, deep thinking, and continuous learning. You might say Megan and I are two peas in a pod or birds of a feather. In my experience, it is easy for birds of a feather to flock together. While we have used our talents for different pursuits, we share mutual respect and similarity in how we see and engage with the world.

As Megan and I have experienced through our own interactions, we tend to gravitate toward people like us. It's fantastic to find people who think in similar ways and who share your way of viewing things. It seems to make things easy. Yet often the most crucial and transformative growth (as organizations or individuals) occurs when we can look past perceived differences to learn from those who on the surface seem incredibly different from ourselves.

With this book, Megan and her coauthors invite young and old alike to connect, communicate, and collaborate with people who see the world through a different lens in every workplace and community worldwide. Rarely do books come out when needed the most, but *Gentelligence* is needed now more than ever.

The generational wars are alive and well both within and outside the workplace. This book directly and accurately ties these workplace tensions to the roots of the problem: a lack of understanding of those who have grown up before or after us, as well as our deeply rooted perceptions about age in the workplace. Thinking back, the impact of my own age has always been in the back of my mind. When I was a young adult, I wanted to look and be older. I've always had a sort of boyish face, and when I became an entrepreneur, I worried that people wouldn't take me seriously. I couldn't wait to turn thirty. My expectations were met (and exceeded) when my thirties and forties were marked with success as my ideas sprang to life and my businesses soared.

As I approached the mid-century mark, I absolutely dreaded getting older. Would I have the health, energy, and vitality to be productive and successful? I had enjoyed a wonderful career for nearly three decades, working on big, inspiring ideas—digitizing the great books of the world, putting the world's genealogy records online, connecting millions of families on the internet—but I seriously wondered, "Will my ideas still matter? Will I fade into irrelevance and obscurity? Will I soon be, as they say, 'over the hill'?"

I'm now looking at age differently. I've started to recognize that my various life stages (younger and older) have brought me different knowledge and perspectives. This fact was clearly demonstrated to me when Google invited me to speak to five hundred employees about personal leadership development outside Dublin, Ireland. I was especially excited about the opportunity because the speech took place near the home of a hero of mine, Charles Handy. Now in his late eighties, Handy is one of the most influential thinkers of our time, specializing in organizational behavior and management. He has published many books, created the graduate business program at the London School of Business, and was featured on the radio for more than twenty years. His work helped me discover the benefits of age in the workplace and, like *Gentelligence*, reveals the opportunities in different life stages: wisdom, perspective, social networks, pattern recognition, knowledge, enjoyment.

Handy is sometimes called the "Peter Drucker of the UK," and I expected many young audience members to know of his work. When I asked about him, I was shocked to discover that not a single Googler had even heard of Handy. While small, this exchange made it clear to me that the wisdom of our past generations and our older leaders was not being passed down as it should be and was in danger of being lost. I have reflected on this realization again and again. For a while, I told people the two most shocking things about growing older for me are (1) how little young people (including my own kids) know about the great thinkers and influencers of my generation and (2) that it is my fault.

The same trend can be found in reverse: It's equally true that older people often know little about young people's lived experience—digital natives who use modern technology as easily as speaking a native tongue. The pace of technological innovation has accelerated to the point that people born just a few years apart can have a significantly different lived experience. In 2008, an older friend told me he would never send a text message—he thought it was ridiculous. He had a large family and more than a dozen grandkids already, so I told him, "Texting is the language of your grandkids, and if you don't text them, you'll miss out on so much." He immediately started texting and later thanked me profusely for how much it had positively impacted his relationships with his family.

Gentelligence is about what I realized through both of those experiences: We all can make efforts to foster connection and understanding across age groups to make our relationships and our organizations much stronger. The world is better when people of all ages can communicate and collaborate, whether it's connecting with our ancestors' stories or taking an extra minute with a co-worker from a different generation.

Many books change minds and hearts, and some books launch movements. I believe *Gentelligence* will do just that. With a timely and powerful invitation to people of all ages to have a profound positive impact on individuals and organizations, this book has the power to improve organizational life drastically. I'm thrilled that it is now available to you.

Acknowledgments

Writing this book has been amazingly rewarding and phenomenally challenging, in equal measure. We want to thank Matt, Zach, and Madeline for their love, patience, and contributions over the hundreds of hours we spent writing this book. We collectively apologize for the many nights spent staring into our computer screens and typing loudly when you were trying to sleep.

Many thanks to our fierce agent, Jessica Faust, at BookEnds Literary for pushing us to create the book she knew we could write and for inspiring us to always ask each other, "What would Jessica think of this?" all the way to the finish line.

Endless gratitude to our thoughtful editor, Kathleen Veslany, for lending us her incredible talents for every chapter (sometimes more than once!), for cheering us on, and for pointing out that *reverse mentoring* was not a Gentelligent term at all.

Our heartfelt thanks to our senior editor, Suzanne Staszak-Silva, and the entire publishing team at Rowman & Littlefield for taking a chance and bringing our book out into the world.

Love and honor to Miami University, where our author team first met six years ago. To Billy Price and all of the teachers and students (past and present) who have shown us the power of Gentelligence, we are so grateful. We send a special thanks to Beth Bjorlo, our extraordinary marketing consultant, and to the brilliant Rebecca Luzadis and

Josh Schwarz for the friendly reviews, nine chapters' worth of insightful feedback, and endless support in all things.

And, finally, to our parents—Marlene and John, Sophie and Johan, Stephanie and Howie—for passing down the most important things between generations: love, support, and unwavering belief in our potential.

Introduction

Each generation imagines itself to be more intelligent than the one that went before it, and wiser than the one that comes after it.

—George Orwell

In March 2019, I (Megan) wrote a provocative editorial for *Business Insider*, declaring that we had failed in leading and managing our Millennials:

> We blew it with the Millennials.
>
> From the start, we viewed them as adversaries. They were confident, bold, and startlingly different from any generation we had seen before. When they entered our classrooms and our boardrooms with a new perspective on how things could be done, we had to make a choice: to welcome them as partners in navigating our changing world or resist them, viewing them as a threat to the way things had always been. We most definitely chose the latter, and there's a price to that choice.[1]

Reactions to the op-ed were predictably mixed. Millennial readers loved it, posting and sharing on social media. I received several positive messages from Baby Boomers and Gen Xers like me, agreeing with the perspective and encouraging me to continue the push toward more progressive and open views toward generational diversity. Of course, not all reactions were that supportive. Several businesspeople (across multiple generations) reached out to say they wished they shared my positive view of Millennial potential, but, sadly, they did not. The most negative reaction came in the form of an anonymous email I received a few days after the op-ed was published:

> I'm not a professor of business, but all I could do was sit there shaking my head the whole time I read your article. As a small business owner myself, I can't imagine ME changing what I believe to know and work, to accommodate a young professional who has different values than I do. I think you underlined the whole issue some of us old geezers have with the new generation. "Hey old guys, accept us for who we are, not what you think we need to be to succeed (or help your business succeed)."
> —Frank Leeput

Our anonymous friend, Frank Leeput (get it?), probably didn't expect his reply to be encouraging, but it was. His entire message is a perfect illustration of the mindset that continues to fuel my passion for generational diversity and inspires me to be a champion for the power that comes with it. Frank's view is one I often see when I speak across industries: an us-versus-them mentality, a belief that he shouldn't have to change just because people of other generations have different perspectives, and a firm conviction that he knows what works and "they" do not. Is it just a case of the old not wanting to make way for the new? Surprisingly, no. This mindset is not limited to older generations who don't want to adapt to the ideas of younger colleagues—it is also very present in Millennial and Gen Z employees I work with. They assume all of their older colleagues are resistant to change and are quick to equate *newer* with *better*.

My editorial was only seven hundred words, and it did what it was intended to do—spark a conversation. However, it wasn't long enough to speak to the potential power inherent in *all* forms of generational diversity. While openness to the ideas of Millennials and Gen Zers is an important part of the puzzle, it is also about how to engage and learn from the experience and knowledge of older generations. It is about seeing the potential of generations as a necessary and powerful form of diversity of thought and approaching them in a smarter way—one that allows us to see them as an opportunity, rather than a threat. It's about developing what we call *Gentelligence.*

We're not talking about simply another strategy for dealing with Millennials. Gentelligence champions *every* generation and is born from intergenerational curiosity. It's a willingness to understand how people who have grown up under different times view things in different and meaningful ways. By viewing generational differences through a new lens, we can start to understand how they can be leveraged effectively.

Gentelligence pushes back on the idea of generational competition, replacing it with the idea that people of all ages can benefit from the potential of intergenerational power. The perspective of seeing other generations as a threat is not new. In fact, these tensions have been around so long that many leaders have accepted them as normal, assuming that nothing can be done to ease them. With an escalation in the speed of change and the increase in global competition, the cost of this tension is now greater than ever before. Ignoring this conflict negatively affects key business outcomes, including attracting the best talent, developing diverse teams, filling the leadership pipeline, and creating adaptable cultures for the future of work.

THE BIRTH OF GENTELLIGENCE

In 2009, there was a knock on my office door at Miami University (where I work as a professor of leadership). It was an administrator from the dean's office. He had gotten a call from a company looking for an expert on generational differences to come speak about how to manage and lead Millennials, and he thought of me. To this day, I am still not sure why. I was a thirty-two-year-old professor at the time, researching employee motivation and individual differences, but nothing I did was focused on generational differences. However, my work did look at differences like gender and personality and the impact they had on workplace dynamics, so, in some ways, I did fit the bill. I was also one of the younger faculty members in the school at the time, so perhaps he thought, "She must know something about this." I was game to give the opportunity a shot.

I dug into the research on generational differences prior to meeting with the group and put together some slides on how to lead a generation that seemed to be making managers pull out their hair. When I finally held the session, the room was filled primarily with managers from the Silent and Baby Boomer generations, but it also had a few Gen Xers and Millennials in attendance. When we turned to the Q&A part of my talk, the managers in the room eagerly shared stories of the confusing attitudes and behavior of their younger employees.

One such conversation focused on how several managers from the Boomer and Silent generations felt their Millennial employees had unrealistic expectations. When I pressed for an example, one Baby Boomer manager shared how she had recently received an email from a Millennial employee, outlining his ideas for a new way to approach a long-standing process. When several days passed without her sending a response back to him, she received a follow-up email. She found many things about this experience irritating: first, that this young employee felt "entitled" to suggest ideas to his manager after being at the company just a few months and, second, that he was bold enough to presume his email warranted an immediate response from his very busy boss.

I asked the manager if the suggestions made had been good ones. She seemed taken aback by my question: "Well . . . possibly. But that's not the point. He just got here. Why does he think he can tell us how things should be done? He doesn't know enough yet." I pointed out that it seemed like her perspective included several assumptions about her relatively new coworker's behavior. While the young employee did lack organizational experience, was it possible he did have experience with the process improvements he had suggested? Could he have learned about a new approach in school or been taught it in an internship? And regardless, if there was potential value in the new ideas, why did it matter how long he had worked there? Was the length of tenure a requirement for trying to add value to the organization?

Our conversation revealed several important issues that influenced her perspective and behavior. The manager shared that during her early career, it was unheard of for young employees to do such a thing. The norm was to keep one's head down and pay their dues, working their way up the ladder and waiting their turn. In other words, she had not been allowed to enact change at that age, and she was continuing to uphold that tradition. In short, she believed her young employees were entitled—expecting things they had not yet earned a right to have because she had not been allowed to have them. Whether the ideas had merit, or could benefit the organization, seemed secondary in importance.

The next issue—one of her young employees expecting an "immediate" response—was also intriguing to me. I thought it might be interesting to try an experiment. I asked everyone in the room to imagine they had just sent an important email to someone else in the company—one that invited the recipient to give feedback. I asked everyone to jot down what they considered a "reasonable" length of time for receiving that response.

The results were eye-opening to everyone in the room. The Baby Boomer managers had all noted somewhere close to a week as an appropriate length of time. The Gen Xers had a slightly shorter timeline, somewhere between three to four days. The Millennials? Twenty-four hours. In that one room, we had a microcosm of different expectations, setting the stage for misunderstanding, frustration, and resentment in every direction. It would be easy for any of those people to assume their expectation was the "right" one, but doing so wasn't going to solve their problems.

I shared with them a story of my then-four-year old, who had recently written a letter to his grandmother, who lived several states away. We had put it in the mailbox at the post office one morning on the way to preschool. When I picked him up that afternoon, he was excited to check the mail on our way home to see whether she had written him back yet. "Not yet, buddy," I told him. "It takes a little longer than that." But this answer made little sense to him—in part because he was four, but also because he was growing up in a time when it wasn't unheard of to get response from a letter in just a few hours (though, granted, it would have needed to be through email, rather than the U.S. Post Office!). His expectations were shaped by the time in which he was growing up, as all of our expectations are.

The Millennials in that room had become accustomed to quick feedback because our technology had evolved to make that possible. The Boomers were comfortable with the switch to email, but less on board with the assumption that it meant they had a responsibility to respond faster just because it was possible to do so. Neither view is wrong—they are simply different. As a result, they needed to uncover and understand these kinds of differences and work together to determine the shared organizational norms that would help prevent such conflict in the future.

This conversation and experience sparked my interest in helping managers better understand generational differences, and ultimately the creation of the term *Gentelligence*. My research began to explore generational dynamics from the academic side. However, that first company I had worked with told other companies, and I began to get more requests to help managers understand "those Millennials." Over time, I became a generational consultant. With every engagement, I realized that I understood something that many others did not: working with those from different generations, while sometimes confusing and frustrating, is fascinating and valuable on both ends of the age spectrum.

One year later, I had my own leadership experience that taught me firsthand about the importance of leveraging generational diversity. I stepped into a new role in co-directing an undergraduate leadership-development program for our business school. The current program was dated, with dwindling membership and a circa 1990s website. I jumped in head first, coming up with new ideas for programming and submitting an urgent request to IT for website updates. I was told it would be put on the list, but due to the backlog, it would likely be six months before anyone could make any changes to the site. Undaunted, I presented my new ideas to the current program members (ages eighteen to twenty-two) and met with a less-than-enthusiastic response.

My ideas just weren't resonating with them—and it occurred to me that I hadn't even thought to ask *them* what they wanted or needed in order to accomplish that goal. I realized I needed their help to understand how to build something that would appeal to them and meet their needs. Frustrated, I invited a few student members of the program to meet for coffee to discuss how to move forward. I asked whether they would be willing to work with me to brainstorm a new shared vision for the program that would be inspiring to all of us.

The table lit up with energy and ideas. I listened, but I also guided. Some of the suggestions weren't aligned with what I knew our university wanted from the program; some were beyond our resources. Rather than shut down the ideas, I tried to ask questions: How would we do that? What challenges would we encounter if we tried that? By the end of the day, we had created a new vision statement and were all brimming with anticipation of what we could build together. As we were leaving, I joked, "Now, if only we could do something about that 1990s website." One of the students turned and casually asked, "Did you want me to build us a new one?" Taken aback, I said, "You can build us a website? When could you do this?" And he said, "Tonight?" And he did. The next day (literally), we had a beautiful, modern website, with our new shared vision statement displayed proudly across the top.

And without realizing it, I had just experienced firsthand the power of Gentelligence. The students took shared ownership of the program—not just the website but also the leadership and the learning. I acted as a guide, a voice for the university when their ideas lacked context or needed revising, and was a sounding board and mentor. I led the program by empowering those whom the program was actually designed to help. The result was an engaged organization, one where the input and contribution of all of us really mattered. This experience became the focus of my 2017 TEDx Talk: "Why I Love Millennials . . . and You Should Too."

In my work as a professor, I work closely with our younger generations every day—not just in the classroom but also in my work co-directing our Center for Business Leadership. I work with teams of amazing students to tackle leadership challenges, and barely a day goes by when I don't ask one of them for ideas on how to solve a problem. I respect their unique kind of wisdom, and, in turn, they are more open to my more seasoned guidance. They seek out my input on the organizational hurdles that often stand in their way and ask my advice when they run into challenges they have not encountered before. By empowering them and valuing their perspective, the entire organization is stronger. It is *our* organization—one where everyone has a voice, regardless of age, and that should be the goal for every leader.

THE BOOK

This book is designed to help all organizations join the Gentelligence movement, leading in ways that empower all generations and create workplaces that view and leverage generational diversity as a strength. We first explore the current reality in business: workplaces full of intergenerational tension and conflict. Chapter 1 reveals that generation shaming is not a new phenomenon, but one that has been newly fueled by changing demographics in the workplace. In the second chapter, we outline both common generational clichés and important shared generational experiences, revealing the complexities of understanding generational identity. We conclude our exploration of the problem in chapter 3 by identifying the roadblocks that prevent Gentelligent leadership, including generational scapegoating, ageism (and reverse ageism), and perceived misalignment in values and knowledge.

In chapter 4, we then present the Gentelligence solution: how to champion the potential of all generations and use this diversity of thought to create stronger workplaces. We discuss the four key practices of Gentelligence: breaking down biases by (1) Resisting Assumptions and (2) Adjusting the Lens; and building strength by (3) Strengthening Trust and (4) Expanding the Pie. In subsequent chapters, we apply these practices, using real business examples to illustrate how Gentelligence is already successfully helping leaders overcome challenges ranging from acquiring and retaining talent to creating strong intergenerational teams and leadership to building culture and navigating change.

BUILDING OUR OWN GENTELLIGENT TEAM: MEET THE AUTHORS

In writing this book, it was vital to have some generational diversity represented in our author team as well. While I am a member of Gen X, my two coauthors (Josephine Nachemson-Ekwall and Brandon Fogel) are both Millennials and former students of mine, now working across different industries. Throughout this book, we will often use first person when referring to examples from my generational consulting, research, or teaching. However, at other times we will use *we* to refer to the views of our author team. Regardless of pronouns, this book has been a collective, intergenerational team effort from start to finish. My coauthors have provided invaluable insight, different perspectives, and hard work, as well as needed motivation throughout the process. Over time, the book has gone from starting with *my* vision to becoming a product of *our* shared vision. As such, this book is a product of Gentelligence.

Our intergenerational chemistry has brought a unique perspective to the project, and I am confident it's better as a result. Over the course of our research for this book, we saw the same effect emerging from the stories and cases of intergenerational learning around the world: the willingness to integrate intergenerational views led to better programs, marketing, and decisions, not to mention stronger organizations.

As this book will explore, the history of generational differences is flush with misunderstandings and tension. While we do not have all the answers for these issues, together, we present a powerful set of Gentelligence strategies to not only move past current challenges but also utilize these differences to improve the culture and success of our workplaces.

1

Blame *60 Minutes*

How Morley Safer Fueled the Generation Wars

A new breed of American worker is about to attack everything you hold sacred: from giving orders, to your starched white shirt and tie. They are called, among other things, "millennials."

—*Morley Safer,* 60 Minutes[1]

In 2007, *60 Minutes* introduced Millennials to the world with the news story "The Millennials Are Coming," framing this generation as some sort of plague humanity would have to survive. Host Morley Safer referred to the brewing generational showdown in the workplace as a "psychological battlefield."[2] The gauntlet was thrown—the business world as we knew it was being turned upside down by these Millennial intruders, and it was up to the older generations to protect it. The Millennials were convenient scapegoats for the strain and chaos that twenty-first-century technology introduced, and this resentment has now raged on for over a decade. Just for fun, do a Google search on things Millennials have killed. The last time we checked, the popular press had blamed them for the end of golf, bars of soap, casual dining, napkins, and American cheese.

Every war has casualties. In the case of generational conflict, the loss is one of talent potential. The ongoing and strikingly one-sided, negative narrative around the multigenerational workforce has led each generation to play into this war. The danger with this mindset is that we overlook potential benefits that come from bringing together people with a diversity of thought and experience. Failing to consider the possible advantages, we have largely squandered the opportunities right in front of us, including the chance to utilize generational diversity to increase innovation and improve problem-solving and to realize how generational understanding can help improve organizational performance in significant ways.

THE LOSS OF TALENT POTENTIAL IN GENERATIONAL WARS

Companies across a wide range of industries are experiencing the consequences of generational wars. The damage they bring to organizational cultures by creating unhealthy competition and sowing mistrust is evident, and the seemingly endless generational tensions have a long-term effect. The road toward intergenerational cooperation has narrowed and is now full of steep terrain.

While the trend of Millennial shaming has received by far the most energy and media attention of any generation to date, this phenomenon began well before Safer's piece on *60 Minutes*. Frustration about the attitude and behavior of youth dates back thousands of years. In 11 BC, a writer named Peter the Hermit remarked, "The young people of today think of nothing but themselves. They have no respect for their parents or old age. They are impatient of all restraint. They talk as if they alone know everything and what passes for wisdom in us is foolishness in them."[3] At the end of the eighteenth century, French philosopher Auguste Comte noted that change in society comes with a change in generations, as it is the conflict between generations that creates unhappiness with the status quo.[4]

We have seen this in our own times as well. Baby Boomers were seen as too revolutionary for the Traditional generation. Gen Xers were labeled "slackers" for their unwillingness to adopt the workaholic tendencies of the Baby Boomers. Millennials were called "entitled" for expecting opportunities at a younger age than those who came before them. Gen Zers, the first of whom just graduated college in 2019, were labeled overly sensitive "snowflakes" even before entering the workforce.

In March 2020, the *New York Times* published an article titled "How Outdoor Voices, a Start-Up Darling, Imploded." Founded in 2014, the athletic apparel brand became a sensation as it carved out space for itself among other major brands like Nike and Lululemon by focusing on everyday people and a mission to "get the world moving" as a way to stay happy and healthy. Yet signs painting a gloomier picture of the company soon emerged, including a portrait of a deeply rooted conflict between its young Millennial founder and the older, more experienced executive team. Ultimately, following a head-on crash with the executive team, the founder was ousted.[5] This example, and the continuing struggles the company is facing, remain a powerful, cautionary tale of what can happen when the generational divide remains unmanaged.

Outdoor Voices is not the only company that has publicly struggled to manage the generational divide. In March 2020, PwC agreed to pay $11.625 million to settle an age-discrimination case that alleged that the company recruited only at colleges for associate-level positions, making those positions unavailable to older workers. Among the settlement conditions, the company agreed to hire age-inclusivity consultants to train those involved in recruitment and hiring.[6] Since February 2018, IKEA has faced five separate lawsuits that alleged the company discriminated against older employees and that the company had created a corporate culture of age bias. The most recent lawsuit in 2019 by a forty-eight-year-old former employee claimed that four employees in their twenties had been given a position he had been denied. The plaintiff alleged that when he asked an IKEA manager why he had been passed over for another promotion, she "told him that the role he applied for was new and required an external candidate who could come up with 'new and innovative ideas.'"[7]

Companies from every industry—including Google, IBM, R.J. Reynolds, WeWork, Citibank, and Marriott—have all been sued for age discrimination in recent years.[8] While these stories represent anecdotal evidence of an ongoing age and generational war in the workplace, research has found additional evidence to support the rage. More than half of employees report they aren't likely to get along with a coworker from another generation.[9] As with any war, there will be fallout as a result. Until we create a sustainable way for generations to not just peacefully coexist but also learn from one another, we will not be able to stop the loss of valuable talent potential or benefit from its many promises.

THE GENERATIONS STRIKE BACK

Most organizations have remained on the sidelines during the generational battle, ignoring (or at best tolerating) the tension it has produced. While the worst-case scenarios involve managerial frustrations and generational blaming, the best case for many organizations currently seems to be having multiple generations working side by side in a fragile peace. Neither instance leverages the possibilities that generational and age diversity can bring. This means there is an immense amount of untapped potential being left on the table as this war rages on.

Left to navigate the struggle on their own, employees have started to find ways to respond, with each generation reacting in their own time and way. Millennials and Gen Z, in particular, have started to openly defend the validity of their perspectives as generational conflict and tension actively continue around them.

"THOSE MILLENNIALS" ARE NOW RAISING THEIR VOICES

The unflattering narrative around Millennials started as soon as they entered the workforce and has continued ever since. This generation has grown up, and they are now fighting back. As the oldest of that generation (age thirty-eight as of 2020) settles into positions of middle management, their response to being framed as the workplace enemy has been sharp. In 2016, Millennial author Caitlin Fisher published a blog post titled "The Gaslighting of the Millennial Generation." Her message went viral and was read by millions, addressing the provocative question: "If millennials aren't a bunch of spoiled brats with an entitlement mentality who needs [*sic*] a trophy just for putting on pants in the morning, who are they?" She argued that who the Millennials really "were" could be seen through both data and the personal narratives of a generation that is greatly diverse, under a great deal of pressure, plagued with significant student loan debt, and driven to improve the world they are inheriting, commenting, "Generations before us completely drove the bus into a lake and it's somehow our fault everybody's drowning."[10]

While the Millennials waited until they were relatively safe in positions of middle management to strike, Gen Zers, the first of whom just graduated college in 2019, have already decided to push back.

"OK BOOMER"—GEN Z HAS SOMETHING TO SAY

The "OK Boomer" trend was born on the social media platform TikTok in fall 2019. The phrase was a proactive response by Gen Z targeting older generations following their initial attempt to mark this generation as overly sensitive "snowflakes." In the inaugural OK Boomer video debut, an unnamed white-haired man, donning a purple polo shirt and a baseball cap, begins to preach in a confident tone, "The Millennials and Generation Z have the Peter Pan syndrome. They don't ever want to grow up. They think the utopian ideals of their youth are somehow going to translate into adulthood."[11] On a split screen, those Gen Zers and Millennials responded to this rant en masse with a simple, dismissive comment: "OK Boomer." The phrase quickly went viral on the platform, spawning a variety of memes and even its own song. The Society of Human Resource Management has equated the phrase to a "digital eyeroll,"[12] and Taylor Lorenz of the *Times* explained, "'OK Boomer' has become Gen Zers' endlessly repeated retort to the problem of older people who just don't get it, a rallying cry for millions of fed up kids."[13]

Millions of fed-up kids, indeed. With their immense social media prowess, Gen Z has spread the rallying cry much faster than Morley Safer ever could with his *60 Minutes* warning about those Millennials. The phrase spread across the globe, even showing up in a New Zealand courtroom, where Chloë Swarbrick (a twenty-five-year-old New

Zealand Green Party politician) used it to respond to heckling from an older colleague in Parliament during her speech on climate change.

While almost every media outlet across the world has published their take on the "OK Boomer" phenomenon, one article in particular stood out to us. In the fall of 2019, the *New York Times* ran the headline "'OK Boomer' Marks the End of Friendly Generational Relations." (We're not sure when those friendly generational relations occurred, but it seems they are already over.) The subtitle to the article proclaimed, "Now It's War: Gen Z Has Finally Snapped over Climate Change and Financial Inequality." Generational war had apparently been declared, and all over two seemingly harmless words.

But were the words harmless? While the phrase has been criticized by many as ageist,[14] Millennials and Gen Zers have been quick to defend it as decidedly *not* ageist, maintaining that this particular use of the word "Boomer" isn't tied to any specific age group. John Kelley, a researcher at Dictionary.com, explains to *NBC News*:

> We're not using "boomer" per se to take down people who were born after World War II in the baby boom. We're using it in an ironic, often humorous, though sometimes malicious way as a catchall or stand-in for a set of attitudes. A "boomer" [in this case] is an older, angry white male who is shaking his fist at the sky while not being able to take an insult. They have close-minded opinions, are resistant to change—whether it's new technology or gender inclusivity—and are generally out of touch with how their behaviors affect other people.[15]

That remark—that a generational name was now synonymous with an insult—set off more alarm bells for us than any of the cheeky memes we had seen on social media. Society had officially reached the point where the name of an entire generation was being used as a sweeping attack. Yet there was a degree of irony in this realization as well, as many of the "Boomers" now being attacked had not had such qualms about using the term "Millennial" in a similarly disparaging way, referring to any young person they perceived as entitled.

In response, I wrote my own article for *NBC News*, voicing my concerns regarding the "OK Boomer" trend, as well as the dynamics that had led up to it. I commented,

> In many ways, these two feisty words represent Gen Z pushing back on the attempts they expect will be made to label and belittle their own generation as they take the place of millennials at the bottom of the pecking order. But in the process of defending themselves, they are unfortunately perpetuating the very age-oriented stereotypes they themselves don't want to be labeled by.[16]

In other words, it might be clever, and it might seem justified, but it's definitely not going to improve generational cooperation. Just as this kind of generation bashing isn't productive when we do it to the Millennials or to Gen Z, the "OK Boomer" retort is definitely not going to make older generations more likely to respect and listen to the perspectives of younger ones. Workers have locked horns in a fight no one is going to win as they continue to paint other generations as enemies in a generation war, rather than as allies.

THE BUSINESS CASE FOR ENDING THE GENERATIONAL WARS

A few years ago, I had given an assignment to my class to think about how increasing diversity might add strategic value to an organization they had worked for in the past. One young woman raised her hand to report that she had chosen to write about her family's agricultural machinery business in her rural southern hometown. She commented that while her family's business was open to hiring more diverse people, the community they lived in simply did not have much diversity at all, and the people interested in working in that area of agricultural machinery seemed to be an even narrower group in terms of demographics. She had concluded that using diversity as part of her family's business strategy was not realistic. I asked her to describe their current workforce, and she shared that they had about twenty employees, all white males. I asked her how old they were. "Anywhere from seventeen to seventy," she replied.

Seventeen to seventy!? While their employees did not represent diversity in terms of other important aspects like gender, race, or ethnicity, it seemed that she had quickly overlooked what did make them diverse in one significant way. I asked her whether a seventeen-year-old and a seventy-year-old view farming in similar ways. This question alone led to several great stories and examples of how different generational perspectives were making waves in their company—from the younger people advocating for the use of drones in farm management to older people sharing best practices for navigating climate conditions. By the end of the conversation, we had uncovered several ways the seventeen-year-olds could learn from the seventy-year-olds, as well as how the seventy-year-olds could benefit from the insight of those who were just seventeen (and everything in between).

There are many workplace stories just like this one, many of which will be shared in the chapters to come. The benefits of successfully managing diversity (broadly defined) are impressive. Companies with stronger diversity and inclusion efforts experience greater market share, enjoy better success in new markets, and have stronger team collaborations and lower turnover.[17] When it comes to increasing workforce diversity, according to the *World Economic Forum*, "The moral argument is weighty enough, but the financial impact—as proven by multiple studies—makes this a no brainer."[18] Countless studies have confirmed that investing in well-managed diversity can lead to more creativity, resilience, effectiveness, and profitability when compared to organizations that don't make such investments.

So where do these positive outcomes come from? It's called the "value-in-diversity hypothesis."[19] When dissimilar people (in our case, it would be those from different ages and generations) work together, everyone ends up with increased access to new kinds of valuable information and perspectives. The Boston Consulting Group argues that this kind of outcome means diversity is "not just a metric to be strived for, it is an actual integral part of a successful revenue generating business."[20]

When it comes to generational diversity, most organizations are far from realizing the value potential.

CHANGING THE MINDSET: FROM GENERATIONAL COMPETITION TO INTERGENERATIONAL COOPERATION

Instead of participating in the endless generational battle, companies need to take action against the very mindset that allows it to continue. It's time to create organizational strategies to foster intergenerational cooperation, allowing them to unlock talent potential rather than perpetuating endless wars over it. Talent is a key source of competitive advantage for almost every organization, one that is increasingly scarce as the struggle over skilled talent intensifies. *Forbes* estimates that employee recruitment alone is a $200 billion worldwide market.[21]

Employees across generations are currently elbowing for generational relevancy, rather than feeling secure in the value they bring to their organizations. Some of the oldest, most experienced members of our workforce are feeling marginalized and undervalued compared with tech-savvy, quick-to-adapt younger employees. Millennials are now beginning to be replaced as the new kids on the block by Gen Z. Our youngest generations of employees are striving to have their voices heard despite their young age and limited expertise. The Society of Human Resource Management explains, "Consider it a major disconnect in hiring: On the one hand, many recruiters put a premium on 'high-performers' with 'proven experience,' while on the other they are increasingly looking for 'digital natives'—members of the demographic raised in the age of online technology and thus by definition too new to the workforce to have proved much of anything."[22] This dynamic can result in a competitive generational gridlock—and navigating these workplace tensions often requires delicate negotiation.

To successfully create a powerful intergenerational talent strategy, we argue that organizations need significant disruption in how they are defining *diversity* to include the vital aspects of age and generational identity. It's time for an increased focus on how these differences can bring value to the workplace, rather than repeating conversations about how they are a headache. The disruption in diversity strategy needs to focus not just on attracting an intergenerational workforce but also on understanding how to develop and retain it. Development and retention require attention to create inclusive organizational cultures where all generations are given a voice and expected to learn from each other. Chip Conley, strategic advisor for hospitality for Airbnb, states in his book *Wisdom @ Work*, "This unprecedented age diversity in the workplace can be confusing as we may have drastically different value systems and work systems at play. But also it can be a wellspring of opportunity that the world has never experienced."[23]

In the end, the existing win-lose perspective creates a mindset of scarcity—one that destructively assumes a finite amount of resources (e.g., opportunities or recognition) and that for one to win, another must lose. This mentality must be debunked and replaced with the idea that working collaboratively together can lead to providing additional resources for everyone. Like most types of organizational change, threats can also become opportunities with the right leadership strategy. JoAnn Jenkins, CEO of AARP, remarked in 2016, "A workplace with Millennials, Gen Xers, Baby Boomers, and the Silent Generation offers a unique opportunity for varied perspectives and approaches to day-to-day work."[24] Now that Gen Z is entering the workplace, we have even more significant input and potential for success—if there is a method to harness and integrate the advantages that each cohort brings to the table.

FROM THREAT TO OPPORTUNITY: UNLOCKING THE POTENTIAL

Effectively managing generational diversity is a significant leadership challenge. We have long known that simply having a diverse workforce without taking steps to manage it effectively is a recipe for disaster, and the same is true when that diversity involves generations and age. The notion that we can simply expect diverse individuals to seamlessly work together without proactive leadership is not realistic. With other types of difference—such as race and gender—in the workplace, this fact has already been made clear.

Without intervention, managers often opt for the strategy that requires the least effort: hiring diverse employees and hoping the differences sort themselves out over time.[25] While working around differences might mean less conflict, it doesn't create the innovation and creativity that is possible. To realize the benefits, a bolder approach is needed—one that involves promoting equal opportunities, valuing cultural differences, and allowing these differences to have a positive impact on organizations and those who work within them.[26]

Easier said than done. While best practices have advanced when it comes to dealing with many types of differences, when it comes to taking a proactive strategy to generational differences, there is little existing guidance on how to do so effectively. What we do know is that taking an approach that assumes any one generation will (or should) adapt to the norms and preferences of another will not be successful.

This lack of best practices in generational leadership may be why early research has shown conflicting results about the benefits of generational and age diversity in the workplace. Left to their own devices, different age groups often refrain from interacting, preferring instead to work with those they perceive as more like themselves. These kinds of divisions can be counterproductive and result in lower productivity. However, when companies take steps to promote and support various age groups working together, age diversity can result in increases in productivity. This is particularly true when the work is complex, because of the increased potential of tapping into the knowledge differences of intergenerational talent.[27] This is why the Gentelligence strategies presented in this book are so important, as they provide specific tools leaders can use to promote healthy and productive intergenerational collaboration.

We argue that Gentelligence, which we define as viewing generational differences as a unique source of diversity of thought, is the strategy that will allow organizations to effectively realize these opportunities. With this mindset, a clever contribution from a Gen Z employee doesn't undermine the experience of a seasoned Baby Boomer, instead enhancing it. Ideas are improved by combining the innovation and wisdom of younger and older employees; the result is something no one employee (or generation) could create alone.

Gentelligence is a movement that encourages intergenerational learning and collaboration. This approach paves the road for younger employees to collaborate with older generations to innovate and solve problems. To successfully turn intergenerational discord into opportunity, the unique identity of each generation must be well understood, and the insight of every generation must be utilized to its fullest potential.

2

Our Generational Identities

A generation is the creation of shared experiences, the things that happened, the things you all did and listened to and read and went through and, as important, the things that did not happen.

—*Rich Cohen,* Vanity Fair[1]

People belong to a particular generation based on the year they were born; yet this alone does not fully represent who they are, what they believe, or why they act the way they do. To assume it does is to misunderstand and mischaracterize the role of generations. Generational membership is one element of a person, and how much it impacts who one is depends largely on the individual. The idea is not to pigeonhole or label generations, as one's age cohort is a single ingredient in the complex chemistry that makes up human behavior at work. However, generational identity is an essential element of who people are at work, and a deeper understanding of different generational characteristics is vital to creating Gentelligent workplaces.

Twentieth-century Spanish philosopher José Ortega y Gasset called the idea of generations "the most important conception in history" and the "vital sensitivity" of society—a "pulsation of its historical energy."[2] In 1952, the German philosopher Karl Mannheim wrote a dense chapter called "The Problem of Generations," asserting that we are all strongly impacted by the context of our youth.[3] Fundamentally, generations were invented as a way to categorize and help us better understand the phenomenon and impact of broad age differences. In this way, they are slightly artificial in their separation but comparable to other created categories of division like political party or religion. As generational researchers Neil Howe and William Strauss write,

> Like most other social categories—religion, political party, income, occupation, race—generations can be imprecise at the boundaries. We define generational boundaries by the calendar year—and of course, some people born just on one side may belong on the other. But a little ambiguity does not keep us from distinguishing Catholics from Protestants, Democrats from Republicans.

Generations are simply one layer of identity. Just as knowing where people grew up can help to explain why they hold particular perspectives, knowing which generation they belong to can illuminate their points of view.

WHO DECIDES A GENERATION?

The criticism that generations are artificial comes from their seemingly arbitrary boundaries. For example, the Traditional and Baby Boomer generational boundaries span nineteen years each, while Gen X and the Millennial generations each bridge only sixteen years. While such groupings may seem random, several factors determine when one generation ends, and another begins. A generation tends to span the length of approximately one "phase of life" (e.g., childhood), and when the oldest members of an age cohort begin to move into the next phase, a new generational division is created for the subsequent cohort being born. Because the length of a phase of life is somewhat influenced by social factors (e.g., at what age society considers an individual to be an adult), this definition fluctuates a bit for each generation but tends to range between fifteen to twenty years.

Social factors are the next element that contributes to the boundaries of a generation. For example, the beginning of the Baby Boomer generation in 1946 was determined by the explosive population growth following World War II. The cutoff for this generation occurred when birth rates plummeted again in 1964. The subsequent generation was initially called the "Baby Bust" generation for this reason. However, this name was soon pushed aside in favor of Generation X.[4] The start of the Millennial generation was determined by considering what birth years would result in the first individuals coming of age in the new millennium—from this, a start date of 1981 was established. When deciding where the Millennial generation should end and Gen Z should begin, formative events and cultural factors once again were taken into consideration.

Formative events are defined as "distinct historical events that shape a generational identity through collective memories."[5] For example, it was decided that 1997 would mark the end of the Millennial generation because, according to the Pew Research Center, "Most Millennials were between the ages of 5 and 20 when the 9/11 terrorist attacks shook the nation, and many were old enough to comprehend the historical significance of that moment, while most members of Gen Z have little or no memory of the event."[6] The shared history of a generation results in what is called a "peer personality"—a story representing an age cohort that results from being born during a common period in history and experiencing significant events and phenomena at common life stages.[7] This peer personality further reinforces the generational groupings, contributing to a stronger and cohesive bond among its members.

The coronavirus pandemic of 2020, for example, affected every generation, but, depending on the life stage, it impacted them differently. For school-aged children and college-aged young adults, it meant unprecedented weeks off from school and immersion in remote learning. For many Millennials, Gen Xers, and some Baby Boomers, it meant an overnight transition to remote workplaces. For older Boomers and

Traditionals, the potential threat of the virus on their health meant a strong focus on limiting their social interactions. The long-reaching consequences of this event on different generations remain to be seen, but as this event occurred during Gen Z's formative years, it will likely have an outsized influence on how they live and work in the future and create a strong bond among members of this generation.

Ultimately, generational groupings help us understand how these historical events influence the attitudes and behaviors of people of a similar age. Growing up, a generation has access to particular knowledge, experiences, and opportunities during its most formative years that prior and future generations do not.[8] Millennials, for example, are often referred to as the first generation of digital natives. This age cohort was the first to have frequent and widely available access to the internet and personal computers as it grew up, creating a significantly different educational and development experience from that of Gen X (the majority of whom experienced most, if not all, of their education without the internet). As José Ortega y Gasset writes, "Unable to find lodging among the philosophies of the past, we have no choice but to attempt to construct one of our own."[9] As the world and its demands shift, each generation adapts its approach to life and work.

As one of the youngest members of Generation X, technology was still a rare part of my education. Videos occurred on days when we had a substitute teacher, courtesy of a film projector and later a TV/VCR rolled down from the school library on a cart. I have vivid memories of dial-up internet emerging when I started college (1994), the same year I hauled my portable word processor to my dorm room to crank out term papers (some of these terms are even confusing to my Millennial coauthors, who had to Google "word processor"). I saw my first PowerPoint presentation as part of my last semester of college in 1998. While this differential access to computers as part of one's education may not seem monumental, it significantly impacts how generations view the purpose of technology as part of school and work. While younger generations don't think twice about pulling out a laptop during a meeting to take notes or access needed information, many older individuals equate technology with distraction and entertainment. This relatively simple example illustrates one of the reasons generational narratives are important to building understanding, as these attitudes stem from which historical periods employees grew up within and have a significant and lasting impact on how they live and work.

Throughout the rest of this chapter, we identify a shared narrative for each generation and pinpoint each cohort's likely collective experiences. We discuss how these tend to lead to certain internalized attitudes and beliefs and how those subsequent attitudes and beliefs may surface as workplace behaviors, and how understanding these identities helps leaders stay away from painting generations with a broad brush based on assumptions.

A WORD ABOUT GENERATIONAL STEREOTYPES

Before we go further, we want to talk about the difference between stereotyping and understanding a generational narrative. Stereotypes at their core are shortcuts in decision making, leading people to assume that all people in a particular group have a set of common characteristics. When it comes to generations, there are interesting and important behaviors and perspectives that tend to be shared by an age cohort due to the shared period of time in which the group was born and raised. While leaders need to understand how the life experiences of different generations may have influenced their viewpoints, they must also remember that generational conversations are rife with clichés, unfounded assumptions, and generalizations that can lead to labeling, judgment, and deep misunderstandings about employees.

Understanding patterns or tendencies unique to particular generations without stereotyping can be challenging, and talking about generational differences without heading down a slippery slope of stereotyping is a conversation that leaders must navigate skillfully to allow employees to achieve their best and communicate effectively across generations. Ironically, many age-based stereotypes toward both younger and older employees are often reinforced in generational training programs in organizations. In other words, training on stereotypes means that workplace education meant to ease any tension between generations ends up making it worse. When done well, such training can instead discuss the increased frequency of certain kinds of behaviors or attitudes among different generations and why they may exist (but is cautious about stereotyping *all* members of a particular generational group).

Today, many generational labels are familiar to both managers and employees, and they affect interactions between co-workers. If generational stereotypes run unchecked, the resulting assumptions prevent a Gentelligent mindset. Instead, they create workplace tensions and can produce a climate that tolerates discriminatory behavior. An article written for *Work, Aging, and Retirement* notes, "Whether objective intergenerational differences are myth or reality, stereotypes persist and have the potential to influence individual perceptions and actions, which may ultimately lead to group conflict in organizations."[10] A Gentelligent mindset suggests that generational identity be used as a valuable lens of understanding: it can help provide important context for different behaviors or higher frequencies of particular attitudes when we compare one age cohort to another. However, Gentelligence pushes back against universal labels and assumptions that *all* members of a generation are always a specific way.

So, what is the difference between a generational stereotype and a generationally intelligent perspective? Stereotyping an individual based *solely* on one's generational identity is lazy and fails to consider other elements that impact an individual's identity and point of view. Within any generation, there are myriad individual differences that influence one's experiences, opportunities, and perspectives. Such elements include nationality, socioeconomic status, race, gender, and even age (being born at the beginning versus the end of a particular generation).

While a deep exploration into the impact of all of these differences is beyond the scope of this book, we do feel they are vital to mention. As such, when individuals do not feel the narrative of their generation particularly applies to them, this disconnect is often rooted in other aspects of their identities. For example, while Millennials are often described as being entitled due to the attention and resources they received as children, this is much more true for those who grew up in higher socioeconomic classes than those with fewer resources to spare, who would not have had the luxury of such additional opportunities. Consequently, individuals born on the cusp of a generation may not see themselves in the typical narrative for their generation, perhaps finding more connection with the neighboring cohort.

We suggest that generational identity is most useful when viewed as just one of many elements of a person, and a *lens* to help us understand differences rather than as an excuse for stereotyping, which more often than not extends generational divides. While we provide some of the usual insights surrounding generationally formative events, we aim to extend the conversation by establishing generational narratives that explore how and why generations matter.

GENERATIONAL LENSES: UNDERSTANDING THE STORY OF EACH GENERATION

Traditional and Silent Generations

Our two oldest living generations are the Traditional generation (born between 1901 and 1927) and the Silent generation (born 1928–1945). While most are no longer active in the workforce, their generational experiences provide important context for understanding current generational contrasts. These generations grew up during the Great Depression and its aftermath and were influenced by America's participation in World War II and its resulting chaos on family life, the economy, and society as a whole.[11]

To illustrate the cause-and-effect pattern that builds the peer personality of a generation, consider what values would be important and constructive for individuals growing up experiencing particular significant events in their first few decades of life. What attitudes would be emphasized at home and promoted in society in order for this generation of young people to not only survive but also thrive in the future? Surging levels of such values help to give a generation its shared persona.

For example, research shows both the Traditional and the Silent generations possess fierce loyalty. This devotion to one's country, family, and organization is logical given the challenges existing during the early years of these generations. Similarly, the emotions and challenges brought by World War II sparked great national loyalty. These generations made and witnessed extreme sacrifice for their country, and, as a result, a collective national pride emerged.

For those experiencing the economic turmoil of the Great Depression, gratitude deepened toward companies that did not lay off their employees or those that gave unemployed workers jobs after long periods without work. Many believed they owed these businesses their loyalty for a lifetime, committing to spending their careers with one organization, working their way up the ladder and remaining devoted to them until the day they were ready to retire. The Traditional and Silent generations are also known for their conservative tendencies toward resources. This is thought to stem from the fact that they grew up with a national collective need to "make do" and "use what you have." Many in these generations also believe in setting aside individual wants for the greater good—a spirit that was necessary to survive and rebuild during and following both the Great Depression and World War II.

Understanding these generations' norms of conformity is also important to appreciate the leadership style of many in the Traditional and Silent generations. As many served in the military and saw firsthand the need to follow the orders of a superior, the idea of "command and control" leadership became embedded in their generational consciousness. Many of the job opportunities of this era were in the manufacturing industry—a place where following directions, rules, and regulations was vital to success. It makes sense that this top-down approach to leadership was what these generations aspired to and had a substantial influence on their subsequent leadership behaviors.

Baby Boomers

Baby Boomers, born from 1946 to 1964, belong to the only generation officially recognized by the U.S. Census Bureau.[12] This age cohort earned its name from the flood of births following World War II, motivated by a nation anxious to rebuild and reversing an ongoing downward trend in America's birth rates that had endured since the 1700s.[13] Baby Boomers were a force to be reckoned with for many reasons, including their sheer numbers (more than 76 million people) when compared to the generations that came before and after. The end of the Baby Boomer generation came during the year population growth dropped for the first time since 1946.

The Boomers represented a new hope for America, symbolizing the victory of the Traditional generation over economic peril and global conflict. As stated by Ron Zemke, Claire Raines, and Bob Filipcza in *Generations at Work*, "The Boom Babies were cherished by parents who had sacrificed and fought a war for the right to bear them, raise them, indulge them, and dream of a new Eden for them to live out their days in."[14] The Baby Boomers grew up in a time of great economic growth and infinite possibility. In 1969, when the oldest Baby Boomers were twenty-three and the youngest were five, a man landed on the moon for the first time in history. The United States was focusing on rebuilding, expansion, and growth to accommodate its bursting population.

Growing up during such a time embedded a sense of optimism and idealism in much of the Baby Boomer generation, and its role as the new hope for a nation was internalized. *Time* magazine even awarded its coveted "Man of the Year" designation to the Baby Boomer generation as a whole in 1967.[15] The idealism and optimism of the Baby Boomers, combined with the magnitude of their age cohort, resulted in several notable progressive shifts and important events in society during their formative years, including the March on Washington, the Vietnam War and protests against it, the passage of the Civil Rights Act, and the women's movement. These events fed the ambition of this generation, whose members took this drive and energy with them in their early careers.

The opportunities available for the Baby Boomers were unthinkable to their parents' generation, and they took full advantage of them, focusing on their ascent up the corporate ladder and determined to make good on the promise they had represented in their youth. Baby Boomers popularized the sixty- to seventy-hour workweek, in some cases doubling the previous work-hour norms. The word *workaholic* was invented in the 1970s but became increasingly popular as the Boomers hit their career stride, capturing their exhaustive dedication to work success. The newly established rights for women created another dynamic in the Baby Boomer work-family balance. A surge of dual-career households, as well as single-parent households (as a result of increased divorce rates), meant greater complexity when it came to childcare responsibilities at home, and the popularity of sixty- to seventy-hour workweeks for both men and women increased this tension.

The Baby Boomers' relationships with leadership are also complicated and a bit of a paradox. While their parents' generation had been content to accept the direction and authority of its government and leadership during the trying times of the Depression and World War II, the Baby Boomers did not follow suit when they faced the impending Vietnam War. Rather than readily accept the U.S. government's position that involvement in the war was necessary, many Baby Boomers openly protested American military action. Those who served came home without the heroes' welcome that World War II soldiers had received. Many veterans were left severely impacted (physically and emotionally) by the Vietnam War with lingering distrust in their government's decision making.

While Baby Boomers established an identity early on as "anti-establishment" and demonstrated a strong willingness to buck the status quo in favor of progress and change, they were working for bosses who came from the Traditional generation and favored the command-and-control bureaucratic style of leadership. Many Baby Boomers succeeded under such leaders, and while they still admired the more egalitarian, anti-authority ideals of their youth, they had worked hard to achieve their career success and wanted to enjoy the power and authority traditionally resulting from such a climb. This resulted in many opting not to challenge the leadership status quo inside the organizations where they had built their careers.

Generation X

In 1965, the birth rate in the United States fell for the first time since 1946, bringing the Baby Boom to a close and marking the beginning of a new age cohort: Generation X. Gen X was temporarily called "the 13th Gen" (officially due to its status as the thirteenth generation since the colonization of the United States) until Douglas Coupland's 1991 book popularized the label "Generation X," and the name stuck.[16] Ron Zemke and colleagues wrote of Gen X in their 2000 book *Generations at Work* that Gen X is defined more by "what it's not than by what it is." Journalist Alex Williams of the *New York Times* concurs:

> What is an X? An empty set, a placeholder, a nothing that fills a void until an actual something comes along. . . . To the extent that we were defined, we were defined in the negative—the first generation in American history to be written off before it had a chance to begin.[17]

If the Boomers were born into an era of optimism, Generation X was born into one of caution and skepticism. While Boomers saw a man land on the moon during their childhood, Generation X saw the explosion of *Challenger*. The Boomers experienced free love and Woodstock; Gen X was warned about stranger danger, "just saying no" to drugs, and safe sex in the wake of the AIDS epidemic.

While formal cautions abounded, many Gen Xers grew up with relatively high amounts of independence. This cohort largely comprised the children of Boomers (and the youngest Traditionals) and consequently faced a very different childhood reality. Gen X was raised by the first generation of parents navigating dual-career or single-parent households at a much higher frequency than before. The women's liberation movement had successfully opened doors for many women to pursue their career goals and become more independent. Divorce rates doubled during the childhood of Gen X compared to that of Boomers.[18] With many Baby Boomers investing heavily in their careers to provide opportunities for their families, those sixty- to seventy-hour workweeks became a norm in some industries. These domestic and workplace trends led to the creation of yet another new term: latchkey kids. Before daycare was widely available (and certainly before it was available in the workplace), many school-aged Gen Xers let themselves into empty houses after school for a few hours until their parents came home from work.

Such circumstances simultaneously gave this generation a sense of independence and self-reliance, but also a sense of disillusionment and disengagement from the forces that motivated their parents. Seeing many of their parents define success as a job title, Gen Xers came of working age with the opposing philosophy that one should "work to live, not live to work," pushing back on the norm that work should occupy such a central focus in life. While the Traditional generation believed in loyalty to one employer and the Boomers defined success in terms of their careers, Gen X rebelled against these conventions. This was the first modern generation to experience firsthand the potential downside of strong parental ambitions at work, which led to the internalized attitude that success could mean more than just career advancement. Carrying the independence forged in their childhoods into adulthood, Generation X members demanded greater levels of balance between their work and private lives. Their Traditional and Boomer managers often perceived this set of reoriented priorities as laziness, quickly rebranding Gen X as the slacker generation.

What has this situation meant for Gen X in the workplace? It's a generation that has stayed largely under the radar, stuck between the overwhelming force of Boomers who have remained in the workplace much longer than expected and the Millennials who have dominated media and employer energy and attention for the last decade. Generational researcher Mary Donahue states, "Gen X is the most misunderstood group in the workforce today. They have been ignored because of the brilliant boomers before them and the magnificent millennials who followed them. Gen X is exhausted. If this were 1950 and a Gen X walked into a doctor's office, he or she would be hospitalized over their stress. Gen X has to manage both Boomers and Millennials, and they are getting really tired."[19]

The forces squeezing Gen Xers from multiple directions have led to a complex dynamic in terms of organization leadership pipelines. Currently, Boomers are starting to retire after longer-than-expected tenures, and the go-getter Millennials are more than ready to take their places in key leadership roles, meaning Gen Xers are once again caught in a void. As of 2020, Gen X is between forty-one and fifty-five years old and in prime earning years. Despite this, recent data have shown that Gen Xers are less likely to receive promotions than both Millennials and Baby Boomers, suggesting they may be getting passed over for opportunities.[20]

The Millennials

The Millennial generation includes those born from 1981 to 1996. Millennial childhoods were marked by a prevalence of technology and the dot-com era, giving this cohort the moniker of "digital natives." They were parented by younger Boomers who wanted more for their children, nurturing their self-esteem and development from an early age. Early opportunities for enrichment and education began to trend, from Mommy and Me classes to foreign language, sports, and music lessons for kids younger than school age. Parenting, especially among higher socioeconomic classes, became somewhat competitive, with parents investing the same level of drive they had given their careers in their children's development. As San Diego State psychology professor Jean Twenge states, they are "a generation of soaring expectations, raised on [the] mantra of 'you can be anything you want to be.'"[21]

From this well-intentioned parenting style came a flurry of labels, including the "Trophy Kids" and "Generation Me." Compared to generations before them, Millennial children were the focal point of the family dynamic. While their predecessors were raised with the long-standing philosophy of "children should be seen and not heard," Millennials were the heartbeat of their families, with their busy schedules often dictating the family plans as children were taxied to and from activities and arranged playdates, rather than wandering neighborhoods looking for pickup games of kickball or impromptu bike rides with friends, as had been done by several generations before them.

In addition to Millennials exerting influence on their family dynamics, research shows that parents were much more likely to be involved in their Millennial kids' lives. The long-range study Monitoring the Future (which, coincidentally, I participated in as a child) reveals several trends that show a change in the direction of the formative years of the Millennials as compared to Generation X.[22] In 1991, 76 percent of kids in eighth grade (the tail end of Gen X) reported regularly spending time at home alone with no adult present; by 2014, this percentage had fallen to below 70 percent. Research reveals Millennials were less likely to engage in many independent rites of passage during their teen years than any generation before them, including being less likely to go out without their parents, get a driver's license, or hold a part-time job in high school.[23]

While Gen X had resulted in the new phrase "latchkey kids," Millennials' parents were referred to as "helicopter parents." As Millennials were attending school and participating in afterschool activities, their parents were often deeply involved in both—regularly interacting with the teachers, coaches, and other adults involved. With such heavy investment and high expectations for their Millennial children, parents increasingly made decisions with (or for) them. This trend set the stage for the outcries of frustration from both college professors and employers when Millennials attended college and started jobs while still closely connected to their parents, relying on them for advice and intervention on their behalf. It was not unusual for professors I knew (or for me) to be contacted by parents of our students, requesting that their son or daughter be moved out of an early class section ("Madison can't have an 8:30; she needs more sleep than most people, or her health will be at risk") or inquiring whether exam dates might be moved to accommodate an early departure for a family trip over Thanksgiving break. In many of my workshops, HR managers would share stories of being contacted by the parents of Millennials who had received job offers, wanting to negotiate on their behalf.

Millennials emerged from childhood as the most highly educated generation ever in the United States, but also the most dependent on adults at a stage in life when society expected them to operate independently. Managers criticized them for lacking self-direction and requiring too much hand holding, but, ironically, many of those managers were Baby Boomers who had also raised their own Millennial children to behave the same way. Having been raised at the center of their families' conversations, Millennials often entered the work world expecting that their voices would matter to the same extent for their bosses, earning them the unflattering reputation of being entitled. From one perspective, this generation seemed indulged and sheltered; from another, Millennials appeared proactive with high expectations for success.

In terms of development, experiences, and education, they were often significantly ahead of where previous generations had been as young adults, often confident that they might be ready for more responsibility at an earlier age. Yet their Traditional, Boomer, and occasionally Gen Xer managers frequently believed that Millennials needed to put their heads down and wait their turn, just as the preceding generation had.

Gen Z (the Zoomers)

The generational identity of Generation Z is still a work in progress. The oldest of Gen Z were born in 1997, with an end date not yet formally established for this generation. (The COVID-19 pandemic in 2020 has emerged as a key factor in when to draw the line for the end of Gen Z, with arguments being made that those too young to have firsthand memories of the pandemic should not be considered part of this generation.)

As the first of Generation Z graduated college and entered the workforce in 2018, the trends that shaped their childhood narrative were also beginning to become evident. Since that time, profound events such as school violence; the educational, social, and workplace turmoil surrounding the global pandemic caused by the coronavirus; and the activism of the Black Lives Matter movement have continued to make up the formative landscape of this generation. Social media has exploded as the primary form of communication for Gen Z, with many kids having their own smartphones before they turned ten (and helping their parents learn to operate their own). While there is great concern that the "always-on" Gen Z will lose the ability (or desire) to communicate face-to-face, research surprisingly has shown that this generation prefers face-to-face communication over any other form, including texting.[24]

The majority of Gen Z were still school age when COVID-19 forced a drastic transition to remote learning almost overnight. During a worldwide quarantine, traditional classrooms were suddenly replaced by online learning, and the face-to-face communication Gen Z craved with classmates and friends was ironically only possible via online technology tools such as FaceTime and Zoom. This reality, along with the rapid pace of technological change being experienced by Gen Z during their formative years, has led me to suggest the formalization of "Zoomers" (a name that had been used occasionally up until that point) as the official name for Gen Z.[25]

The Great Recession hit as the first members of this age cohort were entering middle school, with many witnessing firsthand the effects of this economic turn in the form of relatives and family friends losing jobs and the bursting of the housing bubble. For some, the recession drained their college funds, impacting their future college plans as well as their career goals. The price of college also went up dramatically for Gen Z compared to the cost for Millennials just ten years prior, rising 79 percent from 2003 to 2013.[26] The Millennial child-rearing mantra of "being whatever you want to be" gave way to Gen Z's parental advice to their kids to tread carefully when choosing a path with greater stability and minimal risk. The impact of COVID-19 added a new layer of importance to the risk factor for Gen Z, with many seeing job offers and internships disappear into thin air in the economic aftermath of the pandemic.

However, the invention of the gig economy has presented Gen Z with an entirely new option, redefining what it means to have a career. With its social media and digital prowess, this generation has already spawned countless opportunities to build wealth earlier and earlier in their lives. On TikTok, fifteen-year-old Charli D'Amelio, who became famous for her dancing skills, is about to earn $23,000 per sponsored post and has been able to use this fame to make appearances on Jimmy Fallon.[27] In two years, nineteen-year-old Emma Chamberlain built a strong following of eight million subscribers on YouTube and has completely changed vlogging through her editing style. Estimates claim she makes around $2 million from her videos plus additional advertising income.[28] Thanks to technological advances, options for young people to pursue their interests as entrepreneurs are exploding. While starting a business used to be a long-term dream reserved for those who had achieved financial stability and found investors, today it can require nothing more than a good idea and a solid Wi-Fi connection. However, given the formative experiences brought by the Great Recession and COVID-19, Gen Z members are learning how to balance pursuing their passions via the gig economy with minimizing risk and securing financial stability.

GENERATIONS AROUND THE WORLD: A GLOBAL GLIMPSE

It is important to note that most of the formative events for generations mentioned thus far are rooted in American culture. The Great Depression, the civil rights movement, the *Challenger* disaster, 9/11, and the Great Recession are often cited as significant influences on each of our current generations, respectively. However, other global cultures also manifest the challenges and opportunities of generational differences and would point to somewhat different collective experiences as influential in shaping generational identities. Journalist Salvatore Babones puts it best in an article for *Foreign Policy* when he writes, "Indeed, every country has a different demographic profile, although that doesn't seem to change the fact that intergenerational conflict is as close to a universal phenomenon as human society gets."[29]

There is surprisingly limited work published on how different global cultures view the concept of generations. What has been done has primarily looked at how those born during the birth years associated with Baby Boomers, Gen X, Millennials, and Gen Z differ in terms of attitudes around the world.[30] While this is a start, it still uses a U.S.-centered lens to evaluate and analyze generations around the globe.

This limitation of perspective was obvious when the "OK Boomer" trend recently went viral. As discussed, the very term *Boomer* gets its name from the sharp increase of births in the United States after the end of World War II. While several other Western countries around the world also experienced a spike in birth rates after the war, many other cultures did not. Perhaps it is not so surprising that after pieces I wrote for *NBC News* on "OK Boomer" were published, several news outlets from around the world reached out with requests for interviews to learn more about what a "Boomer" was and also to discuss what connection and relevance it might have for their audience.

The first such request came from Sweden. *Dagens Nyheter*, a morning daily newspaper and one of the largest newspapers in Sweden, wanted to know more about this phenomenon. Although it is more common to refer to people by the decade of the birth year in Sweden, the journalist seemed intrigued by how formative experiences and cultural events drive the creation of a generational peer personality. While the American definitions often prevail in Swedish media, the events and experiences that led to the collective memory most likely differ for generations in Sweden. The journalist indicated that while Sweden shares some historical moments with the United States, distinct historical events in Sweden would likely paint a more nuanced picture of the various generations in Swedish society today.

Morning Wave, a South Korean radio show, reached out next. They shared that while *Boomer* is not a word used in Korea, they do have a phrase used to describe the "Boomer" generation: 꼰대, which loosely translates as a "condescending older person." These conversations sparked our interest in learning more about how various countries define generations, as well as where they draw the lines for birth years and why.

What we found reinforces the importance of social, economic, political, and cultural factors in generational identity. While a complete overview of generational history around the world would require its own book, here's a sampling of some of the interesting global views on generations we discovered:

- *Sweden*: Generations are most commonly referred to by the decade of birth year. *Köttberg*, or "meat mountain," is a term sometimes used in Sweden to refer to the Baby Boomer generation (or those born in the 1940s), who are seen as in the way of the available jobs. The term was coined by former minister of finance, Per Nuder, in 2004.[31]
- *Germany:* Those born in the 1940s are called "Generation 68" because of the German student protest movements during the 1960s that peaked in 1968. This era of activism was seen as a rallying against Germany's past and today is said to have laid the foundation for Germany's modern democratic society.[32]
- *South Africa:* Apartheid ended in 1994, and people born after this date are commonly referred to as the Born-Free Generation, or the "Born Frees." Those born into this generation are now young adults.[33]
- *Zimbabwe:* Zimbabwe experienced a "baby boom" of its own (with families having an average of eight children) after it declared independence in 1963, and this generation is called the "Uhuru Generation," which translates to "freedom."[34]

- *Latin America:* About 20 percent of those born from 1996 to 2005 now belong to what has been called "Generation Ni/Ni" ("no work, no study"). These young people are neither employed nor in school.[35]
- *Australia:* Australia has similar names to the United States for their generations, including Boomers, Gen X, Gen Y, and now Gen Alpha. Emerging nicknames for Generation Alpha include "upager," meaning they are maturing faster than past generations. Other proposed nicknames for this generation include "screenagers" or "Generation Glass" because the glass that they interact on in terms of computers, phones, and watches.[36]
- *China:* The generation born after China implemented their one-child policy in 1979 have become known as "Little Emperors" due to their only child status. They were the sole focus of attention (and indulgence) of parents and grandparents in a family and have earned a reputation for high self-esteem and confidence.[37] The generation following the Little Emperors is known as "Precious Snowflakes" for similar reasons.[38]

As the world becomes more connected, more and more events are experienced globally, rather than just locally. Researchers Eddy Ng, Sean Lyons, and Linda Schweitzer explore this idea in their book *Managing the New Workforce: International Perspectives on the Millennial Generation*, compiling an initial set of interesting global comparisons of how Millennials are both similar and different in countries such as Australia, Belgium, Canada, China, South Africa, and Singapore, concluding, "We have merely scratched the surface in our understanding of the Millennial generation as a global phenomenon."[39] Some researchers have argued that as the world becomes more connected, it will eventually result in what has been called a "global youth culture," where members of particular birth years will become more universally impacted by similar formative events.

While the specifics of each country's generational breakdown are different, the ideas behind them still stand. Generations serve as a powerful tool to better understand how people from a specific age cohort may view the world, and generational stereotypes will still spring up and make working across cohorts more difficult.

GENERATIONS AND LIFE STAGES

Each of the generational snapshots described above is simply a narrative that captures the events, trends, and forces at work for a group of people born and coming of age during a particular period in time. While many people outside of these age cohorts lived through these same events and dynamics, research shows that such forces have the most impact on those who experience them early in life. Generations experience such things together, forming impressions, attitudes, and memories unlike those of others who were already adults, resulting in what has been called a "distinct consciousness."[40] For example, research found that the 1963 assassination of JFK was recalled as "especially important" most often by those who were eighteen years old that year, followed by those who were twenty-three, then those who were thirteen, followed by those who were eight years old at the time. Both those beyond their twenties and those who were not yet born at the time of the assassination rated the event as less important. A similar pattern prevailed for memories of World War II, the Vietnam War, the end of Communism, and the 1991 Gulf War.

One of the great debates in generational research is what importance (if any) should be given to the impact of age or life stage. Many generational studies are criticized for focusing only on generational identity and ignoring the impact of life stage, or confusing generational norms with age-related ones. Admittedly, these are very complicated influences to dissect. Throughout this book, we at times will discuss generational and age diversity as interconnected. The rationale for this lies in the notion that every generation has a "shared age" and life cycle they progress through together. Similarly, at any given time, the identity and challenges of a given generation are evolving in relation to their age and stage. If a "freeze frame" of the workplace were taken today, for example, the advantages as well as the challenges of the Boomer generation would be intertwined with their current status as some of the most experienced members of the workforce, in addition to the reality that members of that generation are quickly approaching retirement age. Similarly, Gen Z is currently impacted by their life stage and status as organizational newcomers with less workplace experience. As time goes by, each generation will move together through different phases. Older generations will exit the workforce, and new generations will come along to add to the dynamics.

So, while we have consciously chosen to use a snapshot of today's workplace and its current generational realities as the context for this book, Gentelligence itself is a timeless concept. It focuses on seeing the potential in the rich diversity that comes from different generations collectively passing through life stages at different points in history. It provides a perspective on how to navigate not just the current generational dynamics in the workplace but also any future ones.

Ultimately, our generational identities are just one part of who we are, but they are an interesting and important element. The peer personalities resulting from the collective consciousness of a generation bring differences in perspective, attitudes, and behaviors. Such differences can be a source of frustration if we don't understand their origins and if we are unwilling to view such perspectives as opportunities to learn and innovate. To unlock the potential diversity that generational identities bring, we need to create Gentelligent workplaces that proactively work to create intergenerational social capital. So, what is standing in the way?

3

Mind the Gap

Roadblocks to Closing the Generational Divide

Be curious, not judgmental.

—*Walt Whitman*

Generational and age diversity have the power to improve performance and strengthen organizations, but it is not a phenomenon that occurs easily or naturally. To realize the potential, it is necessary to first explore the roadblocks that frequently get in the way. According to *Inc. Magazine*,

> With generations being one of the greatest diversities that divide employees, leaders must act intentionally to unite generations to reap the benefits of generational diversity. Fostering an environment of respect, inclusion, open communication, and freedom to create and implement ideas will help organizations capitalize on their generations diverse cognitive power.[1]

Diverse cognitive power? Yes, please! But to access this power, we need to create Gentelligent workplaces that have positive age climates and cultures that develop intergenerational social capital. Unfortunately, there are a number of daunting barriers that stand in the way of this important goal. We have identified four major roadblocks that prevent the development of Gentelligence: generational shaming, age biases, value perceptions, and knowledge differences.

GENTELLIGENCE ROADBLOCK #1: GENERATIONAL SHAMING

An overwhelming number of diversity and inclusion programs have not yet embraced the importance of including generational diversity as a critical component. The most recent data show that only 8 percent of companies include age as part of their diversity efforts,[2] meaning most companies and employees lack insight into how to productively address age differences. As a result, multiple generations are attempting to work together without a solid understanding of their age-related differences, leading to conflict, miscommunication, and frustration. This confusion can rapidly snowball into the generational shaming that seems all too common these days.

One of our recent hobbies is collecting really terrible generational headlines. This pastime keeps us fairly busy, as barely a day goes by without a spiteful clickbait headline making its way across our newsfeed. The media has taken an active interest in egging on a war between the generations, as evidenced by some of these recent articles:

> "OK, Millennial: Boomers Are the Greatest Generation in History" (*Newsweek*, March 2020)
>
> "Gen X Is a Mess" (*New York Times*, May 2019)
>
> "Actually, Gen X Did Sell Out, Invent All Things Millennial, and Cause Everything Else That's Great and Awful" (*New York Times*, May 2019)
>
> "Time's Up, Baby Boomers. It's Gen X's Turn Now" (*Washington Post*, April 2019)
>
> "Back Off, Millennials: Boomers Still Belong at Work" (*Financial Times*, December 2018)
>
> "Why Do Boomers Hate Millennials but Not Gen Z Kids?" (*IGN.com*, December 2018)
>
> "How the Baby Boomers—Not Millennials—Screwed America" (*Vox*, November 2018)

"It Isn't That Millennials Hate Boomers: It's That Every Generation Hates Everyone Else" (*The Wire*, May 2018)

"Millennials Are Struggling. Is it the Fault of the Baby Boomers?" (*Guardian*, April 2018)

"Gen Z Is Coming and Millennials Aren't Too Happy about It" (*Maclean's*, December 2017)

"7 Bad Workplace Habits Millennials Need to Stop Making" (*Entrepreneur.com*, October 2017)

"Gen X Needs to Save America from the Millennials" (*New York Post*, 2017)

"The Real Reason People Hate Millennials" (*Forbes*, May 2017)

"Millennials Don't Suck, You're Just Old and Hate Change" (*Insider*, June 2016)

"Millennials: Are They Really the Worst?" (*Dayton Daily News*, February 2016)

If just an article's worth of generation blaming isn't enough to satisfy, popular recent book titles can also provide support for the trend:

The Gaslighting of the Millennial Generation: How to Succeed in a Society That Blames You for Everything Gone Wrong (Caitlin Fisher, May 2019)

Zero Hour for Gen X: How the Last Adult Generation Can Save America from Millennials (Matthew Hennessey, September 2018)

iGen: Why Today's Super-Connected Kids Are Growing Up Less Rebellious, More Tolerant, Less Happy—and Completely Unprepared for Adulthood—and What That Means for the Rest of Us (Jean Twenge, September 2018)

A Generation of Sociopaths: How the Baby Boomers Betrayed America (Bruce Cannon Gibney, March 2018)

Not Everyone Gets a Trophy: How to Manage the Millennials (Bruce Tulgan, January 2016)

Passed Over and Pissed Off: The Overlooked Leadership Talents of Gen X (Mia Mulrennan, July 2015)

Generation Me—Revised and Updated: Why Today's Young Americans Are More Confident, Assertive, Entitled—and More Miserable Than Ever Before (Jean Twenge, September 2014)

The Pinch: How the Baby Boomers Took Their Children's Future—and Why They Should Give It Back (David Willetts, May 2011)

The titles listed above send the signal to leaders that it's socially acceptable to disparage an entire group of people based on their generational identity and that if we are frustrated that things are changing too much (or not enough), we need to look no further than a particular generation to know whom to blame. This mindset creates an unproductive dynamic, one where the difference is viewed as something negative, rather than a potential asset to new ways of thinking and solving problems.

In 2017, the *Wall Street Journal* made a bold but savvy move and claimed that it would no longer use disparaging Millennial stereotypes in its publication: "'Millennials' has become a sort of snide shorthand in the pages of *The Wall Street Journal*," the editors explain. *Quartz* celebrated the change in its subsequent article titled "The Wall Street Journal Says It's Done Being Snarky AF about Millennials."[3] Clearly, others are fed up with the blame game, too. While the *Wall Street Journal* acted swiftly, others have not, and by reinforcing the idea that our generations are engaged in some kind of ongoing battle, generational shaming stands in the way of creating Gentelligent workplaces. After all, these existing attitudes assume that others must lose so that another can ultimately "win," whether the prize is relevance, power, or resources. Instead, intergenerational collaboration, while complex, can increase the number of resources available, but it must be based on a foundation of trust rather than competition.

The Society for Human Resource Management notes that intergenerational conflict is increasingly significant and has implications for a wide range of issues in the workplace.[4] Generational tensions can substantially weaken workplace engagement and negatively impact turnover, career development, knowledge transfer, leadership effectiveness, and succession planning. Research has found that age differences at work can be related to increased levels of conflict. Shared life experiences (or even the perception of shared experiences) tend to create assumptions of common values and viewpoints among those in the same generation, but can also create distance between different age groups, leading to conflicts that can be tricky to manage.[5]

With the addition of Gen Z to the workplace generational mix, the growing workplace tension that was reinvigorated by Millennials stands to become even more intense. According to Mike North, a professor at the Stern School of Business, "Generational tensions clearly foster more discrimination, and vice versa. The main difference [is that] the perception of generational tension appears to be greater than at any point in recent memory."[6] The forces will continue to rise unless action is taken to deter them.

GENTELLIGENCE ROADBLOCK #2: AGE BIASES

Ageism appears to be one of the last socially acceptable biases, with people of all ages freely using age and generational identity as a form of insult. Today, biases around other types of difference such as gender and race are most definitely taboo, but biases around age and generation seem to be freely and openly tolerated, whether it be an off-handed comment regarding a Boomer's lack of tech savvy or a broad-brush characterization of Millennials' entitlement. According to Libby DeLana, co-founder/creative director of strategic creative agency Mechanica,

> Despite growing mindfulness around the importance of diversity and inclusion in the workplace, one very toxic form of discrimination is often left out of the conversation: ageism. From recent graduates who are "too young to have an opinion," to those who are "too old to be innovative," ageism in the advertising industry is pervasive. It's damaging to both the people within our agencies, and the work we put out.[7]

We are in no way insinuating that discrimination by gender, race, sexual orientation, religion, or any other category is eradicated. One only needs to watch the news for a few short minutes to see national cases where people are discriminated against for one of these categories in some part of their life. Rather, we are struck by how ageism in the workplace seems to be more widely accepted and tolerated when compared to other types of discrimination. While ageist attitudes seem to lack the social stigma of other kinds of bias, the effects of all types of workplace discrimination have been widely documented, and the consequences include a negative atmosphere and decreased employee productivity.[8]

Like other forms of bias, ageism exists in varying degrees and at all levels of awareness. It can be direct and blatant, such as denying someone a position based on their age, or more subtle, such a snide comment suggesting someone is less capable, innovative, or credible based on their age or generational identity. According to Harvard's Project Implicit, "An explicit stereotype is the kind that you deliberately think about and report. An implicit stereotype is one that is relatively inaccessible to conscious awareness and/or control."[9] For example, an implicit bias can be a stereotype that characterizes older workers as less adaptable to change, which would influence decisions regarding their work assignments, promotions, and other opportunities. Even though it may not be explicit, this type of discrimination is just as (if not more) damaging. Whether it be a stereotype or a "harmless joke," all forms of age bias are dangerous and unproductive. The remaining portion of this section will look at ageism and reverse ageism in the workplace.

Ageism in the Workplace toward Older People

Brian Reid, an engineer at Google, was fired in 2004 after being told by members of the organization that he wasn't a "cultural fit" and that he was "too old to matter." Reid was only in his early fifties at the time, and he subsequently sued Google for age discrimination. The Supreme Court of California ruled in favor of Reid, setting precedent that even off-the-cuff ageist remarks can be used as evidence for age bias in the workplace.[10] Creating a workplace that fosters intergenerational cooperation is impossible as long as age discrimination exists.

Age discrimination is most often thought of as a threat to older workers, and there are many common biases about older workers that researchers have found exist in the workplace. Such common labels include being rigid, averse to change, less motivated, harder to train, and tech resistant. A survey on age perceptions in the workplace found that more than half of Millennials, for example, believe that older workers are too rigid or set in their ways, while 44 percent think they aren't as skilled with technology, and 36 percent believe older workers are less interested in training than their younger colleagues.[11]

Surprisingly, these kinds of negative perceptions are not just a matter of younger people being biased against older people. Research has also found that *older* individuals are the most likely to hold negative attitudes about other older people.[12] While the reasons for this phenomenon are not yet clear, researchers suspect it may be that older workers are keenly aware of the ageist views that exist in their organizations and take on these attitudes as a way to fit in.[13]

For every perceived bias about older workers, there's corresponding research that invalidates it. For example, it's trendy to lament Boomer dinosaurs and their unwillingness to use social media along with their fumbling, unhip lack of digital savvy. However, research has found Boomers to be just as technologically capable as younger workers but without the natural confidence in those skills that are second nature to younger employees.[14] Boomers also tend to view technology as a tool and a means to an end rather than a constant part of their lifestyle. As such, they may not be up to speed on the latest tech but can hold their own among workplace mainstays such as Microsoft Word and PowerPoint. Though the stereotypes about older workers are largely unfounded, their impact can be profound. Research has found that even the use of the term *Baby Boomer* promoted discrimination.[15] Recently, as many as two-thirds of workers between ages forty-five and seventy-four indicated that they have experienced age discrimination at work, suggesting that Brian Reid, the engineer at Google, is not alone in his experience.[16]

Ageism in the Workplace toward Younger People

True or false: In the United States, all employees are protected from age-based discrimination in the workplace. The answer is *false*. According to the federal Age Discrimination Employment Act of 1967, only those *over* the age of forty are considered a protected class. In practical terms, this means age discrimination against anyone over forty in any employment decision is prohibited, but there are no federal legal protections for anyone *under* forty. Not only does this make for an excellent exam question in my "Introduction to Management" course, but it also generates disbelief and outrage when those students realize this law wasn't designed to protect them.

Ageism is often assumed to apply exclusively to discrimination against older workers. While the term *ageism* was originally used only to refer to prejudice against older people, it technically refers to bias against *anyone* based on age. A Gen Z employee, therefore, can be a victim of ageism just as a Traditional or Baby Boomer can. Ageist attitudes about younger generations are widespread and can be just as damaging. A study published in the *Human Resource Management Journal* found that discrimination for being too young is at least as prevalent as discrimination for being too old,[17] and reports have found that over 75 percent of hiring managers see younger employees as less reliable than older employees.[18]

Notably, even those over forty lack protection if they feel someone older is being favored in the workplace based on more advanced age: In 2004, a U.S. Supreme Court case known as *General Dynamics Land Systems Inc. v. Cline* took on the question of whether even those over forty could claim they had been discriminated against in favor of a colleague older than themselves. The final ruling declared that even those over forty could not claim this as age discrimination, meaning, "The Supreme Court held that statutorily protected workers older than 40 may not file an ADEA claim alleging that their employer discriminated against them in favor of older employees."[19] The Court observed that "if Congress had been worrying about protecting the younger against the older, it would not likely have ignored everyone under forty."[20]

With no current federal U.S. legislation protecting workers under the age of forty (or even for those over forty who claim that they have been discriminated against in favor of an older colleague) from discrimination based on age, younger workers don't have any formal protection from ageism. This arrangement leaves reverse age bias tolerance and policy largely up to individual states and individual organizations. For example, Michigan, Minnesota, New Jersey, and Oregon have all passed laws preventing age discrimination for those under forty. In Maryland, all age discrimination in employment decisions is prohibited, regardless of the age of the person in question.[21] The wisdom of formally protecting only the older members of our workforce from age-based discrimination remains a topic of debate.

While there is little in the way of protections for younger workers, when it comes to stereotypes about younger workers, there are quite a few. Younger employees have been labeled as disloyal, entitled, narcissistic, selfish, demanding of praise, unable to handle criticism, disrespectful of authority, and lazy, among others. Research has found a majority of Boomers believe that younger workers feel more entitled, while just under half think that younger workers "are not as professional in an office."[22] What Gen Z and Millennials themselves may see as proactive behavior is often seen by those in older generations as entitled. Since they entered the workforce, the view that Millennials are lazy seems to have persisted, despite little to no evidence to support this. Because Millennials are more outspoken than prior generations about what they want from work, especially when it comes to jobs that align with their interests and skills,[23] this is often interpreted by older colleagues as an unwillingness to do work that doesn't fit that vision.

A 2016 report by the Society for Human Resource Management explains:

> Stereotypes about Millennials often lead to misinterpretations about this cohort. Their confidence and idealistic and ambitious outlook are frequently mistaken for arrogance and egotism. Given today's advancements, Millennials may be achieving milestones more quickly than their generational counterparts and, therefore, less willing to stay put for extensive periods of time without promotion. Arguably a bit impatient, Millennials are, in reality, eager to contribute and want to be involved, but their attitude is repeatedly frowned upon.[24]

Who wants to stay in an organization where their desire to contribute is "frowned upon"?

GENTELLIGENCE ROADBLOCK #3: VALUE PERCEPTIONS

Gentelligence requires balancing two realities; failing to do so is a barrier to unlocking its potential. First, even those who grew up during remarkably different periods of time share several fundamental values, and second, generational identities can sometimes give us unique and different perspectives on behaviors. While these may seem like mutually exclusive claims, we assure you they are not.

The good news is that despite what many people believe, we actually have a number of values that are *shared* across generations. These areas of value similarity can set the stage for building Gentelligent workplaces, as they demonstrate that in the end, we are all more alike than we are different. Four workplace values have been found to span all generational boundaries: (1) respect: a desire to feel valued and vital to the organization; (2) competence: being perceived as knowledgeable and skilled; (3) connection: collaborating with colleagues and experiencing mutual trust; and (4) autonomy: having the freedom and independence to exercise judgment and make sound decisions.[25] While people of all ages tend to share these core values, they may end up expressing those values in ways that other generations may not recognize or understand.

1. *Respect:* Consider a Millennial employee and her Baby Boomer colleague. Both want to meaningfully contribute to their company. However, the Baby Boomer (having begun her career during a time when organizations were more hierarchical) may believe respect comes from paying one's dues and putting in the time to eventually earn a position that will allow one to enact change in the organization. The Millennial, growing up in an era when parenting styles favored protecting children's self-esteem and affirming how children were each unique and special, might believe that speaking out and challenging the status quo early on is the most impactful way to earn respect. Both employees want to be seen as adding value to their company but may have very different ideas of how that looks.
2. *Competence:* While a Gen Xer and a Millennial both want to be seen as skilled and knowledgeable employees, the way they seek validation of competence might manifest quite differently. Gen X was the first generation that grew up after both the civil rights era and the women's liberation movement, resulting in a sharp increase of single-parent families as well as dual-career families among this cohort. These circumstances led to a higher level of independence in Gen X than in prior generations; thus, a Gen X employee may believe that being granted freedom in her work is the most important signifier of her competence. A Millennial employee also cares about being seen as capable but grew up with continual feedback and reinforcement from her teachers and parents. As such, the Millennial employee may seek out higher levels of affirmation and approval of her work as validation of her competence.

3. *Connection:* While the value of connection is shared, the definition across generations may be different. A Baby Boomer may define *connection* as having an open-door policy for her direct reports or making a point to know some key facts about her colleagues that help her strike up a conversation during a lunch or company social event. While a Gen Z employee may also appreciate these behaviors, connection for her may mean utilizing multiple channels to interact with her coworkers even when she isn't at work. She may connect with a new team member on LinkedIn as well as share her cell phone number, opening up numerous ways to communicate. The Gen Zer may freely send work-related texts to a colleague after work hours and expect a quick response. For younger generations, connection may mean a level of informality that is uncomfortable for older generations. Nevertheless, all employees are striving for connection, even though they go about it in different ways.
4. *Autonomy:* No one likes to be micromanaged, so perhaps autonomy as a generationally shared value is not much of a surprise. For this example, let's consider the Gen X employee, from a cohort with more two-parent working families and less parental oversight, and a Millennial employee who grew up as the center of their family's life. Watching their Boomer parents work long hours and dedicate themselves to their companies led many Gen Xers to shift to more of a "work to live" attitude (as compared to the "live to work" philosophy that was popular among the Boomer generation). As such, our Gen X employee might define *autonomy* as having flexibility in her work/life balance and having ownership over her time. In contrast, our Millennial employee is a member of the most highly scheduled generation, growing up at a time when parents were dedicated to investing significant resources into the interests and potential of their children. For many, this situation meant extensive lessons after school, athletic games on the weekends, and structured playdates to make friends. This lack of free time and increased involvement of so-called "helicopter parents" resulted in Millennials being much

less comfortable with self-direction than their Gen X predecessors. Therefore, our Millennial employee may very much value autonomy but may seek more assurance and direction than a Gen X employee before feeling comfortable enough to act independently.

These examples all illustrate how generationally shared values may manifest in slightly different ways and impact work-related attitudes and behaviors. At the core, we share many common values, and with a bit of work, we can develop a greater understanding of how these values may show up differently in our colleagues across generations. While understanding shared values is essential, it is also vital to appreciate the different values that researchers have found salient across generations.

Dr. Jean Twenge, author of *Generation Me* and *iGen*, has identified several value differences between older and younger generations. Older employees view work as more central to life as compared to younger employees; they also possess a stronger self-reported work ethic. In contrast, younger employees put a stronger value on leisure time as well as individuality in the workplace.[26] These are important value differences that can clarify cohort-related priorities, but even these supported differences need to be carefully considered to avoid risks of stereotyping.

For example, although younger employees self-report valuing leisure more than older ones, this does not necessarily equate to a reluctance to work hard. Recent research[27] has examined the workaholic tendencies of young Millennials and their risk for early career burnout, which directly counters the long-held assumption that this generation is lazy. Alarm bells have sounded about Millennials being afraid of taking lunch breaks or sick days in order to prove themselves to their leaders. While Boomers may assume "valuing leisure" means sitting on the beach or taking a nap, *leisure* may be defined by Millennials or Gen Zers as having time to exercise after dinner, with plans to work afterward until late at night. Constant access to technology has created the ability to be continuously connected to work (for better or worse), and for a younger employee, *leisure* may mean being able to work on a presentation from their couch rather than from a cubicle. In other words, even when we consider research-validated generational differences in values, we must be careful not to make assumptions about how those value differences might translate at work and manifest within the individual employee. Failing to both understand and appreciate the shared values and meaningful differences that exist between each generational cohort obstructs any attempt to create Gentelligent workplace environments within our organizations.

GENTELLIGENCE ROADBLOCK #4: KNOWLEDGE RELEVANCE

In 2007, Facebook CEO Mark Zuckerberg famously said, "Young people are just smarter."[28] The quote hit a nerve, unleashing a debate about the kinds of knowledge twenty-first-century businesses need most. Did the wisdom of youth now trump decades of experience? In his article "Why Ageism Never Gets Old," journalist Tad Friend captures this phenomenon:

> This sharp shift in the age of authority derives from increasingly rapid technological change. In the nineteen-twenties, an engineer's "half-life of knowledge"—the time it took for half of his expertise to become obsolete—was thirty-five years. In the nineteen-sixties, it was a decade. Now it's five years at most, and, for a software engineer, less than three. Traditionally, you needed decades in coding or engineering to launch a successful startup: William Shockley was forty-five when he established Fairchild Semiconductor, in 1955. But change begets faster change: Larry Page and Sergey Brin were twenty-five when they started Google, in 1998; Mark Zuckerberg was nineteen when he created Facebook, in 2004.[29]

This shifting dynamic has bred tension between generations, as it threatens our shared core values of competence and respect. If the rules of the game are changing, does someone have to lose?

Once again, generations have found themselves locked into that fixed-pie mindset, believing that if one generation has highly valued expertise, the other clearly cannot. Unproductive competition and generational struggle create invisible barriers between generations and prevent any knowledge from being exchanged between the age cohorts. The missing variable in this standoff is the acknowledgment that even in the twenty-first century, different kinds of knowledge are needed for organizational success.

The truth is that Mark Zuckerberg should have known better when he made that comment. By working with Sheryl Sandberg, someone from a different generation with years of experience leading multiple organizations, he has seen firsthand that older people are every bit as smart, just sometimes in different fields. Many of these kinds of expertise complement each other—a new, revolutionary idea from a Gen Z employee still needs to receive feedback and navigate the organizational landscape to have its intended impact. Sophie Nachemson-Ekwall, a researcher at the Stockholm School of Economics, enjoys partnering with age-diverse individuals on projects, explaining, "I know I have to listen to the youth to understand how they see the world. They don't always have the knowledge or the experience to do something 'productive' with what they see but combined with my knowledge and experience, I know we can create something new together."[30]

Knowledge in the workplace can take many shapes. There are five different types of knowledge that can be valuable to an organization: *know-what*, *know-how*, *know-when*, *know-why*, and *know-whom*. *Know-what* is considered declarative knowledge, related to facts or information. *Know-how* is procedural in nature, giving us insight into method or approach. *Know-when* is also called conditional knowledge, or insight as to when the timing is right to use certain skills or facts. *Know-why* provides insight and reasoning into causes and explanations. Finally, *know-whom* is a relational kind of knowledge that focuses on insight into communication and connection.[31]

This framework is useful in understanding how a range of knowledge may show up in different ways for employees across generations and how they can be used together productively. In table 3.1, we have provided additional examples of the ways both older and younger workers may contribute to all of these types of knowledge.[32]

Table 3.1. Application of Knowledge by Age Groups

Types of Knowledge	*Older Workers*	*Younger Workers*
Know-What	Job-specific knowledge of older and retiring workers; knowledge about the industry, customers, and products and services	Digital and technological knowledge of emerging tools and trends
Know-How	Knowledge that is needed to perform well at a given task, such as problem-solving skills as well as social and communicative competencies	Digital native natural technology skills, talents at social media, advanced views on diversity
Know-When	Organizational culture and red tape, timelines, and the general functioning of the organization	Awareness and adaptability to change
Know-Why	Knowledge about the development of and reasoning behind existing organizational processes and systems	Ability to match new solutions to existing business challenges
Know-Whom	Awareness of organizational politics, internal and external social networks	Extensive virtual social networks with broader global and cross-industry reach

By realizing the importance of different forms of insight, one kind of knowledge can start to be seen as a complement rather than a threat to the importance of any other. This opens the doors for intergenerational knowledge exchange.

Airbnb executive and author Chip Conley has popularized the concept of a modern elder, suggesting that older generations can exchange their emotional intelligence for the digital intelligence more inherent to younger employees. He argues that now more than ever, older generations can play a crucial role in organizations if they are empowered to do so, bringing mentorship and wisdom to younger employees. While younger generations are hungry to disrupt and innovate, Conley speaks to the power modern elders have in providing deep and necessary organizational knowledge to these younger employees, giving them context that explains the current realities.

Regardless of age, people differ in their willingness to share and transfer their knowledge. Failing to consider these differences in motivation might result in the loss of valuable insights currently hidden in a generationally diverse workforce. Some older employees are highly motivated to mentor younger colleagues, and others are more protective of their accumulated expertise and wisdom. While it's tempting to get out that broad brush and paint all older workers as natural sages and willing mentors, research shows that some are more comfortable with that role than others. In his popular TED talk "Good Leaders Make People Feel Safe," Simon Sinek argues that leaders and organizations must create feelings of security and appreciation for their employees and cultures to facilitate mutual wisdom and idea sharing in the workplace.[33]

If older workers feel threatened and undervalued by younger ones, they will be far less likely to share their vast organizational wisdom in the latter stages of their careers. Baby Boomers are now eligible to retire at a rate of ten thousand employees per day. This situation means vast amounts of organizational experience stand to be lost if leaders do not encourage the passing down and transfer of certain kinds of vital knowledge. Once it is gone, it cannot be replaced. Recognizing the need for generationally positive atmospheres in the workplace is also needed for younger workers to be willing and interested in transferring their unique knowledge, as well as for them to be open to learning what older generations have to teach.

In his book *Originals*, Adam Grant discusses the idea of young geniuses and old masters. While young prodigies and twenty-year-old entrepreneurs tend to be more newsworthy, Grant highlights important creative value that older employees contribute.[34] For example, older employees submit more and higher-quality ideas to suggestion boxes (which raises the question of whether younger employees are paying as much attention to "suggestion boxes" as they might to newer ways of collecting feedback). Many famous artists, scientists, and other great thinkers contributed their greatest work in the latter part of their careers. Just as important, there are extensive examples of young entrepreneurs and innovators who have disrupted industries with their new ways of thinking. Gentelligence acknowledges and appreciates the value of a young genius and an old master (and everything in between) but is particularly interested in what happens when the two sit down at a table and share ideas together.

With no end in sight to the impact generational differences are making in our workplaces, it's time to change how we are viewing this disruption, moving our perception from one of a threat to one of immense opportunity for growth, innovation, and learning. With a clear set of best practices to follow, we believe Gentelligence can improve how organizations approach talent strategy, fundamentally shift the dynamics of teamwork, change how we define *leadership*, and transform capabilities to navigate change for the future of work.

4

The Gentelligence Solution

Four Key Practices

The question is not what you look at, but what you see.

—Henry David Thoreau

Let's return to the year 1974. Baby Boomers were then the dominant generation in the United States, overwhelming any other with a staggering 78.8 million members.[1] A sociologist and American media studies instructor at New York University named Jib Fowles (who was not a Baby Boomer but a member of the Traditional generation) penned an article for a little-known magazine named *Futures*. In his article, he described a persistent human tendency he called *chronocentrism*: the belief that "one's times are paramount, that other periods pale in comparison."[2] Inherent in this belief, journalist Tom Standage later explained, is "the egotism that one's own generation is poised on the very cusp of history."[3] While Fowles's term caught on in small circles, it never quite took off, but now might be the right moment to return to it.

Gentelligence, or the deep understanding and appreciation for the value in meaningful differences between generations, is the antithesis of chronocentrism. Every era of history has important value, as do the perspectives of those born and coming of age during those periods. Chronocentrism, like any other kind of bias, is dangerous and stems from the idea of ethnocentrism, or the sense that our way of doing things is the right one and superior to others. Discounting a different generation as wrong simply because it is not our own is misguided and suggests the damaging and unproductive "us versus them" mentality that can damage our relationships and organizations long term. Contrary to chronocentrism, Gentelligence champions *every* generation and is born from intergenerational curiosity. It is a belief that prevails over the sense that one way of doing things is the right or only way; it is the product of two broad goals that can, if achieved, unlock immense human potential.

THE GOALS OF GENTELLIGENCE

Gentelligence is the result of achieving two broad goals: the first is to *break down* the barriers of generational tension and bias, and the second is to *build up* the capacity to leverage intergenerational strength and power. The first goal focuses on eliminating existing biases, including the roadblocks of generational shaming, age bias and stereotypes, value perceptions, and knowledge relevance discussed in the previous chapter. These mental roadblocks can result in a competitive mindset, resulting in a view that operates from a perception of scarcity. Those who cling to this perspective tend to be defensive, not wanting to consider the input of other age cohorts. This belief also leads to lack of interest in sharing knowledge or resources and a general unwillingness to help those older or younger to succeed. Ultimately, the barriers of generational tension and bias limit the vision of what is possible by casting colleagues as generational adversaries. To move companies forward, these roadblocks of bias and misunderstanding must be eliminated.

Once the breaking down of barriers is accomplished, the focus can turn to *building up* the capacity to leverage intergenerational strength and power. To do so, organizations must actively focus on creating cohesion and cooperation across generations.[4] To realize the potential in generational diversity in the workplace, employees of all ages must believe that they have more to gain than lose by partnering with those across generational gaps. This task demands that organizations devote resources and attention to strengthen the abilities and potential of those

TEXTBOX 4.1

THE FOUR PRACTICES OF GENTELLIGENCE

To break down barriers of intergenerational tension and bias:

1. Resist Assumptions
2. Adjust the Lens

To build up the capacity to leverage intergenerational strength and power:

3. Strengthen Trust
4. Expand the Pie

from all generations and create opportunities for mutual learning and benefit. Ultimately, the successful transfer of knowledge and insight from older to younger, and vice versa, requires a *specific set of best practices* designed to minimize conflict and encourage collaboration between generations.

We have developed four key practices (as seen in textbox 4.1) to help achieve the broad goals of Gentelligence: Resist Assumptions, Adjust the Lens, Strengthen Trust, and Expand the Pie. Breaking down biases can be accomplished through Resisting Assumptions and Adjusting the Lens, whereas the building up of intergenerational power is the result of Strengthening Trust and Expanding the Pie. By using these four practices, Gentelligence can be established at all levels of an organization.

GENTELLIGENCE PHASE I: BREAK DOWN BARRIERS

We have already discussed several roadblocks that stand in the way of seeing generational diversity as a source of strength and opportunity. Recognizing these biases and misunderstandings, and actively taking steps to dissolve them, is a critical first step in becoming Gentelligent. There are two essential practices needed to help break down such generational barriers: Resist Assumptions and Adjust the Lens.

Gentelligence Practice #1: Resist Assumptions

To begin breaking down the bias and misunderstanding that currently exist between generations, it is essential to consciously Resist Assumptions. Resisting Assumptions means pushing back against human tendencies to draw automatic connections based on stereotypes about someone's generational identity. While this may seem straightforward, most assumptions are made at an unconscious level, meaning most people may not even realize they are falling into the habit. As a result, preventing them can be difficult. Assumptions are a part of human nature (and a kind of unconscious bias) and help people process the mass amounts of information encountered in everyday life. In short, these automatic connections are a shortcut in decision making that allows us to draw conclusions about people based on their membership in particular groups. Furthermore, it is also true that our subconscious mind prefers familiarity over the unknown and any form of uncertainty. As Jib Fowles (the man who coined the term *chronocentrism*) would remind us, members of a particular generation carry with them a set of comfortable norms about what is "right," just as people do regarding, for example, their home culture. Associating what is familiar as "right" and what is unfamiliar as "wrong" is a deeply ingrained human tendency, and one that becomes evident when working with other generations.

As we've discussed already, ageism is one example of common biases standing in the way of becoming Gentelligent. One of the most dangerous parts of ageism is that it can operate without conscious awareness.[5] One might, for example, assume that all Baby Boomers hate change or that all Millennials are entitled. A scroll through daily headlines often reinforces these connections. For example, when the phrase "OK Boomer" began trending online in 2019, it soon was the title of hundreds of articles, perpetuating many negative stereotypes about

Boomers. The prevalence and popularity of this expression suggested an immediate linkage between being a Baby Boomer and being out of touch with current times. Similarly, the popular press has worked to make the term *Millennial* synonymous with *entitled* for over a decade, using "Generation Me" and the "Selfie Generation" as synonyms for this younger cohort. Each time one of these articles seems accurate or relatable to someone in real life, they push us toward conclusions about a person before developing a more complete picture. These automatic connections are trusted, and therefore any indications that suggest they may be incomplete or unfair are ignored.

Gentelligence requires an active effort to suspend such hasty judgments. To push back against these kinds of damaging conclusions and successfully Resist Assumptions regarding generational differences, several key strategies can be used to raise awareness (both our own and those around us) and become more conscious of judgments being made.

Strategies to Resist Assumptions

To break the habit of making automatic assumptions, it is necessary to pause and analyze what unconscious connections might be being made. When it comes to age or generational identity, is there an automatic assumption that the Baby Boomers in the office won't have innovative ideas? Is it assumed Gen X (slacker) employees won't be interested in putting in the extra work needed for a promotion? Are younger coworkers' ideas in meetings dismissed because they have fewer years under their belts? Recognizing, calling out, and replacing these assumptions is a first step in breaking down biases that prevent us from being more Gentelligent.

1. Conduct an Assumption Audit

To raise awareness of these unconscious biases, we suggest conducting a self-study throughout the day. When attending meetings, reading emails, or even in casual interactions around the office, pay attention internally to the automatic connections that might be occurring. Take notes on the connections being made. Notice what patterns begin to emerge over time—are certain thoughts more frequently associated with interactions with older or younger colleagues?

My work as a university professor has allowed me to regularly interact with those both younger and older than I am, and such regular interactions have proven invaluable in pushing back against generational stereotypes. By becoming aware of the automatic associations you're making, you can begin pushing back against your own generational stereotypes, as well as bringing attention to when others are making the same mistake. For example, when I do an industry workshop on leading across generations, it's common to hear older managers complain about how Millennial or Gen Z employees don't want to work hard. Every day I see evidence to the contrary, with my students taking on heavy course loads, part-time jobs, extensive extracurricular activities, and multiple internships to learn as well as expand their career opportunities.

My role also allows me a forum to push back against stereotypes in the other direction. Students often enter my classes with preconceived ideas about the "old-school nature" of the decisions made at our university or in their internships, convinced that older people in charge are not open to new or different ways for things to be done. Whenever possible, I try to pause to dig deeper, helping them to Resist Assumptions, by asking them to consider other possibilities and sharing my own experience.

When I provide these contrary examples as a way to call out assumptions that are being made, it prompts managers and students to think about why they make generalizations in the first place and helps us explore the challenges and hurdles people face when trying to collaborate effectively with coworkers from other generations. Raising awareness of automatic associations (ours and those we see from others) is a habit vital to master the first Gentelligence practice of Resisting Assumptions.

2. Replace Assumptions with Personal Connections

In her TED talk "The Danger of a Single Story," world-renowned author Chimamanda Ngozi Adichie states, "The problem with stereotypes is not that they are untrue, but that they are incomplete. They make one story become the only story."[6] To Resist Assumptions, we need to go beyond the "single story" that has been told regarding a particular generation. An effective strategy to accomplish this is to reach out to family members or friends who belong to different generations. Ask them what misperceptions exist about their generations and what they wish others understood. Also ask them for "untold" or forgotten stories about their generation to paint a dynamic picture that goes beyond the "single story."

Starting with the relative safety of family and friends is a low-risk way to realize our unconscious biases and automatic assumptions. From here, try to get to know younger or older colleagues at work on a one-on-one basis. Research shows that having personal familiarity with individuals is a powerful way to break down and reject the automatic assumptions we may otherwise be tempted to make. The more opportunities an organization has for intergenerational communication, the greater the likelihood that stereotypes can be successfully broken down.[7] It's human nature to gravitate toward people of similar age, limiting our opportunities to spend time with coworkers from other age cohorts, but by creating these relationships, you'll begin to replace assumptions about an age cohort with personal connections.

The importance of familiarity in breaking down bias was recently demonstrated in an *American Scientist* study titled "Scientists Who Selfie."[8] To break down a common stereotype that scientists are knowledgeable but not particularly warm or friendly, thousands of scientists uploaded selfies on social media with the hashtag #scientistswhoselfie, giving (smiling) faces to the unfamiliar and often-misunderstood world of science. Even this small action helped to broaden the perception of scientists, as every individual we know in any particular cohort makes it harder to broadly generalize about an entire group of people. In their book *The Gen Z Effect*, Thomas Koulopoulos and Dan Keldsen state, "Define community by your age, and the generational gap will be very wide. Define it through a deep understanding of people's interests and behaviors, and it will be far narrower."[9] Getting to know those older and younger can help shatter the single story about a generation and instead reveal valuable perspectives hidden among the people around us.

Gentelligence Practice #2: Adjust the Lens

Learning to Resist Assumptions is key to becoming Gentelligent, but it's just a first step to building our understanding. The next practice, Adjust the Lens, aims to better illuminate the intent behind the actions and behaviors of those from other generations. It is not meant to determine *which* workplace behaviors are acceptable as much as it is to understand *why* colleagues may behave in particular ways in the first place.

In many ways, generations simply represent a unique kind of cultural difference. Just as travel can bring challenges in correctly understanding language, norms, and behaviors, interacting and working productively with those from other generations can be similarly confusing. Imagine someone from the United States walking into a café in Italy. She enjoys a coffee and waits patiently for the server to bring the check. Minutes pass. The server walks by her table multiple times. Soon she becomes irritated that the server isn't dropping off the bill. After more time goes by, she begins to make assumptions about her server's behavior: he must dislike Americans; he's giving preferential treatment to local patrons. Eventually, the customer catches the waiter's eye and asks for the bill. The waiter brings it promptly. Now imagine an Italian tourist sitting down at a coffee shop in the United States. He orders his coffee, and before he can even take a sip, the server sets the bill on his table and rushes off to serve other customers. The Italian is offended. Is the server trying to rush him out of the café? Is he not welcome to sit and enjoy the coffee?

This is a common scenario of misunderstanding and frustration for most people who have traveled abroad. In both cases, the travelers are interpreting the behavior of their servers using their own cultural norms and preferences. In Italy, as with most places in Europe, it is typically considered rude to bring the bill before it has been requested. Food and drinks are often savored and enjoyed with friends and family for as long as one likes. Conversely, Americans tend to be much more rushed and expect the bill to be available whenever they are ready to leave. Servers often leave the check after the customer has ordered so it is there when they want it. Neither practice is wrong; they are just different.

While cultural intelligence is most often thought of in terms of interacting with those from different geographical regions, the concept has been used to help improve interactions across many kinds of differences.[10] When applied to generations, cultural intelligence means that the norms and behaviors of colleagues from other age cohorts could be better understood with a new frame of reference. Developing cultural intelligence involves having the drive, knowledge, and tools to more effectively interact and work with those different from ourselves.[11] Research shows that cultural intelligence is greatly needed when it comes to understanding those in other generations, with a startling one-third of research respondents reporting that they have been offended "often" or "a lot" by what someone from another generation does or says.[12] To enhance our understanding of others, we must apply actionable strategies to help Adjust the Lens to see more clearly where others may be coming from and increase our ability to relate to their experiences.

Strategies to Adjust the Lens

We have long known that the interest and ability to both understand and adapt when interacting with those from different global cultures is essential to developing business relationships and learning how to work together effectively. Researchers refer to this ability as "cultural strategic thinking" and argue that, over time, it can significantly improve our interactions with others.[13] The same kind of insight is needed when we are working to bridge generational divides.

1. Use the DIE Approach

The *Describe-Interpret-Explain* (DIE) exercise is often used when training employees to work abroad, but it can be used to develop the habit of Adjusting the Lens as well. It helps strengthen our ability to recognize subjective interpretations (assumptions) to objective behaviors and consider other explanations (lenses) for the actions of others.[14] In the example of the Italian server, it would look something like this:

- *Describe* the behavior: The server isn't bringing the check, even though I have been done eating for quite a while.
- Note the automatic *interpretation*: He is ignoring me because this restaurant doesn't like Americans.
- Consider alternative *evaluations* for what is being experienced: Maybe I need to signal the waiter and specifically ask for the bill. Now that I look around, no one else seems to have their checks brought without requesting them either.

Now let's apply the DIE pattern to a common workplace behavior that causes generational conflict:

- *Describe* the behavior: Olivia is pulling out her laptop and typing, even though we are having a team meeting right now.
- Note the automatic *interpretation*: She's being rude. She isn't paying attention to what's going on and is probably working on something else instead.
- Consider alternative *evaluations* for what is being experienced: She does seem to be engaged in the meeting—she's asking questions and offering input. She seems to type when others are talking. Maybe she's taking notes to use later.

By working to better understand the intentions behind the actions of others, miscommunication and misunderstanding are far less likely to occur. Using the DIE exercise regularly can help strengthen the habit of Adjusting the Lens, replacing the ingrained tendency to use only our own norms as a frame of reference.

2. Understand the Disconnect

Working to Adjust the Lens represents a personal motivation to understand those who are different from ourselves and to discover what might currently be misunderstood between them and us. It is easy to lack awareness that our own behaviors and preferences are confusing or frustrating to others, as they make perfect sense to us. One effective strategy is to gather a group of colleagues of mixed ages and generations together to discuss everyday workplace actions and behaviors that trigger different associations depending on age cohort. Consider the following actions, and individually write down what your typical initial reaction would be to each:

- Typing on a laptop during a presentation
- Insisting on hardcopy documents
- Receiving a work-related text from a colleague after hours
- Leaving a voicemail rather than sending an email
- Questioning the decision of a manager
- Insisting on keeping personal pictures of family and friends on the desk

After individually recording the responses, share those reactions within the group. Without commenting, pay attention to the places where reactions to everyday actions are notably different. These are all actions that are neither inherently "good" nor "bad" but tend to be evaluated differently across generations. Some of these disagreements may not follow generational divides, while others may clearly reveal a split between older and younger colleagues.

After reactions have been revealed and recorded, there is still more work to do.

Adjusting the Lens involves going further to explore the intent and meaning of others' actions by asking questions. The goal is to understand the underlying "why" behind the initial responses that were split among generational divides. For example, in the case of the colleague insisting on hardcopies of documents, asking him why this is his preference can reveal important insight beyond the initial assumption that "he isn't comfortable with technology." Pose a simple, nonaccusatory question: "Jim, I noticed you have a preference for printed documents versus electronic ones. Why do you think that's the case?" Many people, regardless of their age or comfort with technology, find that reading hardcopy documents allows them to focus more without distractions that can occur when working on a computer (including the lure of incoming emails), resulting in better-quality feedback or reactions to the materials being shared.

This strategy of asking questions nudges colleagues to think more deeply about interpretations being made by themselves as well as others. Cultivating a habit of asking questions regarding actions or attitudes that differ from our own can develop intergenerational curiosity and can also help us create a set of shared norms through a better understanding of why particular preferences exist. The example below is relatively long but provides deep insight into the power of Adjusting the Lens and represents one of the most valuable and rewarding experiences I have had as a generational consultant to date.

A few years ago, I was conducting a Gentelligence workshop with a group of emergency department physicians and nurses. They had reached out to better understand the many ways Millennials had turned the healthcare industry upside down, from patients who seemed to expect a higher degree of customer service during their emergency room visits to doctors and nurses who were pushing back on the long-standing expectations to work nights and holidays and for extended shifts. The nursing director who originally contacted me summed up these challenges by stating, "This is an emergency department. I'm not sure what they thought they were signing up for, but this is how we do it here."

After our initial discussion about Gentelligence, I divided the crowd up into smaller groups and passed out some common workplace scenarios. Each group was instructed to read them aloud and talk about how each member would likely react. The examples include calling a supervisor by a first name, engaging in a conversation with colleagues about salaries, opting to work at home, and taking out a laptop during a meeting—all common workplace situations that can produce different reactions across generations.

One group was discussing the scenario of a colleague pulling out a laptop during a meeting, and the conversation turned quickly to Gen Z and Millennial patients using their cell phones in the exam room while they were meeting with doctors and nurses. I eavesdropped on the table's exchange. When we came back together as a large group, I asked them to share what they had discussed.

One of the women at the table (a Baby Boomer) began, "It drives me crazy. Millennials take out their phones and don't pay attention when we are trying to talk with them about important things—their diagnosis, instructions for aftercare. It's just disrespectful."

I stopped her. "Okay, I think we can all agree young people are frequently on their phones. But why are you assuming that means they aren't paying attention?" She looked at me, surprised by the question, and contemplated her answer. To her, those things automatically went together. But is that necessarily the case? I asked the group, "Can anyone think of something a patient (Millennial or not) might be doing on their phone that might be *helpful* to the situation?"

A hand shot up in the back of the room. It was another nurse (who also happened to be a Millennial): "They could be taking notes on the conversation on their notes app on their phone, so they don't forget the instructions." More hands were raised: "They could be checking the hours of the nearest pharmacy." "Texting their roommate to let them know they were contagious." "Texting their parents or significant other to give them an update on their diagnosis." "Googling their condition."

I returned to the table that had started the conversation. Admittedly, some patients might be disrespectful and inattentive to the doctors and nurses by being distracted by their phones, but there did seem to be other possibilities that were equally valid. I then asked the group what other challenges the tech-savvy Gen Z and Millennials had brought to the healthcare field. One gentleman at a table in the front of the room spoke up: "WebMD. I hate WebMD."

I asked him to tell me more. "Young people come into the exam room already sure they know what is wrong with them because they've spent twenty minutes on the Internet. I spent nine years in medical school, and they are sure they know more than I do. It drives me crazy."

A hand went up in the back of the room. It was an emergency room doctor (also a Millennial): "I love when my patients have been on WebMD and tell me what they think is wrong with them. It helps me know where to start in terms of explaining my decision making. Most patients come in thinking they know what's wrong with them—Millennials are just more likely to tell you their opinion. I'd rather know their assumptions from the beginning, so I can engage them in the discussion and help them understand why I have come to a potentially different conclusion than they did." This was a perspective many in the audience had not considered before and was a powerful example of our second Gentelligence practice. I stepped back and let the conversations among colleagues continue. This was an opportunity to witness the impact of Adjusting the Lens unfold.

GENTELLIGENCE PHASE II: BUILD UP INTERGENERATIONAL POWER

When it comes to generational relations, there are two schools of thought: one that believes competition between generations is inevitable, and another that alternatively believes generational cooperation will lead to greater benefits for all involved. A person's mindset is an essential factor and plays a critical role in the outcome of generational cooperation. The competitive belief will never result in Gentelligence, while the cooperative one is truly crucial to its success.

According to the management journal *Academy of Management Review*, "A distinguishing element of intergenerational interactions lies in the potential for transmitting skills, knowledge, experiences, and resources that one generation develops in virtue of its location in a chronological order. However, the successful transfer of these resources across generations cannot be taken for granted."[15] Once steps have been taken to break down the barriers, age diversity must then be proactively leveraged for mutual advantage. When this happens, such generational diversity can benefit productivity and improve outcomes. To accomplish these goals, we must learn and master both practices in phase II of creating a Gentelligent organization: Strengthen Trust and Expand the Pie.

Gentelligence Practice #3: Strengthen Trust

To help others understand the importance of team trust, I often ask them to think about a favorite toy from childhood. Maybe it was Legos or a favorite doll (the answers alone can reveal some great generational differences among coworkers; I once had a Gen X workshop participant say her favorite childhood toy was a Monchhichi, much to the confusion of her Millennial and Gen Z coworkers). When heading to a friend's house, we had to decide whether we would take that beloved toy with us to share with them. If our friend understood how much it meant to us, he or she was careful with it, and together we might have had even more fun playing with it than we would have alone. But if instead our friend smashed our Lego creation or dropped our Monchhichi on its head, that was probably the last time we took those toys over to share. In other words, we want to make sure our workplace is one where people are confident they can share their valuable perspectives without fear of having them stomped all over.

The third Gentelligence principle, Strengthen Trust, is vital to helping people at all levels in an organization see the potential in depending on and collaborating with those across the perceived generation gap. When we work with people we perceive as being different from ourselves (generationally or otherwise), we tend to view them as adversaries whose ways of doing things threaten our own goals and survival rather than seeing them as dependable partners. Ultimately, teams composed of members who view themselves as different in incompatible ways (such as Baby Boomers with a great deal of organizational experience and Gen Zers with very little) struggle with building mutual trust and respect. Older generations may have a difficult time believing that younger employees have enough experience or insight to fully understand organizational challenges. Younger generations may wonder whether older colleagues are serving the best interests of the future of the organization, or if they are offering advice instead in defense of self-preservation and protecting the old ways of doing things.

Trust stems from positive expectations about someone's actions: believing that what they say and do will be in the best interest of everyone involved, including ourselves. Demographic differences often create fault lines within a team that naturally form around similar characteristics such as age.[16] As a result, when it comes to working with colleagues from other generations, trust between generations does not come naturally, which is why leaders must intentionally invest in developing it within their teams and organizations.

I hear these concerns again and again in my workshops: "Why in the world should I listen to some twenty-five-year-old kid who knows nothing about our business?" or "What they are saying might have worked twenty years ago, but it's not going to work today!" These negative attitudes signal doubt that others have something valuable to offer. As Cornell professor Michele Williams states, "When people believe that they are not trusted or think that they are under evaluative scrutiny, they dedicate time to ruminating over this lack of trust and are more likely to interpret ambiguous behaviors as sinister acts."[17] When a member of the team holds such beliefs, that individual may become increasingly wary of any action taken by a teammate, further eroding those relationships.

Therefore, trust is vital for teams to flourish. Not only does a high level of trust positively correlate with team performance and satisfaction, but it's also linked to lower levels of stress and better problem solving.[18] To foster and strengthen this feeling, it's necessary to believe our colleagues don't mean us harm. While older and younger employees often sense they are striving for scarce resources in the workplace, including opportunities, attention, and recognition, strategies can be deployed to navigate these roadblocks and proactively Strengthen Trust.

Strategies to Strengthen Trust

Using the strategies below, leaders can create environments where employees across age groups can learn to depend on one another. By providing specific opportunities for employees from different age cohorts to spend time together in the context of accomplishing a shared task, colleagues of different generations can connect beyond the surface level and discover the different complementary strengths they bring to the table.[19]

1. Measure and Build an Intergenerational Psychological Safety Zone

To Strengthen Trust between colleagues across generations, organizations must develop what Harvard professor Amy Edmondson calls *psychological safety*, defined as "a climate in which people are comfortable being and expressing themselves."[20] To Strengthen Trust, we suggest first measuring the current levels of psychological safety in the team, department, or organization to obtain a baseline and snapshot of the current reality. One valuable open source for these tools is Google's re:Work website, which provides customizable surveys on psychological safety, as well as other important team dynamics. Sample survey questions are also available to begin creating such a measure, including items that employees from different generations may find particularly relevant. Examples of such survey questions include "People on this team sometimes reject others for being different" and "Working with members of this team, my unique skills and talents are valued and utilized."[21] Psychological safety comes from feeling comfortable sharing ideas and perspectives and believing they will be fairly considered.

While the first goal of this strategy is to obtain a current-state snapshot of trust and safety levels in the organization (and how those may differ by generation), there's more to be done when the baseline has been created. Once this snapshot has been taken, the group-level results should be shared with all involved as a way to encourage further discussions and open up the conversation regarding the importance of an environment where everyone, regardless of age, feels comfortable and confident to contribute. Building strong psychological safety is vital for sparking innovation and encouraging risk taking, and it can drive higher levels of performance for everyone on the team.[22]

I experienced a powerful example of this early in my career. I joined the Department of Management faculty at Miami University at the age of twenty-six. After introductions at our first department meeting, one of the senior faculty turned to me and the other new junior professor joining the department and said, "We want you to know that this is not a place where we only care about the input of the older members of the department. Please speak up with any ideas or perspectives you have—they are important to us, and we want to hear what you have to say."

While I'm not sure he would even remember saying it, his comment had a profound impact on my confidence to contribute to discussions and decisions from the very beginning of my time at the university. He was a well-respected member of the department, and his message was important for both the younger and the older faculty, as it clearly signaled what kind of culture we wanted to have: one of mutual respect, regardless of age or tenure.

2. Establishing Shared Goals and Complementary Roles

Leaders are powerful change agents when it comes to modeling desired behaviors, and when they show interest in working collaboratively across generational boundaries, it begins to create a norm and an example for others to follow. To continue to Strengthen Trust, we suggest building initial levels of trust by engaging in deeper-level discussion on shared goals and complementary roles. The Gallup Organization suggests asking four specific questions to move these conversations forward and strengthen a culture of trust[23]:

- What can we count on each other for?
- What is our team's purpose?
- What is the reputation we aspire to have?
- What do we need to do differently to achieve that reputation and fulfill our purpose?

This strategy requires leaders to serve the role as facilitator, grounding the discussions in the challenges at hand and helping build agreement on a collective goal. The subsequent discussion aims to generate the widest range of ideas possible and exchange information within the team.

Once a shared goal has been established, discussions around complementary roles can then occur. The aim of this process is to raise awareness of how each person's individual knowledge and expertise can allow them to add unique value and play a vital role. It's vital during this stage to be careful to avoid the pull of generational stereotypes. (This means not automatically assigning social media responsibilities to the Gen Z team member or delegating client interaction exclusively to the oldest team members on the assumption that they are most comfortable or well suited for that role.)

Rather, the leader should ask who feels most adept or prepared for particular roles, allowing the rest of the team to hear why each person is stepping up for different tasks. Hearing that an older colleague has a great deal of experience interacting with start-ups or that a younger coworker has recently completed a class on a new analytic technique can demonstrate what value others can bring to the collaboration. Some of the skills may exist in spite of generational identity, and other values may thrive because of it.

Whether it's role modeling from leadership that demonstrates that the organization values the input of employees at all levels across generations or a formal strategic commitment to leveraging age diversity to meet the company's goals, workplaces must convey that intergenerational cooperation is both expected and in the best interest of the organization.

Intergenerational power can only be unlocked once a strong foundation of mutual respect and rapport spanning across generational boundaries occurs. By showing support for and interest in members' skills and knowledge (regardless of generation), leaders can initiate the development of the trust that is needed for Gentelligence.

Gentelligence Practice #4: Expand the Pie

There's an amusing T-shirt slogan that states, "Equal rights for others do not mean fewer rights for you. It's not pie." It is on this note we introduce the last of the Gentelligence practices: Expanding the Pie. It's a term we shamelessly swiped from the field of negotiations, which uses it to describe two parties creating a win-win solution from what was previously seen as a win-lose situation. To do this (in negotiations or anywhere), we must resist the notion that we are competing with one another and instead trust that effective collaboration might produce more pie for everyone involved. And who doesn't like more pie?

According to negotiation expert Max Bazerman, "The mythical fixed pie mindset leads us to interpret most competitive situations as purely win-lose. For those who recognize opportunities to grow the pie of value through mutually beneficial trade-offs between issues, situations can become win-win."[24] By encouraging two-way knowledge sharing and balancing the natural strengths of one generation against the weaknesses of others, organizations can frame problems through a collaborative focus on collective success. Ultimately, successfully Expanding the Pie requires cooperation and reciprocity, as well as a belief that we can build something greater together than any generation is capable of on their own.

Strategies to Expand the Pie

To Expand the Pie, it's important to cultivate the habit of proactively searching for those win-win opportunities. In other words, there must be a way to identify opportunities where a gain for one person might also mean a gain for another. At first, both older and younger employees may be skeptical that such opportunities exist, but we have found that once people experience the benefits of such an interaction, they are eager to seek out ways to create that synergy again.

1. Focus on Interests for Mutual Gain

One effective strategy for this search comes again from the area of negotiations: focus on interests rather than on positions.[25] For example, if a younger employee tells her older boss that she feels like she is stuck in her current role, and her more senior boss responds by pointing out the company timelines for promotion, both are focusing on their individual positions that seem to have no common ground and are headed toward a stalemate. To change this dynamic, each person should shift to share the *interest* behind their position.

The younger employee could instead say, "I really want to learn as much as I can during these first few years of my job. I feel like there is so much I don't know yet." The result? This reveals to her older boss that she is less concerned about getting a promotion and more interested in opportunities to grow her experience and knowledge about the business. In turn, her boss could respond, "I'd love to teach you more about the way some of these areas of the business function, so when the time comes, you are ready to take the next step." In other words, the boss is happy to teach her younger employee now that she understands her employee's primary interest is to learn as much as she can, and, in fact, the boss enjoys passing on her knowledge. Focusing on interests allows people from different generations (who may be more likely to misinterpret one another's positions) to find common ground for mutual benefit.

2. Encourage Intergenerational Learning: The "Ask Me About" Exercise

To further Expand the Pie, we recommend the strategy of trying an easy icebreaker designed to create a conversation about areas of unique expertise, known as the "Ask Me About" exercise. This activity prompts each person (ideally in a room of organizational colleagues from across departments, levels, and ages) to identify a unique kind of expertise they possess and welcome others to ask them about. While valuable for intergenerational learning, this approach can be a great way to reveal different kinds of knowledge than what we tend to associate with a generation.

There are two ways this exercise can be done. One option is to leave the instructions wide open (if so, expect to learn that Bob from Accounting has tried all the flavors of Ben & Jerry's and Janet from HR is an amateur magician). The other option is to guide the discussion toward more work-relevant expertise. Because our goal is to build trust and encourage learning across the organization, we recommend following up on the sharing of areas of expertise with a discussion question: *How might sharing this expertise help our organization?*

I used the "Ask Me About" exercise in one of my recent workshops. Within the first half hour, everyone learned that one employee could teach how to double one's Twitter followers in less than a week, another employee had a tried-and-true technique to close even the toughest sale, and yet another enjoyed doing virtual-reality programming in her spare time. While the technique to close a sale, for example, might seem like a fun party trick, the opportunity to hear about his method ended up Expanding the Pie: several workshop participants asked whether the employee would share his technique with them, many of whom were younger employees still developing their sales skills. Furthermore, the exchange made the man who had mentioned it feel respected and needed by his younger colleagues. By the end of the session, they had set up a time to meet later in the week over coffee to hear his approach.

The "Ask Me About" exercise can lead to all kinds of unexpected win-win opportunities. While some organizations might discover that one of their own could help them double their Twitter followers, helping fill a need for greater outreach and communication, other companies may be anxious to pick the brain of the newly discovered virtual reality expert as they work to understand how such technology might benefit their business. At a minimum, everyone in the room can appreciate the wealth of interests and expertise around them, and in the best-case scenario, it exposes new opportunities for intergenerational learning and collaboration that will strengthen relationships and lead to organizational growth.

A more formal, long-term version of the "Ask Me About" exercise can occur by creating a living database within your organization that allows employees to identify their areas of strength and expertise. The European Agency for Safety and Health recommends creating a catalog of skills and experiences across employees of all ages as a tool to promote knowledge transfer.[26] Such a resource highlights the unique experiences and abilities of employees at all levels, and it also signals their interest and willingness to share their expertise with others interested in learning from them. This can be a transformative workplace investment that can continue to reveal opportunities for intergenerational learning and win-win collaborations.

HOW GENTELLIGENCE ENABLES LASTING ORGANIZATIONAL SUCCESS

Together, the four practices of Gentelligence can move individuals and organizations from a generational battle toward intergenerational cooperation, an approach to work and life that views each generation as equally important. Striving to bring together different age cohorts builds respect, promotes understanding, and encourages mutual learning.[27] By creating habits to Resist Assumptions, Adjust the Lens, Strengthen Trust, and Expand the Pie, leaders and organizations can transform their multigenerational talent into a strategic competitive advantage, by minimizing conflict and maximizing the potential for collaboration and growth.

Subsequent chapters will explore further how to build and apply these Gentelligence practices across all aspects of work. We demonstrate proof of concept and share stories of leaders across industries who use these strategies to tackle current challenges in filling the leadership pipeline and enabling effective intergenerational leadership, creating strong teams, attracting and retaining top talent, and transforming organizational cultures. Beyond this, we discuss how a Gentelligent approach can help prepare organizations to succeed in the future of work.

5

Filling the Pipeline

Leading Up (and Down)

Leadership and learning are indispensable to each other.

—John F. Kennedy[1]

Mark Zuckerberg is everyone's go-to example for the changing age of leadership. Kylie Jenner was named the youngest self-made billionaire by *Forbes* in 2019. Evan Spiegel, the founder of Snapchat, made his first billion at age twenty-one. At age forty-five, Stefan Larsen had already served as CEO of the Ralph Lauren Corporation, global president of Old Navy, and then as head of the parent company of Calvin Klein and Tommy Hilfiger. Those leaders are impressive, no question. But our favorite *wunderkinds* make that group appear wrinkled in comparison: Mikaila Ulmer, CEO of Me & the Bees Lemonade, made an $11 million deal with Whole Foods when she was just eleven years old; Shubham Banerjee invented an affordable 3D braille printer and became CEO of Braigo Labs at age thirteen; Moziah Bridges of Mo's Bows launched his company at age twelve and recently landed a seven-figure licensing arrangement with the NBA for his bespoke bow ties.

These examples make it easy to conclude that the future of leadership now belongs only to the young. Taking a closer look, the story of age and leadership is less clear. Despite great examples of innovative young leadership, the average age of a CEO in the United States is *increasing*, climbing from forty-five in 2012 to fifty years old in 2017.[2] Leadership responsibilities are not universally transferred to the young and hip, nor are they solely held by the older and more seasoned. Regardless, perceptions of age do impact leadership dynamics in many important ways. Research has found that age cues, or the assumptions about someone based on their age, influence how we view them as leaders. According to *Leadership Quarterly*, "Age is one of the most basic and easily accessible cues of face perception. It can be assessed fairly accurately at first glance, and it has major consequences for a range of social goals such as collaboration, competition, leadership, and successful organizational behavior at large."[3] To become Gentelligent leaders (and followers), we have to acknowledge the reality and the attitudes that exist around age and leadership.

Years ago, when I was a young faculty member, I found myself in a committee meeting where we were making decisions about which applicant to hire to teach a class. All of the final candidates had come in to teach a short sample class, and one in particular impressed us all. It seemed like a clear choice to me, but then one of the committee members commented, "I just wish he looked older."

He didn't say, "I wish he *was* older." He said, "I wish he *looked* older." I found this comment both horrifying and fascinating, and I couldn't help asking out loud why his appearance mattered. My colleague replied, "I just don't think our students will see him as an authority figure. He looks about eighteen." Now, perhaps because I was about twenty-six at the time (and was mistaken for a student myself at least once a week), I took personal issue with the statement. Was I viewed as less of an authority figure because I was much younger than many of my colleagues? Probably so. But by whom? Only by students? By my coworkers? My boss? Questions abounded.

Did my students (early Millennials at that time) factor in age when considering whether they should listen to someone? I doubted it. I could see age cues mattering more in prior generations but found it hard to believe that my Millennial students were equating advanced age with expertise or respect. Many of them felt confident in their *own* knowledge and expertise at their young age, and I suspected they would take even more of an issue than I had with the comment about someone needing to look older to convey authority.

I honestly believed that although my youth, and that of our job candidate, might initially have given some of our students pause, once we demonstrated our competence and expertise, whether we looked like the stereotypical professor would cease to matter. Yet hearing an older colleague express concern that looking young could undermine one's perceived authority opened my eyes to the importance of age cues in the workplace and also introduced me to the generational differences that exist in the importance we assign to one's age.

The importance society has traditionally placed on age cues can be traced back to the days when tribes had to decide who they should follow in order to survive.[4] When seeking out a safe place to shelter or deciding how to protect themselves from the threat of predators, the older members of the tribe had more experience, and following them seemed like a more reliable bet. However, younger members of the tribe had more energy and were more willing to take risks, meaning followers looked to them if the challenge was about where to explore or ways to invent something new. A wrong choice about leadership had dire consequences. Research published in *Leadership Quarterly* in 2014 summed it up as follows: "[F]ollowers prefer younger faces for leadership in the context of change, and older faces in the context of stability."[5] Historically, who we chose to follow depended on what challenges we faced: Did we need to stay put and use our resources in a wise and time-tested way? Or did we need to make a change and seek out something new to survive?

THE EVOLVING NATURE OF ORGANIZATIONAL LEADERSHIP

As the world has changed, advanced age (or the appearance of it) continues to be a reliable cue for some types of experience. However, it is now a less reliable proxy for others, mainly the types of digital and technological knowledge that younger generations have grown up with that older generations have had to intentionally master later in life. For example, the advent of the internet has forever changed the way we find information and whom we need to rely on to access it. My students no longer need me to be their sole source of information in the classroom—they can Google the answer to any question they might have faster than they can ask and receive a response from me. As a result, age alone is no longer the reliable cue to determine who has access to the needed expertise that it once used to be.[6]

Faced with unprecedented and even unknown challenges, leadership in the twenty-first century belongs to every generation. Conventional norms about who should lead and when are being challenged at every turn, with recent data revealing that at least 40 percent of employees report to a boss who is younger than they are. This phenomenon is known as "leapfrogging"—when younger individuals jump over those older to assume an organizational leadership role.[7] Two factors can explain this role reversal.

The first factor is the staggering number of Millennials paired with the relatively low amount of Gen Xers in the workplace. In 2016, Millennials took over as the largest generation in the workplace,[8] while Gen X has always paled in comparison to both Boomers and Millennials, often referred to as the "sandwich generation" or the "middle child." As these labels imply, Gen Xers are stuck between two generational giants and overshadowed by the attention and interest in both. There are simply not enough Gen Xers to replace retiring Boomer leaders, even if it were just a numbers game. In March 2019, the *Washington Post* cautioned, "In many industries, employers also face significant uncertainty as to who or what will replace a retiring Boomer."[9]

The second factor contributing to the new leapfrogging leadership phenomenon is rooted in generational reputations. As we've discussed, those Gen Xers grew up witnessing the long hours and steadfast organizational loyalty of their Boomer parents, leading to an increased interest in making their own rules and living life on their own terms.

The Boomers viewed Gen Xers' desire for independence as a sign that they were going to be succeeded by a generation of slackers, which has resulted in Boomers perceiving that Gen X won't want to lead once they exit. For some Gen Xers, this assessment is accurate; fewer people in this generation equate leadership positions and status with success to the same degree that prior generations did. Yet for other Gen Xers, being independent might result in a desire for leadership roles, allowing them to write their own rules and foster a different kind of organizational culture. Unfortunately, the long-standing reputation of Gen Xers may preclude their consideration for open leadership roles. Gen Xers' promotion rates have been 20–30 percent slower than Millennials'. The latest data show that Gen Xers hold about half of the leadership roles in the United States, which should arguably be much higher given that this cohort is currently in the mid to latter stages of its working life.[10]

In contrast, the Millennials, long labeled as entitled and hungry for advancement, are perceived as eager to jump into leadership roles as soon as they have the green light. This generation took on internships to gain experience before graduating from college, with many feeling ready to lead from their first day in the office. Millennials were raised with a strong emphasis on the importance of completing higher levels of education and an increased emphasis on internships during their college years, leading to the potential for this generation to "feasibly rise to positions of power in organizations more quickly than others have in the past."[11] Fueling this trend is a substantial amount of media attention on Millennials, causing many companies to invest heavily in attracting and retaining this generation, including the invention of leadership-development rotations and programs designed to fast track Millennials into the advanced roles they supposedly crave.

This perfect storm of demographic and generational forces has changed the leadership dynamics in many organizations, a shift that has been called a "new organizational order" where more and more older employees are being led by younger ones.[12] Despite these changes, the fundamentals of effective leadership remain the same: leaders of any age must find ways to successfully establish leader-follower relationships on a foundation of mutual trust and credibility. Building this trust may require a different approach for those who oversee employees older than themselves as opposed to the more familiar dynamic of older leaders guiding younger workers. In all cases, the end goal is the same: regardless of age, leaders and followers need to work together to find ways to accomplish their goals. Gentelligence can create awareness of the strengths different generations may bring to leadership roles, as well as the unique challenges they might need to overcome.

THE LEADER-FOLLOWER DYNAMIC

For almost seventy-five years, researchers and managers alike have searched for the magic recipe for leadership success. Is it a set of certain personality traits? Specific behaviors that we can teach anyone who wants to lead? Both of those suggestions have proven too simple—there is not a one-size-fits-all approach to leading effectively. Successful leadership requires that one be *self-aware* enough to understand their strengths and weaknesses and *socially aware* enough to understand the strengths and weaknesses of their followers. Beyond this, effective leadership requires adapting one's approach to the needs of their followers and the environment in which they are leading. Understanding those needs has become much more complicated in a workplace filled with multiple generations.

Gentelligent leadership in the twenty-first century is about empowering followers from every generation to achieve something extraordinary together that cannot occur alone. Leader-follower trust can be further complicated by age, generation, and status. It is not uncommon for leaders to prefer people just like them as their followers, resulting in age polarization (as discussed in chapter 6). Those not part of our in-group (or "inner circle") find themselves on the sidelines, and over time, the lack of closeness with and attention from the leader tend to result in lower levels of satisfaction and performance and, in the worst cases, result in the employee leaving altogether. Gentelligent tools and

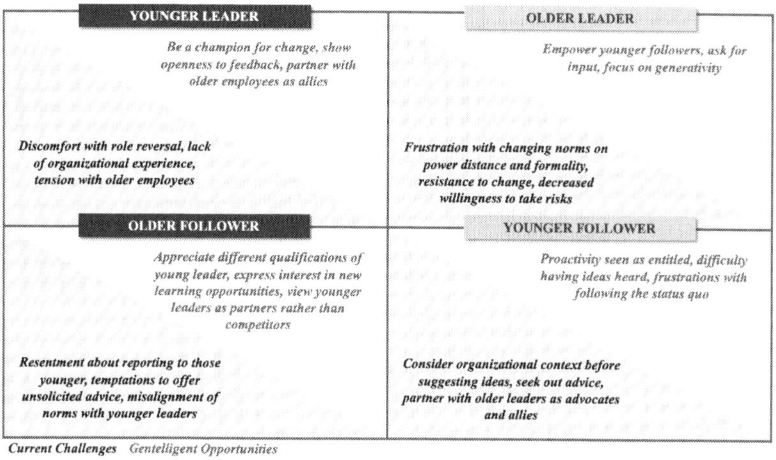
YOUNGER LEADER
Be a champion for change, show openness to feedback, partner with older employees as allies
Discomfort with role reversal, lack of organizational experience, tension with older employees
OLDER LEADER
Empower younger followers, ask for input, focus on generativity
Frustration with changing norms on power distance and formality, resistance to change, decreased willingness to take risks
OLDER FOLLOWER
Appreciate different qualifications of young leader, express interest in new learning opportunities, view younger leaders as partners rather than competitors
Resentment about reporting to those younger, temptations to offer unsolicited advice, misalignment of norms with younger leaders
YOUNGER FOLLOWER
Proactivity seen as entitled, difficulty having ideas heard, frustrations with following the status quo
Consider organizational context before suggesting ideas, seek out advice, partner with older leaders as advocates and allies
Current Challenges
Gentelligent Opportunities
FIGURE 5.1.

strategies are needed to create the mutual trust necessary to overcome these kinds of natural biases that can occur between leaders and followers from different ages and generations.

We have identified two key relationships where Gentelligent strategies are now needed more than ever: the "Younger Leader–Older Follower" dynamic and the "Older Leader–Younger Follower" dynamic. In figure 5.1 and in the remainder of this chapter, we highlight the unique challenges that must be overcome for each of these roles, as well as the value-added opportunities that may be present for these pairings, providing advice for both leaders and followers navigating these complicated generational waters.

THE YOUNGER LEADER–OLDER FOLLOWER

Years ago, I was invited to speak at a board chairman's retreat. When I walked into the room, I realized that I was, by far, the youngest person there. The average age of the attendees was close to sixty-five, and I was in my late thirties. While everyone was polite, I sensed that many of them were wondering what in the world I could teach them about leadership; they had most likely held leadership roles before I was even born. Yet in that room, I *was* the expert on the particular leadership topic I was speaking about, and I was confident that I had interesting and valuable perspectives to share with them. My approach to speaking is always interactive, but in this particular case, I decided to engage the audience even more than usual. After my introduction, I immediately called out the elephant in the room by noting how many years of combined experience were in the place and letting them know how much I was looking forward to learning more about their industries. I gave them some background on my expertise and told them I wanted to hear how the issues and challenges we would be discussing were impacting their businesses. In other words, I invited them to partner with me in a shared learning experience, one that reflected my expertise but also respected theirs.

While this represents a success story, research has found that the outcomes of this particular leader-follower dynamic are often problematic.[13] Because the younger leader–older employee dynamic is a new phenomenon, its success requires a new approach. Below, we identify the unique challenges of leading those who are older and outline how the opportunities that exist in this dynamic can enable a younger leader to overcome these challenges.

The Younger Leader

For younger leaders who find themselves in charge of older colleagues, the role can feel awkward. Research in the journal *Human Resource Development Quarterly* summarized the tension by explaining,

> Older workers feel uncomfortable taking instructions from supervisors the same age as their children or grandchildren. Younger supervisors are reluctant to give orders to workers as old as their grandparents. Similarly, younger supervisors with older subordinates may contradict status and age norms that suggest older, more experienced supervisors should supervise younger, less experienced subordinates.[14]

The traditional workplace norm assumes that leadership belongs to the oldest and most experienced members of the organization, and the role reversal can initially be uncomfortable. By approaching this relationship through a Gentelligent perspective, young leaders can become more aware of the inherent challenges, as well as work toward proactive and constructive solutions.

The Current Challenges

The role of the younger leader who is guiding and managing employees who are older than them is daunting. Given this is a relatively new phenomenon, there hasn't been much of a roadmap provided in terms of potential pitfalls. If a Gen Xer learns his new manager is a Millennial, what baggage does that bring before that leader has a chance to even walk in the room? Any negative perceptions about a generation make it difficult for members of that cohort to earn workplace respect and credibility from their generationally different coworkers when stepping into leadership positions. These negative perceptions make it challenging for Millennials to earn the respect they crave from their generationally different coworkers.[15]

While research in this area is relatively new, early evidence shows that overcoming negative perceptions can be a challenge for a younger leader. Older workers often perceive younger leaders as not possessing the needed wisdom and experience. As a result, younger leaders believe older employees show them less loyalty and are less willing to make contributions.[16] The problematic perceptions don't end there. While effective leadership hinges on mutual trust, younger leaders lack the automatic confidence that older leaders often enjoy and find their judgment more often questioned. This skepticism also translates to younger leaders, particularly those under the age of thirty, not being perceived as role models.[17]

To Strengthen Trust, a leader must be authentic, and this is particularly true for young leaders. Authenticity requires a high degree of self-awareness. Part of this awareness requires identifying one's strengths, including how one earned this position of leadership. If a leader lacks self-assurance, her subordinates—especially those who are older—will lack confidence in their abilities. However, being confident is not the same as being cocky. Younger leaders often overcompensate for their age or inexperience by pretending to know more than they do, which can, in turn, create distrust and resentment among older employees.

The Gentelligent Opportunities

While the challenges can be daunting, the unique value younger leaders can bring to their role creates immense Gentelligence opportunities as well. Before things get too discouraging, keep in mind that particularly in today's business world, younger leaders possess a great deal of valuable insights that organizations desperately need. These opportunities can also be harnessed and become natural strengths that can be leveraged to overcome the challenges ahead.

Youth does bring with it a certain number of age cues and assumptions, some of which might work in a young leader's favor. When it comes to age cues and leadership perceptions, younger leaders are assumed to be innovative and energetic with a take-charge style. Younger bosses are believed to be more enjoyable to work with, more strategic, and more persuasive.[18]

Younger leaders tend to also embrace change, a critical talent in the rapidly evolving twenty-first-century business landscape. Their comparably shorter organizational tenure can become an asset in terms of challenging outdated processes and nudging the business ahead. Young leaders are more optimistic than older ones, for better or worse, and, as such, they tend to take on the crucial role of change champions and advocates for continuous improvement.[19]

Another critical opportunity for young leaders is to take advantage of feedback and ask for insight from colleagues as well as followers in areas where they may lack experience—something younger leaders are much more open to compared to older ones. Traditionally, older leaders believed that having a leadership role meant they were expected to know everything, or at least present the appearance of it. However, this notion that the leader knows all—and therefore knows best—is not an effective way to gain respect or motivate followers.

Brene Brown's groundbreaking research on vulnerability in leadership supports the impact of a leader admitting that he or she is aware of the areas where they need help and the power of being willing to ask for it.[20] Young leaders need to Resist Assumptions that their lack of years of experience is necessarily a weakness and instead view this as a vulnerability that can be a source of strength. Whether it's an issue such as lack of experience with a particular client or matter, or a general area where the leader would value input from someone with more organizational context, when a younger leader acknowledges what she does not yet know and communicates an openness to learning to her team, she creates openings for her employees to step up and help. Adjust the Lens to view your older employees as vital partners, not as followers. This strategy empowers them to be part of a shared vision rather than merely doing what they are told without investment in the process. Vulnerability is a powerful leadership tool regardless of age but especially important for younger leaders—it demonstrates to a team that their leader knows both her own limitations and the strengths of others.

To Expand the Pie, leaders need to focus on identifying team strengths. In the case of younger leaders with older employees, think about how the experience of older employees could be a valuable asset. Where might that knowledge and wisdom be valuable? When leaders acknowledge that older colleagues bring unique value to the team and ask them for help or advice that is genuinely needed, older employees can become valuable allies as well as more productive team members. Tobius Lucke, the thirty-seven-year-old founder and CEO of Shopify, says he directly told his board, "I am not going to pretend to know things I don't know, and I really hope you are going to help me in this journey."[21] While this approach may seem risky, the balance of confidence and authentic vulnerability creates a powerful leadership impact, especially for younger leaders.

The Older Follower

When someone with more experience learns that she will have a younger boss, it can hit a nerve and raise questions about process and fairness. The entire notion of being led by someone younger is known as "status incongruence," and it represents a violation of career norms that can be difficult, especially from the perspective of the older employee. Traditionally, status congruence is considered intact when the oldest members of an organization are paid the most and have the highest positions in the organizational chart. When this is not true, a feeling of status incongruence occurs, which can result in a wide range of potential difficulties in the workplace.

The Current Challenges

Research shows older employees working for younger bosses are more likely to report higher levels of anger and fear.[22] Questions often surface regarding the validity of a younger leader's readiness and qualifications to lead. According to research from *Human Resource Development Quarterly*, "Older subordinates with a younger supervisor often feel their supervisor does not have the knowledge, experience, or training to lead and mentor. Even when younger supervisors have advanced education, older subordinates believe they lack experience and, as a result, support them less."[23] This combination of doubt and negativity can breed resentment that becomes toxic to the leader-follower dynamic over time.

Adding to the challenges for older employees is the potential misalignment of preferred workplace norms in critical areas like communication channels, speed of response, and preferred levels of formality. While such differences are relevant regardless of whether an employee is older or younger than their leader, for an older employee needing to make a good impression on the boss, such differences need additional attention. Examples of such disconnects include preferred titles (calling your boss "Ms. Smith" when she prefers informality and would rather you call her Alison) and modes of communication (calling versus texting). Several unexpected generational conflicts tend to arise regarding speed and timing of expected response, especially in the younger leader–older follower dynamic. If a younger boss messages after regular work hours and expects an immediate response, older employees may react negatively, as they are often less comfortable with being contacted at home when they are "off the clock," particularly through something like a text message.

Regardless, any instances of misalignment such as these can create tension and frustration for both leader and follower. Addressing these issues head-on is vital. Working together to establish practical norms can go a long way to smoothing the road. Resist Assumptions that younger leaders will automatically prefer certain types of communication, and make it a point to ask them what they would prefer. While some may love the informality of texting or want all employees to embrace Slack for teamwork, some young leaders may prefer to pick up the phone for a quick call. Just as older employees don't want to be stereotyped as unwilling or unable to adapt to new ways of communicating, younger leaders run the gamut in their preferred methods of reaching out as well.

Finally, one of the most significant challenges for an older employee working for a younger leader is the temptation to offer unsolicited advice. While such input is usually well intentioned, having an employee provide his or her two cents on how a younger leader "should" handle an issue is likely to come across as condescending. While strong leaders (of any age) will reach out to their team for input, offering it without being asked lacks Gentelligence and suggests to the leader that they are not seen as capable in their role.

The Gentelligent Opportunities

Given the increasing frequency of the younger boss–older employee reality, what role can older employees play in changing this dysfunctional dynamic to one that is more productive? While the older employee may feel like it is not his or her job to help solve these challenges, keep in mind that doing so can be mutually beneficial for the performance and relationships of both the leader and the follower involved.

To seize the Gentelligent opportunities of this dynamic, first Resist Assumptions about why and how the younger boss obtained her leadership position, especially when those assumptions may lean toward presuming she doesn't deserve the role. While she may be leading at a younger age than was typical in the past, try to objectively evaluate the skills and talents that may have led to that decision. Adjusting the Lens in this kind of dynamic might mean considering the potential differences in pre-career and early career opportunities that the younger leader may have experienced, and how such experiences may have helped her develop and prepare for the current role. For example, multiple internship experiences during college have now become the norm for many students, allowing them to gain experience in their chosen field before they even graduate. Additionally, leadership-development programs have become popular only in the last decade, providing accelerated exposure to multiple areas of business during the first years of one's career. While such programs are not a substitute for years of organizational experience, they provide alternate ways to acquire essential knowledge and skills.

Another opportunity for older workers is to express interest in new learning opportunities. While organizations often invest resources into training for early career employees, less attention has traditionally been given to continuous learning for those in later stages of their careers. As we will discuss in chapter 7, reskilling and upskilling are becoming vital at all career stages. An older employee who is proactive in approaching their leader about ways to learn new skills and competencies will stand out as someone invested in continuous improvement.

Gentelligence can also help turn the younger boss–older worker dynamic into a powerful partnership. To Strengthen Trust, seasoned colleagues can share their experiences while being thoughtful about how and when to do so. A friendly offer to talk through a situation over coffee signals respect for a superior's role and a willingness to be helpful. Providing unsolicited advice in front of colleagues, in contrast, can come across as an attempt to undermine leadership, and too many trips down the organization's memory lane can start to feel like an unwelcome history lesson. To avoid coming across as stuck in the past, older followers should focus on supporting the organization as it moves into the future by productively empowering and helping the team and their leaders.

To Expand the Pie, think about the mutual benefits possible when an older employee views his younger boss as an ally rather than a threat. According to John Boitnott of *Entrepreneur* magazine,

> Both you and your manager have relevant knowledge that is more valuable when put together. You probably have accumulated wisdom from on the job experience, and your manager might have a fresh perspective or innovative new ideas. Together wisdom and innovation can form a valuable pair that propels both you and your manager to success.[24]

By focusing on the potential benefits of learning from a younger colleague, older employees can gain valuable skills to propel themselves to leadership positions of their own.

THE OLDER LEADER–YOUNGER FOLLOWER DYNAMIC

Several years ago, I conducted a workshop with a group of finance employees in Indiana. When I arrived for the event, the older gentleman who hired me met me at the door. He pulled me aside and said, "My biggest issue with these young people is that they all keep calling me by my first name. I never invited them to call me by my first name. Is this something you can fix?"

I'm reasonably confident that his young employees did not intend to be disrespectful. It seems unlikely they had gotten together and crafted a malicious plot to call him Bob when he preferred to be called Mr. Jones. However, Millennials have grown up with much less separation between themselves and authority figures than prior generations. Both Millennials and Gen Zers likely have had relationships throughout their lives with adults who encouraged them to call them by their first names. As such, these younger generations considered the informality acceptable and inoffensive. In contrast, the Indiana boss viewed this behavior as disrespectful, which affected his willingness to build relationships with these young employees. This mutual misunderstanding of generational norms and practices led to conflict and resentment within their organization. They needed some Gentelligence.

The Older Leader

Research shows that based on nothing more than a number, people are more likely to perceive an older leader as calm, collected, and even keeled, as well as more structured and more conservative than a younger leader. Older leaders are also assumed to be more cooperative, empathetic, and possessing greater respect for authority.[25] Yet there are assumptions around advanced age in leadership that can be considered barriers as well.

Traditionally, many firms have placed age limits on their top executives, suggesting that age can become a detriment to effective leadership at some point. According to Jeffrey Sonnenfeld, senior associate dean at the Yale School of Business, "We've reset the clock on the chronological age barriers in all sectors."[26] A majority of companies in the S&P 1500 require their CEOs to retire at age sixty-five, including General Electric and Intel.[27] However, fewer and fewer companies still adhere to this rule. In 2017, 3M eliminated the mandatory retirement age for its current CEO, and pharmaceutical company Merck eliminated its own in 2018. Companies cite many reasons for this mindset shift, including evolving perceptions about when people should retire.

The Current Challenges

Leadership has traditionally been the privilege of the oldest members of an organization, meaning it may seem counterintuitive that there are now new challenges to such a role. The oldest members of the workplace are today primarily Baby Boomers, who are bucking past organizational trends and remaining in their leadership roles (and their jobs overall) much longer than prior generations did. The increased longevity of Boomers, the impact of the Great Recession on their retirement accounts, and the high levels of importance they have placed on building their careers have combined to create a bit of a bottleneck in terms of the leadership pipeline, and not everyone is happy about it. This tension can create a challenge for older leaders.

Younger employees who desire leadership roles are frustrated by the Boomers' lack of interest in retiring, as they perceive them as wearing out their welcome. Gen Xers, Millennials, and Gen Z may also stereotype Boomer leaders as "coasting"—enjoying their paychecks and merely biding time until they decide to retire, rather than being necessary change agents or long-term visionaries. Baby Boomer leaders who are met with these kinds of assumptions from their followers may find themselves struggling to prove their commitment and interest in the long-term health and vitality of the organization.

Age barriers have changed, and so have the norms about what it means to lead. Boomers grew up in an age when holding positions of leadership meant you received unquestioned respect. But younger generations are less likely to listen to someone simply because they have a title, and this dynamic has led to many older leaders feeling frustrated by what they perceive as a lack of respect for authority and a lack of understanding of workplace norms. In today's multigenerational workforce, older leaders are challenged by younger workers who have differing workplace attitudes and norms, and these clashes can impact the ability to build necessary trust with their followers.

Through my own research, I found the same result. In a study I published in *Studies in Higher Education* in 2016, I dug into how individuals of different generations determined whether a leader was "credible." I found that regardless of generation, people considered competence and character relevant to overall leader credibility.[28] Competence comprises intelligence, training, and expertise, whereas character consists of honesty and trustworthiness.

Millennials, however, placed a significantly higher value than Gen X and Boomers on leader sociability (talkativeness, friendliness, and good nature) when determining whether a leader was credible. This finding means that younger employees may be more likely than older ones to view a leader's social interaction and willingness to personally connect with them as critical parts of whether they respect and trust a leader. Once again, this finding stems from the impact of the time in which Millennials were raised, including parental styles that promoted a more participative approach to family decisions, and the constant presence of technology that allowed for quick and endless amounts of feedback. As a result, Boomers may experience unexpected difficulties if they assume respect from younger colleagues is guaranteed based only on their leadership position.

Another challenge for older leaders is their own assumption that there's not much they have left to learn, especially from younger employees on their team. However, this presumption is just as dangerous from an older leader as it is from a younger employee, as it can prevent exposure to new ideas and lead to a resistance to change. Research in this area shows a negative relationship between CEO age and risk taking and innovation, which can be particularly damaging in today's rapidly changing business landscape.[29] Regardless of their years of experience, older leaders should be proactive in seeking out new learning opportunities.

The Gentelligent Opportunities

While older leaders likely have the upper hand in organizational experience, staying open to things they may not know or understand as well as younger colleagues can be a powerful leadership tool. It doesn't have to be as cliché as asking a younger employee how to use the latest social media—though I will admit this is how I learned to use Twitter and Instagram. Older leaders may be hesitant to ask for help directly, as doing so violates more traditional notions of leading. Instead, we suggest using one powerful question: "How would you do it?"

With this one question, leaders demonstrate their interest in new and different viewpoints, and respect for the ideas of their younger colleagues. Empowering younger employees signals enough confidence to share power and enough self-awareness to seek help where it's needed. Beyond all else, sharing power demonstrates valuing employees and trusting in their abilities. In turn, they begin to internalize that their leader is acting in their best interests and for the good of the business. At the very least, being willing to ask younger employees how they would approach tasks helps to Strengthen Trust and mutual respect. In the best cases, this approach strengthens the leader-follower relationship and Expands the Pie by creating innovative approaches to solving problems.

Younger generations value strong connections with their leaders, which can subsequently open up lines of communication to allow for two-way exchange and learning. After younger colleagues suggest ideas, leaders can ask them to think through potential challenges and offer suggestions. If the idea has merit, they can continue to work with the younger employee to strengthen its potential. Asking for input also allows the older leader to provide needed coaching and development that younger generations crave.

For example, take the situation of a Gen Z employee questioning his Gen X boss about a work assignment he was given. On the surface, it would be easy for the Gen X supervisor to interpret that behavior as insubordinate, entitled, or disrespectful, especially if that Gen Xer would never think to question her own boss when given a work assignment. However, after Resisting Assumptions, learning to Adjust the Lens allows the boss in this scenario to engage with her employee to better understand why he was asking the question.

To be more Gentelligent, the supervisor could say, "Tom, I asked you to enter this data for all of our accounts this month and send me a summary of the results. You've asked me repeatedly if this needs to be done each month. Help me understand your concerns." The phrase "help me understand" does not mean the boss is condoning her employee's actions; it means she is willing to take the time to explore the meaning behind Tom's statement. It might be that Tom shrugs, apologizes, and puts his head down to do what he was asked, suddenly realizing that regardless of whether he likes it, he needs to complete the work. Or imagine this response: "I know it's important we have these reports available whenever you need them. I was just wondering if it might work better if I created a program that automatically connected to our database, so we didn't have to enter the information manually every month. Then if you wanted the reports more often or needed them on a moment's notice for a client, I would be able to run them a lot faster for you."

Tom could have been lazy and thought he knew better than his boss, hoping to get out of the work he was being given, or he could have very much understood what his boss needed. In this case, his desire to be seen as competent and gain respect had generated an idea that he thought might be even more helpful to her and the company moving forward. By stopping to adjust her lens to consider the possibilities, Tom's boss demonstrated that she is open to understanding where he is coming from and showed Gentelligence. If she agreed with the intent of his actions but not necessarily the way they were communicated, she has now opened the door to coach and mentor him on a different way to get his ideas across.

Because many older leaders have decades of leadership experience and career success behind them, the purpose of their leadership can begin to evolve to become more about mentoring and developing others. Research in the journal of *Psychology and Aging* found that the key to success for older leaders was a phenomenon called "generativity." Generativity is leading to guide and develop members of a younger generation, with less focus on one's own gain from the relationship.[30] Research has shown that older leaders who practice generativity are considered more effective than those who do not. Younger employees expect more experienced leaders to be willing to mentor and share their wisdom.

The idea of generativity is also vital for older leaders in terms of pursuing their values of meaning and connection. Boomers can conceive of mentorship and their subordinates' development as ways to find continued meaning in their work and to connect with future generations of leaders. Studies have also shown that practicing generativity leads to stronger feelings of well-being and happiness. Dan McAdams, a professor of psychology at Northwestern University and the leading expert on generativity, says that it comes out of the desire of human beings to do good. McAdams believes the generative mindset is important for all: "I would say that one should not wait until the latter part of a career to be generative. I would say that it is a moral challenge as well. It involves deciding if you are going to live your life for trivial and selfish reasons or if you are going to try to make a positive difference in some way."[31]

For some leaders, moving to a generativity mindset may require a shift in priorities. During the latter part of their careers, leaders may find that personal career accomplishment is not as essential or motivating as it once was. Focusing on generativity will allow them to engage more effectively in their work and leadership roles with a renewed sense of purpose and meaning. According to Marc Freedman, author of *How to Live Forever: The Enduring Power of Connecting the Generations*, generativity has profound effects in "engagement with others that flows down the generational chain will make you healthier, happier, and likely longer-lived."[32] Rather than feeling that their careers are waning, older leaders should instead focus on how to pass along their valuable experience and organizational wisdom in a way that will strengthen their company and those who will someday be charged with its success.

The Younger Follower

Years ago, I conducted a workshop with eighteen- to twenty-one-year-old students to raise awareness on how managers were struggling to manage Millennials. I put up a few slides describing common scenarios we see these days in a university setting and asked them how they would react and respond. The first example involved taking an exam for a course that they felt was confusing and tricky and receiving a low grade. I asked what action they would take in that situation. Responses ranged from a few who suggested they would "go ask the professor how to better prepare for the next exam" to the overwhelmingly popular answers of "go to the professor's office and tell her the exam was confusing and tricky" or "see if I can negotiate for a better grade." I have personally seen all of those responses after a difficult exam. I asked them what they thought the professor's reaction might be to a student criticizing his or her test and received responses like "I think she would want to know! It's doing her a favor to tell her it's confusing!"

I paused, trying to process the responses. They weren't necessarily *wrong*, but they also weren't necessarily *correct*. Student participants were simply considering the scenario using the lens they had grown up with: *Go after what you want. Speak up—your voice matters.* However, I wondered if they realized that prior generations had not grown up believing they had the right to challenge authority (even respectfully). Did they know this behavior was new? That the professor they were going to see most likely would *never* have spoken up about a difficult exam when she was a student? Was that the right way? Not necessarily, but every generational cohort has its own sense of acceptable protocol. I asked that group of students what percentage of their parents they thought had challenged a professor or teacher about a grade when they were in school. They guessed 90 percent.

Many had never thought about it before, and when they did, they failed to Adjust the Lens and instead assumed prior generations were just like them. We had a great discussion on the shifting norms involving questioning authority, and many admitted to me afterward that they had never realized their behaviors were unique or considered how someone with a different life experience might interpret their actions. Now, this was a student sample, but every single one of those eighteen- to twenty-one-year-old participants is now someone's employee—a boss has replaced their professor.

The Current Challenges

Younger employees won't be surprised to have leaders who are older than they are. Still, Millennials and Gen Zers in particular may be surprised that an older leader can misinterpret their more proactive approaches to work as being entitled, pushy, or disrespectful. Because these younger generations have been raised to speak up and express their opinions and ideas to parents and teachers, these behaviors are not likely to switch off once they reach the workplace. However, for older leaders who believe it's important for an employee to pay his or her dues before being allowed input, this kind of bold behavior on the part of a young employee can trigger alarm bells.

This disconnect represents a significant challenge for young employees who are working on standing out and making a difference in the early days of their careers. They want to be heard and often feel their older bosses are uninterested or dismissive of them, leading to frustration and, in the worst cases, leading them to leave their organizations in the hope of finding a place where their voices will be heard. We also hear from older leaders who are taken aback at the "presumptuousness" of young employees, offering ideas and suggestions for better ways to approach work.

In other words, while younger generations are motivated by a strong drive to contribute and make an impact, they may risk stepping on the toes of older leaders in their quest to do so. What younger employees view as proactive behavior can be interpreted as entitlement by their older boss, and this kind of misunderstanding can erode relationships quickly. From the perspective of the employee, she may feel her input is not valued and that the company is not interested in engaging her in meaningful work. These are issues that are significant for younger generations and often lead them to start looking elsewhere for employment.

A related challenge for employees working for older leaders is feeling stifled by requirements to approach their work in ways those younger generations may feel are outdated or inefficient. For example, younger employees who have grown up being able to complete work from everywhere at any time may balk at the insistence of their older manager that they log a certain number of physical hours at their desk.

While this kind of "face time" has traditionally provided managers with the assurance that their employees are present and accounted for in terms of their commitment to work, younger employees may feel they are not as productive behind a desk in an office as they may be elsewhere. This requirement to do things the way they have always been done even when employees feel it is ineffective can erode the older leader–younger employee dynamic.

The Gentelligent Opportunities

Older leaders often feel the younger generations haven't taken the time to look into relevant organizational history and context before presenting new ideas. It's the same problem that many companies have with consultants coming in to fix a problem. How can we trust that these new or young people understand the specific situations at our organization? Gaining that context takes research and respect for what came before you. Regardless of age, it's essential to have respect and understanding of what has been done before. Consider Adjusting the Lens to ask *why* things are the way they are, rather than presuming that no one has thought of those ideas before. It very well may be the case that the ideas are novel and revolutionary, but it's tough to know that right out of the gate, and it's not wise to start with this presumption.

We have found more often than not that it's more of the *presumption* that's considered entitled than the *ideas* themselves. That's why it's crucial to do the homework. Talk to mentors and leaders, and ask about the history of a practice and what has been tried in the past. If those are productive conversations, it will demonstrate a level of interest in really making a substantive change. Refine thoughts and communicate with others before announcing an idea. Doing this goes a long way to Strengthen Trust and earn respect from older colleagues. Along the way, those people that have been consulted can potentially become advocates to help you move those ideas forward.

Let's imagine that a Gen Z employee has a new idea for how to handle company records more efficiently. Despite several emails and even popping her head into her boss's office to try to move this idea forward, her attempts have fallen flat. Her boss has been polite but not encouraging. Before casting blame on an older boss for not being receptive to new ideas, Gentelligence would suggest she stop and think more about why her manager might not be reacting to her thoughts in the way she hoped. When her boss was at her same career stage, what were the norms around younger employees giving unsolicited input? (If she isn't sure, reaching out to a mentor, family member, or friend who may be able to provide context can be helpful.)

Another key question to consider is what organizational history may already exist around the issue at hand. It's possible that her idea has been tried before or that there is a charged history around the topic that she isn't aware of given the brief amount of time she has been working for the company. Asking coworkers who have longer tenure at the organization may provide necessary background. Discovering what she doesn't know or understand can be key to not only gathering valuable context but also earning the buy-in of others.

Frustrated young employees can often interpret generational disconnects in norms and work attitudes as negative attributes to an organizational culture, leading them to consider finding other places to build their careers. Gentelligence requires a change in perspective and a realization that such disconnects are possible in any organization. Rather than seeing such roadblocks as a sign to immediately jump ship, finding ways to navigate these initial disconnects can be a much more productive and successful strategy for long-term success.

TOWARD GENTELLIGENT LEADERSHIP

Years ago, I had a participant in one of my workshops provide a deceptively simple definition of the word *leadership*. She defined it as "the process of getting people from point A to point B." I've returned to that definition again and again because it is both simple and complex. While a useful definition, it does not mention *how* leaders do this. Explaining *how* to be a productive leader is a critical component in effective leadership.

Gentelligence suggests that the "how" of effective leadership now requires a high degree of awareness of the role that age and generational dynamics may play in vital elements such as communication, learning, and decision making. Beyond this, both leaders and followers must practice Gentelligence to overcome the barriers of bias and misunderstanding that may erode trust and look to the unique opportunities inherent in a multigenerational leader-follower dynamic. Such opportunities take on a new dimension when they involve leading multigenerational teams, as we will explore in our next chapter.

6

The Secrets of Gentelligent Teams

None of us is as smart as all of us.

—*Ken Blanchard,* The One-Minute Manager[1]

This book is co-written by three people. Two of us are Millennials; one is a Gen Xer. While many of the stories are written in the first person, the work is the collective product of hundreds of hours of debate and discussion among three people with a sizable age gap between them. When I decided to write this book, I thought a lot about the best approach. It immediately became clear that writing a book about the power of intergenerational diversity by myself or with an author team of colleagues with similar ages and experiences would be hypocritical. So, despite a twenty-year age gap between myself and my two coauthors, we decided to give it a try. In the end, this book itself is a case study in the power of Gentelligence.

When looking at research on team diversity (other than age), the results tend to be positive. A recent analysis revealed that companies in the top quartile for ethnic and cultural diversity on their executive teams were more likely to experience above-average profitability.[2] However, to date, research on age-diverse workplace teams is scant, and the research that has been presented suggests a divided view of the potency of age-diverse teams within organizations. We strongly believe that intergenerational teams are an untapped source of this valuable cultural diversity within companies today. Deborah DeHaas, chief inclusion officer and national managing partner of Deloitte, commented on the opportunity to create intergenerational teams and increase age diversity in the workplace in an article published in the *Wall Street Journal* a few years ago: "There is a great and largely untapped opportunity for boards to seek younger directors to gain perspectives of a generation that is redefining technology, consumer preferences, business strategy, business models, and even business risk."[3]

Companies across industries are just beginning to implement programs that leverage the potential of age diversity to facilitate real intergenerational learning, creativity, and problem solving. By actively preparing for a generationally diverse workforce, organizations can ensure that age-diverse prospective employees are interested in their organizations. But how do they guarantee the same level of openness once these people become employees? By creating intergenerational teams to leverage the strengths of each member. But creating intergenerational teams by leveraging the principles of Gentelligence requires more than launching a new program; while it may seem simple, this task demands that we change how teamwork is executed daily, on every project, and in every team.

THE TEAM EFFECTIVENESS TRIFECTA

We have identified three key ingredients of effective team collaboration: support, structure, and significance. This trifecta of elements matters for *all* types of teams, regardless of age or field. They allow employees to feel secure in their contributions, clear in their direction, and valuable to the collective work of the group. These three elements push team members to take necessary risks, work efficiently toward shared goals, and realize the collective power of creating something together that could not be achieved by an individual.

Structure

Years ago, I was running a team workshop for a group of early career professionals. At the start of the day, I asked how many people enjoyed working in teams. One woman had a conflicted look on her face, tentatively raising her hand partway only to put it down again. I asked her what was behind the hesitation: "Well, I would like working in teams . . . if people would just do things the right way." Amused, I asked her what the "right way" was. As you might have guessed, she defined the "right way" as *her* way. This is one of the biggest hurdles to building effective teams: agreeing upon how members will work. Whether it's about when to meet, how to communicate, or what processes and deadlines to use, people cling to their own tried-and-true methods that work for them, and it would be wonderful if those techniques were exactly the same ones that worked for others on their team. Rarely is this the case, which then leads to frustration and sparring about whose way is the best way and who will eventually give ground in the interest of moving forward.

A well-structured team, in contrast, invests in developing a set of clear operating procedures, creating a scaffold to minimize confusion and mixed messages about how to collaborate. While the temptation may be to jump right into discussing ideas, teams that first establish *how* their members will work together end up saving themselves a lot of headaches down the road. Discussing individual roles, agreeing on how everyone will communicate (e.g., email, Slack, group texts), and setting up norms for decision making all create a clear path to and higher likelihood of team success.

Support

Successful teams are built on collective trust and a feeling of support from their members. As mentioned in chapter 4, psychological safety creates an environment that makes it easier for teammates to share ideas freely, take risks, and put in the time that is critical for teams to produce innovative, original work.[4] A revolutionary study done at

Google, known as Project Aristotle, found that the most effective teams had little to do with *who* was on the team. Instead, success was the product of *how* that team worked together. What factor was most directly tied to those effective teams? Psychological safety.[5]

Teams bring a kind of forced interdependence, raising questions about whether members can count on others and whether they want their successes tied to their colleagues' willingness to work hard. Because continuous, effective teamwork requires a more significant investment of time and energy than individual endeavors, team members need to believe that putting in the extra energy is going to benefit both the process and the performance. Coworkers need to be able to count on their team members to behave as dependable contributors. Therefore, dependability is a critical component of team effectiveness and signifies that team members will reliably deliver the work they promise to produce, on time, and at a high quality. The assurance that others are putting in similar degrees of effort and energy makes one's own investments seem worthwhile. In short, all members of the team need to feel like they are getting an emotional return on their investments.

Significance

We've established the universal need every employee has to be respected. Teamwork gives us a front-row seat to where others shine and where they are vulnerable in terms of knowledge, skills, and abilities. The team context also creates the possibility of getting lost in the crowd and that individual contributions won't be acknowledged or appreciated. The most productive teams find opportunities for all members to utilize their complementary talents and share leadership. By providing opportunities for teammates to contribute in their own way, the team builds what we call significance.

Significance represents the purpose people find in their work, allowing for the full and varied range of how individual team members may define this concept for themselves. Some may value the opportunity to speak for the team to an outside audience. Others may be energized by seeing their ideas brought to fruition through the collective effort of their colleagues. When teams give their members opportunities to contribute and develop in the areas of their interests, those coworkers become more invested in helping the overall team achieve its goals.

Believing one's contributions are impactful and seeing how teamwork matters to the organization are also essential to building significance. If employees feel that their roles are negligible or that teammates view them as replaceable, it undermines their internal motivation to put in the work required. Subsequently, the extra effort needed for a high-performance team may no longer seem worth it. As such, a team must understand how the work it is being asked to do fits into the bigger picture.

These elements of structure, support, and significance are vital for all teams. When it comes to diverse teams, and age-diverse teams in particular, there are a few more secrets to success we want to share. Today's workplace teams have greater age diversity than ever before, increasing the likelihood of intergenerational challenges while also Expanding the Pie with the possibility of innovative and transformative team collaborations.[6]

THE PARADOX OF INTERGENERATIONAL TEAMS

Diverse teams, in general, can be a bit of a double-edged sword. According to the *Harvard Business Review*, "Diverse teams are prone to dysfunction because the very differences that feed creativity and high performance can also create communication barriers."[7] Our promises throughout this book regarding the potential of age diversity, and now age-diverse teams, might sound idealistic to some, especially to those who have been frustrated with past intergenerational collaborations. In fact, existing research presents a divided view of the efficacy of age-diverse teams. Some of this research confirms what many reading this book may have already experienced: many age-diverse teams *aren't* successful. One explanation for this failure is that increased age diversity within teams can lead to more age discrimination, significant team conflict, and ambiguity in expectations and roles.[8] However, other research has shown the opposite effect due to increased perspectives, an extended pool of talent, and greater potential for creativity and innovation.[9] Ultimately, intergenerational teams are a paradox. They can be an utter disaster, *or* they can be a transformational breakthrough in the diversity of thought (or somewhere in between) depending on how these teams are led and managed.

To help steer the leadership of these teams in the right direction, we need to understand what drives this paradox. Underlying the dynamics of intergenerational teamwork is a phenomenon known as age polarization. This term describes peoples' preferences to associate with those who are similar in age. This concept stems from the idea of similarity-attraction, where people assume that those close to their own age will share attitudes, opinions, behaviors, and shared experiences; as a result, there is a comfortable familiarity in sticking to their age cohorts. In doing so, in-groups are naturally formed and become a source of ease, because people tend to interact with other in-group members regularly. People prefer their in-groups so much that they often distance themselves from those in the resulting out-group.

This tendency is deeply ingrained, particularly in American society. According to Dr. Elizabeth Lokon of the Scripps Gerontology Center at Miami University, multigenerational interaction used to be much more common. Over time, our societal structure has changed to become more segregated by age. Our schools divide people into age categories, and older adults are separated and often live together in retirement homes. As a result, people have gone from interacting with different age groups daily (we lived with our grandparents and attended school with students of many different ages) to rarely interacting with people from other generations. The long-term effect of this age segregation is in the subsequent inability to understand, relate to, and interact with people from different generations both in and beyond the workplace.[10] This separation means colleagues from different generations tend to lack regular interactions, which impedes their abilities to Strengthen Trust and Expand the Pie, and leads us back to that problematic us-versus-them dynamic that precludes Gentelligence.

INTERGENERATIONAL TEAM CHALLENGES

The secret to a successfully Gentelligent team, therefore, is to effectively reduce age polarization. Leaders can accomplish this task by proactively considering how the elements of structure, support, and significance can ensure that team members from different age cohorts interact in meaningful and constructive ways. Intergenerational teams must fully understand how to create effective team dynamics with Gentelligent tools and insights that allow colleagues to navigate the potential pitfalls of team generation gaps. To fully understand these dynamics, let's look at some common challenges of age-diverse teams.

Team Challenge #1: The Power Struggle

Power struggles play out in all aspects of our lives: between a parent and a child, across various political parties, among our organizations, and, of course, within teams. In our quest for significance, team members must recognize individual members' value and respect what they bring to the table. Jennifer Deal, a researcher at the Center for Creative Leadership, argues that most intergenerational struggles can be tied back to a concept known as *clout*, which represents power, authority, control, and position—all issues that are magnified when working in a team context.

According to Deal, "Most conflicts have to do with the natural desire of older people to maintain their clout and the desire of younger people to increase theirs. As organizations increasingly promote younger people over older people, elders naturally work to maintain the balance of power—in their favor—by appealing to their greater experience."[11] Consequently, instead of working together, the desire to maintain or acquire power divides teams. Separations between age cohorts can create subgroups within organizations (or age polarizations). Eventually, these dynamics trigger in-group/out-group behaviors, preventing psychological safety and trust from developing, dividing age cohorts from each other, and obstructing any chance for true collaboration. In some cases, this kind of age polarization can lead to conflict and age-based discrimination.[12]

These team dynamics are even more challenging in the context of the organizational change prevalent across companies that are preparing for the future of work. The perception that organizations have changed and are readying for a new, more technologically savvy workforce has left some Baby Boomers feeling that their previously secure positions might be imminently vulnerable. However, younger generations perceive the Baby Boomers staying longer in their jobs as obstacles to reaching their own full potential and advancing in rank. The natural response for both of these groups is to dig in their heels and stand firm, either asserting that experience is the most valuable asset or seeking a promotion because change is coming. In this generational sparring for clout and power, team trust and the essential element of support is damaged. Uncertainty and change increase the pressure on individuals and cause emotional stress among team members. Rather than Expanding the Pie, the us-versus-them mentality kicks in as a survival mechanism in the fight for relevance.

To address this counterproductive dynamic, leaders can proactively build the structure, support, and significance necessary for a successful intergenerational workplace. Before diving into a new team assignment, leaders can provide opportunities for teams to discover each contributor's strengths, how they add value to the team, and why no team member is replaceable. It is essential to emphasize why teamwork matters to the organization and why everyone on the team is vital to the desired outcome. Leaders should articulate how particular work fits into a broader context and overall organizational strategy. Team leaders should also work to create psychological safety.

As mentioned previously, creating psychological safety is essential for intergenerational teams to Strengthen Trust and do their best work. Aaron Hornbrook, customer service manager and vice president at

Wells Fargo, builds team safety by holding monthly meetings to bridge generational perspectives among his team members. According to Hornbrook, "These create opportunities to regularly bring together a diverse cross-section of team members to talk about a variety of workplace topics. It also serves a purpose that isn't obvious to most attendees. These meetings illuminate common ground when members of multiple generations can talk about their viewpoints or interpretations of the same issue."[13] As a leader, Hornbrook guides discussions and helps team members understand why one colleague might interpret the same thing differently from another. As a result, the contributions of all intergenerational members are viewed as equally valid, reducing the perception of threat and insecurity and replacing the quest for individual clout with greater team cohesion.

Team Challenge #2: The Struggle of Managing Team Needs

Recently, I worked with an intergenerational team to resolve conflicts and underlying tensions to address counterproductive dynamics. I conducted one-on-one working sessions to understand the root causes of the tension and how the team could come together to overcome it. One team member told me that the team leader had put all the project goals on the table in front of the team and said, "This is what needs to get done. It matters less to me how you do it." Then he walked away, leaving half of the team blankly staring into the room and unwilling to raise their hands, afraid that the team leader would think less of them if they questioned his minimal direction. In some cases, such hands-off leadership can empower team members by giving them autonomy to make decisions without the need to jump through hierarchical hoops before moving ahead. However, the hands-off approach that appeals to some members can create confusion and discontent in others. This outcome is especially common for an intergenerational team representing a wide range of expertise and experience.

Imagine a Baby Boomer, now a senior leader, who found success managing Gen Xers through a more hands-off leadership style. This autonomous approach likely developed over time as the Baby Boomer adjusted to Gen X employees expressing their need for flexibility and independence. Now that same Baby Boomer is leading a team of both Gen X and Millennial members. The Millennial colleague has quickly risen in rank and has a reputation for "getting things done," always busy but adamantly moving on to the next action item as soon as one task on the to-do list is complete. She doesn't shy away from going into the office on Saturday mornings to get ahead. Occasionally, the senior leader reminds her that she doesn't need to go into the office on Saturdays, but the Millennial shrugs her shoulders, telling herself that the team leader doesn't understand how much work she has on her plate. At the same time, a Gen Xer on the same team is getting frustrated. What is this Millennial doing? Why is she involved in everyone's work all the time? Is she trying to make the rest of them look bad?

Almost as soon as they reached adulthood and full-time employment, Millennials have been leapfrogging into leadership positions. Their execution-oriented and results-driven approach may cause distress within a team, especially when the team leader is not involved in day-to-day activities. Without a clear leader to provide structure, guidance, and feedback to the team members who need it, lines between individual job responsibilities become blurred. Consequently, a potentially empowering, autonomous type of leadership may backfire within an intergenerational team. With so many different work styles, motivations, and priorities, a lack of structure can expose the group to vulnerabilities, resulting in individual team members overlapping into others' responsibilities, potentially leading the team to fatigue and disintegration.

This example captures a number of the valid generational differences that can cause headaches for age-diverse teams (and their leaders). As discussed in chapter 3, Dr. Jean Twenge, a professor at San Diego State and author of *Generation Me* and *iGen*, has found that generations show significant differences in how they prioritize work, work ethic, and individuality at work.[14,15] These differences, if not actively managed, can trigger undesirable behaviors among team members, resulting in team dysfunction. Once fault lines appear, team culture can still be rebuilt if the appropriate steps are taken. A team member may need to seek out the "hands-off" leader to let him know that while the group appreciates his faith in the team, its members would work more effectively if they could develop clear roles and task ownership. Activities shouldn't be shared unless the team establishes operating procedures for how work will get done.

Team leaders must address the issue head-on. Ultimately, the goal of any team should be to successfully share responsibilities as well as leadership, which only happens after the team has the necessary structure, support, and significance in place. A Gentelligent team discusses norms that go beyond defining the team's mission, scope, key objectives, and time frame by also considering individual working styles, personal preferences, and needs. The potential of intergenerational teams can be realized by providing autonomy and leading at a distance, as long as team members know where to find their leaders when they need additional support.

Team Challenge #3: The Struggle of Decision Making

As a child, your parents probably set the rules in your home. And if you're reading this book and are a parent, perhaps you try to create rules to protect your children from hurting themselves. If you have siblings, you probably remember the oldest being allowed to make certain decisions. These relationships influence how we tend to experience decision making in our lives. In both of these examples, the oldest person has the final word. For intergenerational teams, automatically conferring authority to the oldest team members can quickly lead to team dysfunction.

Intergenerational workplace conflicts are often rooted in "one group's notion that it gets to make the rules and that the other group has to follow these rules."[16] In most organizations, older people make up the group that gets to make the rules and set the standards. This hierarchy might not have been a problem when Baby Boomers were the new kids on the block, as they expected to put their heads down and work their way up the ladder, but younger generations view things differently. Millennials and Gen Zers not only intend to bring their full, authentic selves to work every day but also expect to be able to share their views and experiences with their team members.

The failure to invite younger colleagues to the table when the rules for teamwork are being established can create tension before the work even starts. Team leaders may have good reasons for not inviting their entire team to these discussions. Asking only people with experience directly related to the task at hand to have these conversations might feel natural. But when leaders opt to exclude the junior members of their teams from these initial discussions, they send a stark message that the junior employees' input is valued *only* when they provide ideas that fall within a general framework. Even when younger members of the team are encouraged to share their opinions after the initial rule-setting stage, those junior team members know that the rules guiding the engagement favor the group that developed those guidelines. Ultimately, as usual, the group that made the rules has the final say and can also change those rules whenever it sees fit.

To overcome this team challenge, we propose various strategies for how to make the decision-making process within an intergenerational team as effective and inclusive as possible. First, team members need to clarify the structure and supporting operating procedures to guide how the team works, including *how* it will make decisions. The decision-making process within a team is arguably one of the most challenging aspects of any kind of teamwork because it requires all elements of team effectiveness to come together. In an intergenerational team, these elements become even *more* critical. Teams want to utilize their members' resources and potential to the fullest, and a well-designed decision-making structure will allow us to do just that.

Knowing that team members of varying ages, tenures, and experience levels may differ in their comfort and willingness to speak up, an established decision-making process is essential to ensuring that all voices are heard. Several best practices in group decision making can help with this dynamic. One we have found to work well is the nominal group technique, which helps to both generate and evaluate all ideas fairly.[17] This is how the approach might look in a Gentelligent team:

Step 1: After a problem/challenge is identified, all group members individually and privately brainstorm ideas.

Step 2: Members of the team take turns sharing their ideas with the rest of the group, with no preferences given for issues like seniority or title. All ideas are recorded, but no discussion occurs during this step.

Step 3: Once all team members have shared their ideas, a thorough discussion of all ideas takes place. Team members have a chance to further explain their input and ask their colleagues clarifying questions.

Step 4: Using a predefined procedure, team members vote for the strongest ideas. The vote can be done via private ballot or through a more transparent process such as voting with sticky notes for the concepts that people like the best, to rank the most viable ideas.

The nominal group technique aims to overcome the kinds of barriers many intergenerational teams face today. Not only does it provide a clear structure for making decisions, but it also addresses significance by allowing each team member's ideas to be heard and given fair consideration, regardless of one's age or position. Over time, such an approach can also help multigenerational teams build support, as members begin to trust that others will listen to their input; consequently, they'll become more willing to share their ideas. Once a healthy level of support exists, the team may no longer need a highly structured approach. Teams should determine when they have built the trust required to communicate and make decisions effectively without the detailed structure.

Another decision-making process we recommend for intergenerational teams is the stepladder technique.[18] This approach begins by pairing two team members together; for Gentelligent teams, we suggest pairing two members who have a significant age difference. These two members discuss their initial thoughts on the challenge at hand, and then a third team member is invited into the discussion and shares their idea. This process continues until all team members have joined, and then a final consensus is reached. The stepladder technique has four rules that keep the process on track:

1. *Preparation:* Before joining up with the core group, team members need adequate time to think through their ideas and questions and formulate what they will say.
2. *Speak on Arrival:* When "new" group members join the discussion, they should individually share their ideas with the existing group before hearing what the core group has already discussed. This approach ensures that the preexisting group won't dominate the discussion and that new ideas won't be lost.
3. *Timing:* The stepladder technique requires careful timing to make sure each new member has the same amount of sufficient time to share their fresh input when joining the preexisting group. As the group expands, teams may want to rush through this step as more and more ideas are available, but it's critical to fully consider and respect the input of each new member.
4. *The Final Decision:* No decisions are made until all members have joined the discussion, and the preexisting group ultimately includes every member of the team. Once all perspectives from each member have been heard and considered, the group makes a final decision.

The stepladder technique is a powerful strategy for decision making in intergenerational teams, as it gives a structure to the process by putting each member on equal footing (subsequently providing significance) and requires every participant to provide input. The gradual technique of adding members can preclude individuals from being overwhelmed and from inadvertently dominating discussions. By the end of the process, there is less individual ownership of ideas as they evolve and are absorbed by the team as a whole, creating interdependence and the ever-important aspect of support.

Team Challenge #4: The Struggle for Shared Communication Norms

Stephanie Korey, the cofounder of the travel luggage and lifestyle brand Away, credits the communication tool Slack (an instant messaging platform that blends elements of Skype for Business and GroupMe) for the company's success. Ultimately, she says, "If the decision is not in Slack, it might as well not have happened."[19] At Away, using Slack is a common and well-accepted form of communication. Still, for some organizations, the lack of established communication preferences can prevent close collaboration and disrupt teams. Establishing norms for information sharing is essential to team effectiveness. When colleagues miscommunicate or when the team members talk past each other, performance suffers. To truly overcome the many stumbling blocks for intergenerational teams, we need to broadly assess the norms of communication, or how various types of interactions with coworkers should occur. Such protocols reflect what is proper and respectful in the workplace environment.

In multigenerational workplaces, teams must recognize the different preferences that members of each cohort might have toward communicating. The Fung Fellowship at Berkeley, which connects diverse undergraduate students with community and industry partners through its unique, impact-driven innovations program, had this realization with one of its programs. The project placed undergraduate students with retirees on a team to collaborate on technology solutions for seniors. Susan Hoffman, the director of Osher Lifelong Learning at UC Berkeley (a partner in the Fung Fellowship program), believes that while the partnerships between the older members and undergraduate students in her program have been tremendously beneficial, the need to articulate communication norms also became apparent as the program progressed.[20]

One such rule limited letting any one member "overshare" about general experiences instead of selectively drawing out insights, preventing one person in the team from dominating the discussion. Hoffman says this adjustment led to more profound lessons in active listening in both directions, allowing older and younger adults to listen to one another without interjecting or interrupting. Listening to each other more fully allowed them to build on each other's ideas, rather than speaking past each other. She believes that intergenerational partnerships should aim for reciprocal learning, rather than limiting the exchange to older adults expecting to teach younger participants.

During her time managing the program, Hoffman has also observed different habits regarding technology: Young people texted older team members at night, expecting quick responses or feedback; more senior members of the program did not immediately respond, feeling no urgency to respond at that time (if at all).[21] Younger members perceived the absence of a response as a signal that older team members didn't sincerely care about them or the program. Open dialogue subsequently revealed that the older members did care deeply about the program, but they did not think they had to respond to text messages at night to demonstrate their commitment.

In some organizations, the norms of communication are disseminated from the top down. They become an intrinsic part of the organization, guiding how things are done; as a result, individual teams don't change or alter those rules for smaller projects. But in most cases, a new team leader or project means a reset for communication protocols and team energy. Establishing ground rules and norms for sharing information goes more smoothly when done at the beginning. Team leaders should consider sharing their expectations, methods, and preferences for team communication. While the specific standards of communication will change to accommodate each team's individual context and composition, we offer the following as starting points for developing shared norms of communication:

1. *Give the Team Space:* Acknowledge that sometimes work may be hectic, but establish that texting or emailing team members on their days off will not be the norm. Instead of encouraging long hours, create a "work smarter, not harder" team culture.
2. *Listen and Learn:* When someone is speaking, resist the urge to interrupt, give advice, or judge. Instead, create a norm of fully listening and building on each other's ideas. Active listening and intellectual exchanges between team members promote intergenerational learning and creativity, enhance team effectiveness, and improve performance.
3. *Share What You Know:* Establish a norm that promotes transparency and open communication, encouraging team members to share information with their colleagues. This mindset will prevent team members from becoming territorial and protective of their work and knowledge.

Lastly, leaders should share what they want their team members to expect from them as well as what they expect from the group. Invite members of the team to share their reactions to the team norms and expectations, and emphasize that rules are malleable, with the possibility for adapting standards as circumstances change.

Team Challenge #5: The Struggle for Knowledge Relevance

A few months ago, I was giving a talk on Gentelligence to a local chapter of a community organization. The audience was primarily older, a mixture of individuals in the latter stages of their career or already retired. After the presentation, I opened up the conversation for questions. One gentleman raised his hand and said that while he appreciated my perspective, he found it hard to believe that he was supposed to place as much value on the input of a twenty-something as he placed on the wisdom of a colleague his age. After all, he commented, "They don't even know anything yet." His perspective allowed us to have a conversation about Resisting Assumptions and the different kinds of wisdom that Gentelligence can bring. Not recognizing the value and unique knowledge of individual contributors can damage teams and weaken their effectiveness. For most individuals, the lack of support and significance diminishes their intrinsic motivation as their contributions are not asked for or valued.

We have previously explored the different types of knowledge that exist in the twenty-first-century workforce and the limitations of assigning knowledge and expertise to people based on their ages. We now want to reiterate the importance of recognizing and appreciating different types of knowledge, specifically in a team context. Remember the divisions of *know-what* (job-specific knowledge), *know-how* (skills, talents, and competencies), *know-when* (organizational history, context, and adaptability to change), *know-why* (reasoning and rationale for decisions), and *know-whom* (wisdom on politics and social networks)?[22] This way of classifying knowledge can be a powerful tool for teams trying to recognize and leverage complementary skills and expertise and facilitate leadership sharing.

Consider how different kinds of knowledge would help to determine the right roles for the members of a team. Within several of the Fung Fellowship's intergenerational teams designing wearable technologies for seniors, the younger team members bring the *know-what* aspects of emerging technology and engineering trends. Older members complement this with their *know-how* knowledge of how the consumer demographic will use the product. The younger team members also bring the *know-why* knowledge regarding what technologies would offer the best solutions for particular problems, and the older members bring their own *know-why* and *know-when* insight of why such solutions may or may not appeal to the target audience, and whether such ideas have been tried before. Understanding these differences can help generations identify the roles they can play (idea generator versus troubleshooter) and how they can add unique contributions, and it also allows them to respect and appreciate the roles and contributions of other age cohorts.

The Open Sustainability Technology Lab at Michigan Technological University experienced this dynamic on an even grander scale. In 2017, lab leader Dr. Joshua Pearce (a Gen Xer) talked to *Science* magazine about his team, which included Traditional industry experts, Baby Boomer researchers, and Millennial interns. This age diversity allowed the lab to see the power of intergenerational knowledge in action. Pearce says the key is to recognize the unique contributions each generation brings to the mix, illustrated through an example from when his team needed an electrical adaptor to make its equipment work. Dr. Pearce had the *know-what* to realize what part they needed and the *know-how* to head to Amazon to place an order for it. His colleague, several decades older, took a different approach and used his own version of *know-how* to piece together a version of the adaptor from existing parts available in the lab. According to Pearce, "That skill doesn't come until you have a pretty in-depth knowledge of technology developed over a long time."[23]

We followed up to see whether the Open Tech lab is still leveraging intergenerational talent. Dr. Pearce recently lost his two most experienced team members to retirement, and that loss of wisdom and experience has been a challenge:

> Losing my two most experienced team members in a few years was a major hit. We have just about rebuilt, both our diversity of technical competencies and our intergenerational team. We have a young Baby Boomer re-joining us while on his sabbatical, along with our new cohort of 20-something Ph.D. students, Gen Z, and younger undergraduates.[24]

When tackling any challenge, we suggest having a team discussion about which members could have relevant complementary knowledge. It's helpful to start this conversation by grounding the team in the basics of *know-what*, *know-how*, *know-when*, *know-why*, and *know-whom*, establishing the coexistence of multiple kinds of valuable knowledge and contribution. Dr. Pearce echoes this suggestion:

> For getting the most out of an age-diverse team, I think it is important to create an atmosphere where everyone feels comfortable asking for

> help in areas they are less familiar (whether it is me having the new students explain Instagram and Twitter for outreach and recruiting, or younger students seeing older researchers show them mental math tricks that are faster than digging out your cell phone for calculations). We function as multigenerational and multi skill-set mini-teams for every project, and everyone is expected to have in addition to their baby (core project) at least one if not several projects that they help other team members complete.[25]

When members of an intergenerational team recognize the significance of the work of their teammates and themselves, they have begun to experience Gentelligence. This realization of mutual value and importance also leads to higher degrees of support within the team. When we are secure in our contributions and roles, it becomes easier to feel safe. When employees see value in their teammates, the psychological safety essential for taking risks and trusting the team is more likely to form.

THE TEAM TRIFECTA AND FIVE STRUGGLES

Creating and managing diverse teams can be a challenge. The team trifecta of structure, support, and significance provides the tools necessary for overcoming *any* team challenge. If effectively implemented, these strategies can prevent team conflicts and tensions from ever manifesting themselves. The intergenerational dimension can make team harmony daunting but not impossible. The German Marshall Fund (GMF) of the United States, a group dedicated to strengthening transatlantic relationships, utilizes intergenerational teams to ensure it considers the broad themes that may impact its work. The GMF comments,

> As we each strengthen our intergenerational competency, we also strengthen our organization. As lifespans lengthen and people work longer, this becomes even more critical. Different events and influences shape each generation, causing distinct motivations, communication styles, and skill sets. Teams can leverage these different approaches in order to excel.[26]

Despite the potential benefits, in reality, there is much more to be done to build Gentelligent teams. Most organizations have not yet understood the myriad of intergenerational possibilities inherent within teams. We argue that the paradox of intergenerational teams should be looked at as one of our greatest challenges *and* one of our greatest opportunities. Organizations tend to recognize and reward strong individual performers effectively but are less likely to understand how to truly support teams. Voices can easily get lost in the noise of a group, and some views can be harder to hear than others. Teams require more work, more time, and more energy to succeed, and both leaders and team members must receive the support they need. Through the tools and strategies of Gentelligence, the rewards of intergenerational teams can outweigh the risks, opening up unrecognized opportunities for growth and learning across all generations and for the organization as a whole.

7

A Gentelligent People Strategy

People are not your most important asset. The right people are.

—*Jim Collins,* Good to Great[1]

When I began my first job after graduate school in 2003, a senior colleague made a point of mentioning that our department was one that valued face time (and not the kind on the iPhone). He said simply, "We want to see you here." For many years, I kept that in mind and made sure to log as many hours as I could at my desk. However, much of the work of a professor (research, writing, reviewing papers) required a great deal of focus, and it soon became evident that while the office was good for many things, concentration was not one of them. It was a great place to meet with students, sit down for a research meeting with a coauthor, or catch up with colleagues. But if I needed to really think and concentrate, I had to work elsewhere. Over time, I noticed that more and more of my colleagues were moving away from the tradition of face time and toward a broader view of what working could look like.

Seventeen years later, I make a point of telling my new colleagues that our culture has changed. While we're all still expected to work hard and be in the office when necessary, we've come to recognize that work can be done in a myriad of places and want people to decide for themselves where they will be most productive.

The U.S. workforce will continue to experience significant changes in the next twenty years. A new generation is coming of age (Gen Z). Many of our mid-career employees (currently Gen Xers and Millennials) are becoming fatigued by demands coming from multiple directions. The oldest workers (currently the Baby Boomers) are expected to both work and live longer. By 2030, people aged sixty-five and older will outnumber those under the age of eighteen for the first time in U.S. history.[2] Already, many organizations have begun to embrace and prepare for these changes. Startups are designing their organizations from the ground up to meet the needs of the evolving workforce, while well-established businesses have turned to organizational redesign and restructuring to survive. To effectively navigate the challenges ahead, we ask five core questions about the evolving workforce:

1. Who will your talent be?
2. What will they need to stay committed?
3. When and where will they work?
4. Why will they work?
5. How will they work?

The answers to these questions will form the foundation of a Gentelligent people strategy, unlocking the potential of an intergenerational workforce and preparing your organization for some expected (and unexpected) challenges of the twenty-first century. Table 7.1 provides a summary of the key strategies we will discuss in this chapter.

WHO WILL YOUR TALENT BE?

Traditionally, maintaining and cultivating the talent pipeline largely focused on young recruits who would progress through the organization and pick up the baton from their older colleagues to lead when it was their time to do so. Shattering conventional norms, many younger workers with contemporary skillsets are currently leapfrogging into leadership positions requiring them to manage older colleagues, as

Table 7.1. Talent Questions and Gentelligent Answers

Key Talent Questions	*Gentelligent Answers*		
Who will your talent be?	Older and Returning Workers	New Category Workers	Gig Workers
What will they need to stay committed?	Continuous Learning and Career Development Opportunities	Retraining and Upskilling	An Internal Gig Economy
When and where will they work?	Flexible Work Schedules	Time Agnostic Work	Remote Work
Why will they work?	Employees Seek Purpose		Brand Resonance and Employee Pride
How will they work?	Embrace Multiple Views on Work-Life Integration	Understand the Socioemotional Needs of Employees	Provide Unlimited Paid Time Off (PTO)

senior employees are often working well past the traditional retirement age. Additionally, unprecedented fields of new knowledge and expertise are emerging that demand new categories of jobs to fill. These shifting dynamics are fundamentally changing the workforce composition; to compete for talent in the future, companies must be willing to search for the strongest candidates in less-than-familiar places.

Older and Returning Workers

As a result of the aging workforce and returning retirees, seasoned employees are now the largest workplace cohort. The number of older workers is growing more rapidly than their younger counterparts in the United States and around the world.[3] Today, Baby Boomers are more likely to stay in the labor force longer than previous generations, and many are postponing their retirement as a result of the 2008 global financial crisis as well as the disastrous economic fallout from the COVID-19 pandemic, both of which had a catastrophic impact on their household and personal finances.[4] Even when Boomers have retired, some are reentering the workforce, out of both choice and need.[5] With the number of Boomer retirees set to explode in the next decade, the talent pipeline of retirees returning to employment may increase. This represents a potential new talent opportunity for organizations, but only for companies ready to seize it. To do so, companies across industries should actively develop restart and returnship programs, Resisting Assumptions that the only place to find new talent is by recruiting those at the beginning of their careers. Such programs target older professionals reentering the workforce after taking time off, allowing them to once again make valuable contributions. These initiatives resemble the restart programs offered to professionals who have been out of the workforce for caregiving, but are focused on a different age cohort.

Goldman Sachs was one of the first companies to offer a returnship program, focusing on sharpening skills and competencies in a work environment that may have changed since individuals left the workforce.[6] Many financial institutions quickly followed suit as the war over talent intensified. Credit Suisse, a Swiss bank, launched what it called the Real Returns Program, which gives senior professionals who have been out of the workforce for an extended period a clear path back. Among other things, the participants are promised opportunities to network and support to upgrade their technology skills. The program has experienced great success, and many returning workers received full-time jobs following their participation.[7] Returnship programs that teach older workers new skills ensure that these employees remain engaged at work while building new, alternative talent pools for the organization. Other programs like Deloitte's Return to Work, Ford's Re-Entry program, and LinkedIn's REACH prove that well-known companies are investing in the benefits of such initiatives.

New Category Workers

In the future, organizations will hire from entirely new categories of workers or create unprecedented talent pools using a novel set of criteria. The creation of New Collar jobs is one such example. Unable to fill open positions requiring technical expertise, IBM's former CEO, Ginni Rometty, created this new job category to solve IBM's talent shortage. New Collar jobs demand high-tech skills in areas of rapid growth but don't necessarily need the same traditional degree that professional jobs typically have required. New Collar jobs call for workers with a technical mindset, an eagerness to learn, and a willingness to continuously grow. Companies often assume they should look primarily to our younger generations, the digital natives, for these higher-tech jobs (and, indeed, many Gen Z members are open to alternative kinds of in-demand skills training to avoid the high costs of a traditional college path). However, organizations must Resist Assumptions, as initiatives like New Collar jobs also provide engaging opportunities for older employees; as such, employers should make these opportunities widely available.

Companies like Apple, Google, IBM, Bank of America, and Hilton recognize the evolving nature of the workforce, and all offer jobs that don't require college degrees. In doing so, they acknowledge what Gen Zers have long known: the development of high-tech in-demand skills also occurs outside the classroom, and many colleges today may lag in technological innovation. Apple's CEO Tim Cook has been outspoken on this topic and says that there is a "mismatch between the skills learned in college and the skills that businesses need." In 2018, half of Apple's U.S. workforce consisted of employees without a four-year degree.[8] Organizations like the Thiel Fellowship, founded by PayPal's co-founder Peter Thiel, even award young people who skip or drop out of college $100,000 grants to explore their entrepreneurial ideas.[9]

Organizations that determine they don't urgently need to create new job categories should instead focus on reevaluating the traditional job criteria currently outlined in their job postings. Identifying the *critical* job requirements and corresponding attributes may help eliminate archaic qualifications that are no longer relevant or predictive of success in rapidly changing organizations. For example, how important is a specific college major, a particular GPA, or a preset arbitrary number of years of experience? No job qualifications should be considered sacred just because they have always been there. Instead, Gentelligence requires organizations to Adjust the Lens. If the job were created today, what would be considered essential for success? As CEO of Tesla and Space X, Elon Musk is admired for his entrepreneurship, creativity, and innovation. Musk has one simple rule for hiring: he looks for "clear evidence of exceptional ability" and pays little attention to whether someone has a college or even high school degree.[10]

While screening for the number of years of experience once ensured that new hires had enough expertise for the jobs they were being hired to do, it no longer carries the same weight as it once did. As technological innovation drives the pace of change and the time between breakthroughs shortens, screening for years of experience won't identify the "right" people in the future. Hiring managers and recruiters should instead focus on alignment between job requirements and essential skills to find the employees they need both within and outside their organizations.

Gig Workers

Today, contingent workers make up a sizable portion of the U.S. workforce, with 36 percent of American workers participating in some way in the freelance economy (including employees like Lyft drivers, seasonal workers, graphic designers, app developers, and independent consultants).[11] This kind of temporary, flexible work appeals to all generations, but it is most popular with Millennials (37 percent of whom have taken on gig work) and Baby Boomers (at 35 percent). Interestingly, Gen Xers are less likely to gig, with only 28 percent reporting having done so.[12] Undoubtedly, with many industries experiencing talent shortages, it will become increasingly important for organizations to look beyond their traditional full-time employees and Adjust the Lens to meet the changing needs of generationally diverse gig workers to thrive in the twenty-first century. In some ways, the freelance economy has already transformed *how* we work, but "gigging" will continue to impact *who* our companies engage in future work.

Traditionally, gig workers were viewed as short-term, temporary resources who were easily replaceable. Companies that maintain this perspective will fail to attract the most in-demand freelancers in the future. In addition to offering these employees benefits, organizations need to rethink how they can retain gig workers who seek meaningful projects and job fulfillment and, while maintaining their sense of autonomy, feel membership with the organizations they work for.[13] Today's skilled freelance workers have more resources to find jobs and new opportunities than ever before. They can also review available projects as well as compare terms and benefits before committing to their next projects. A quick internet search yields numerous articles listing the top fifty gig economy apps or top ten websites for landing freelance work. Undeniably, gig workers today are looking for diverse experiences, and their needs, such as working independently while simultaneously feeling membership within a workplace community, can be challenging to meet.

WHAT WILL THEY NEED TO STAY COMMITTED?

The era of lifetime employment appears to be over. The Work Institute, a leader in workforce consulting, estimates that over 42 million U.S. workers left their jobs voluntarily in 2019, costing employers more than $630 billion in one year (an increase of $30 billion during 2018).[14] To effectively implement programs that lead to long-term commitment, organizations must work to better understand and meet their employees' evolving expectations and preferences.

Continuous Learning and Career Development Opportunities

A few months ago, I had dinner with several friends who work in consulting, all of whom were older Gen Xers or young Baby Boomers in charge of teams of younger workers. Over the meal, the conversation turned to the struggle they were having with retaining their Millennial employees. One remarked, "Eighteen months. That's the reality. You can't get a Millennial who will stay with you longer than eighteen months before they are out the door to the next thing that comes along." Younger generations have developed a reputation as job-hoppers who believe they deserve raises and promotions within a year of working.[15] Recent headlines illustrate this point: "The Office Rookies Who Ask for the World" (*Wall Street Journal*, April 2019); "Why 'Lazy,' 'Entitled' Millennials Can't Last 90 Days at Work" (*New York Post*, March 2019); and "Millennials: The Job-Hopping Generation" (Gallup, May 2016).

Yet the reality is much more complicated than the headlines suggest. The most straightforward, simple, and widely shared narrative is to depict them as fickle and disloyal by showing that compared to older generations, higher percentages of the Millennial generation have left jobs or intend to do so within the next year. However, this is a textbook example of the misconceptions that can result when we forget to consider the importance of life stage when we try to understand generational differences.[16]

Yes, there are many studies showing Millennials are currently more likely to switch jobs than their older counterparts, but they are also now between twenty-four and thirty-eight years old, the period of life when *everyone* is most likely to change jobs. Research supports this idea. The Pew Research Center compared data from Gen X at the same life stage that the Millennials are in now (circa 2002) and found the results were comparable: 69 percent of Gen Xers stayed with an employer for at least thirteen months, compared with 70 percent of Millennials. A third of both groups during this age span reported staying with an employer for at least five years.[17] When we Adjust the Lens and look from this perspective, data suggest that Millennials are not more fickle when it comes to jobs than the generation before them.

Yet employers are convinced there's something afoot, as they are struggling more to retain the Millennials than they have with generations in the past. This situation may stem from Millennials expressing their expectations directly to their employers, including strong desires for meaningful work experiences, coaching and development, and opportunities for work variety and challenge.[18] While prior generations arguably hoped for the same things, they were less likely to ask for them; instead, they assumed such opportunities would come with time. Millennials have pushed back on that norm, letting their employers know that they only want to stay with organizations that are willing to invest in and develop their potential. Demonstrating this point, Millennials are more likely than previous generations to cite a lack of career development as a reason for quitting their jobs.[19] Therefore, while Millennials may not be changing jobs any more frequently than Gen Xers at the same age, they are putting greater demands on what they require from their employers to stay.

While much has been said about younger generations demanding new opportunities, less has been said about the need for development for older generations. However, an overwhelming majority of Boomers report a lack of opportunities to learn and grow during the latter part of their careers. This situation is not only a waste of knowledge and potential for the impacted employees but also potentially damaging to the entire business, as these workers possess valuable institutional knowledge. According to the Gallup Organization, "When Baby Boomers are deeply invested in their work, they can better inspire younger workers. They can encourage creativity, innovation, and excellence—enriching the development of future generations."[20]

To stay engaged, twenty-first-century workers across generations will need continuous learning and career-development opportunities. Whereas previous generations focused primarily on promotions and status, today's employees expect their employers to also provide opportunities to learn and grow. The difference between these priorities is essential. A company that focuses only on rigid requirements for climbing the next rung on the corporate ladder risks being viewed as focusing solely on the short term. Comparatively, employees who see their organization is providing continuous learning and growth opportunities are more likely to feel they are being invested in for the long term. To improve retention and drive engagement, employers should focus on helping their junior *and* senior workers develop new, transferable skills to strengthen their employability rather than focus on incremental status increases. In the end, the desire for fulfillment and the fear of not keeping up with technological changes are driving many workers toward organizations that promise continued long-term career development. When done right, showing that an organization is willing to invest in all workers regardless of age and generation is vital to Strengthening Trust, and this investment in employee growth can become a competitive advantage for the organization. Employees want to feel confident in their company's willingness to prepare them for the future.

Retraining and Upskilling

With an eye toward preparing their workforce for the future, Amazon announced in 2019 that it would invest $700 million to retrain one hundred thousand of its existing employees, representing a third of its U.S. workforce. Due to the impact of rapid technological change on jobs, companies like Amazon are starting to recognize the need to retrain and reskill their existing workers to keep them engaged and prepared for future industry requirements. There are generational differences in who employees believe to be responsible for reskilling and upskilling. Many Millennial and Gen Z workers feel more personally responsible for developing new, in-demand skills, while Baby Boomers are more likely to believe that their employers should retrain and update the skillsets of the workforce.[21] Effective reskilling and upskilling programs will become increasingly important as the talent shortage for skilled workers increases.

As discussed in the previous section, well-executed employee development can become a competitive advantage and driver of long-term success. Thus, it is not surprising that upskilling and reskilling of employees have moved up on executive agendas. Finding talent with the right technical expertise and social skills (and keeping that talent engaged with the company for the long term) is becoming more difficult, but retraining and upskilling existing workers can meet that challenge. By Resisting Assumptions and Adjusting the Lens, we can train and reskill all workers, equipping them with skills needed for the dynamic, contemporary workplace.

The other benefit of retraining and upskilling is that organizations may find that the people they are looking for are already in-house. The benefits of promoting employees from within the organization are well documented. Promoting from within means filling open positions more quickly and with less disruption to organizational culture. External hiring, in contrast, increases stress among existing employees and burdens the peers training new hires as they learn company culture and expectations. Employees who see their current organization relying primarily on external hiring to fill higher positions may also begin to doubt their own ability to move up in the company and begin to focus their energy on positioning themselves for future opportunities elsewhere, hurting overall engagement and work satisfaction.[22]

An Internal Gig Economy

In 2016, PwC launched the Talent Exchange, a platform where the company can post work it needs for internal projects, and freelancers can apply to complete the job. The process is simple: First, the freelancer creates a profile on the Talent Exchange (which only requires the individual to share some basic details). Next, they share their skills, project preferences, availability, and rate with PwC through the platform, who then matches the profile with open roles and available projects. Finally, if the individual accepts the opportunity, they get to work.[23] The CEO of PwC, Bob Moritz, says the platform helps the company "bring in the right talent in the right place at the right time."[24] The platform gives the organization the ability to quickly scale up in needed knowledge areas by bringing employees who may not be attracted to a full-time job. While this platform targets independent talent, it's easy to imagine that PwC (and other companies) could allow existing employees to supplement their primary position with additional project-based opportunities. This arrangement would enable their employees to be in control, increase their pay when necessary, and grow in areas they choose.

To avoid losing existing talent to the gig economy, we recommend that companies develop their own internal freelance platform: a company-owned marketplace with available projects matching employee availability, interest, and skills with the organization's key strategic priorities. This kind of internal tool allows employees to identify and select projects in their areas of interest.

An internal gig economy will result in greater autonomy and an increased sense of control, as well as flexibility, and has the potential to Expand the Pie by increasing employee satisfaction across generations, drive engagement, and enhance productivity. Although a majority of Gen Zers are interested in freelancing, they are also concerned about its lack of stability (a dependable paycheck and job security). As a result, many Gen Zers hold multiple jobs and use freelancing as a way to supplement their traditional full-time employment. However, an internal gig economy might make satisfying the needs of this new generation easier, as the promise of gigging (increased autonomy and flexibility) still appeals to them. This kind of platform may also meet the needs of other generations. Baby Boomers and Gen Xers who have reached mid-to-late career stages often reach occupational plateaus and seek new roles or opportunities. An internal gig economy may provide both generations with new paths to recharge and recommit to their existing workplaces. By developing such a resource, companies can merge the best of two worlds and engage top talent in the future.

WHEN AND WHERE WILL THEY WORK?

We've already offered several new approaches to managing talent, all of which are based on a fundamental need to stay agile and be willing to adapt as the needs of our multigenerational workforce continue to evolve. In many ways, the strategies discussed so far, such as developing new job categories, retraining and upskilling existing workers, targeting gig workers with thoughtfully designed programs, and deploying internal gig economies, will also influence when and where people will work in the future. For example, gig workers represent a novel employee category and challenge the status quo by introducing new ways of thinking about when and where work will get done. Other unexpected events, such as the COVID-19 pandemic or a breakthrough development in technology, can force organizations to evaluate existing workplace norms and work arrangements in the blink of an eye. These are just a few examples that represent a "seismic shift in how we think about and participate in work."[25]

Remote Work

Millennials and Gen Zers are driving many of the workplace changes that are underway. For both of these younger generations, technology has always made it possible to work from anywhere, enabling their constant connectivity to people and resources. Thus, needing to always work in a physical office makes little sense to them, and policies requiring them to do so may be unwelcome. As a recent PwC survey notes, "They view work as a thing and not a place."[26] The *New York Times* captures the generational influence on more flexible work in its 2019 article "Young People Are Going to Save Us All from Office Life." The authors note that while younger generations have been labeled lazy and entitled, they may be helping older cohorts rethink the role that work should play in their lives: "That's how Millennials and Gen Zers are playing the game—it's not about jumping titles, but moving into better work environments. They're like silent fighters, rewriting policy under the nose of the Boomers."[27] In other words, younger generations are nudging their older coworkers to Adjust the Lens when it comes to norms about when and where we work.

In the spring of 2020, the COVID-19 pandemic did more than nudge organizations to think more about where work could be accomplished. Almost overnight, the majority of employees across industries and professions suddenly became remote workers. This global health crisis soon became a case study in the importance of applying the four practices of Gentelligence to people strategy. Leaders (in both workplaces and classrooms) quickly realized that many long-standing assumptions about generational preferences and abilities did not hold when work needed to go virtual, proving that generational preferences and abilities did not fall along generational fault lines.

For instance, many assumed our youngest generations would be least impacted by the shift to working and learning from home. Their earlier efforts to expand acceptable norms about where work could be done could have easily led to the belief that they would thrive when switching to remote work. However, it soon became apparent that while younger generations may not view an office as the only place work can be done, they still viewed it as an important fixture of their professional and personal lives. An initial survey showed that Gen Z felt the *least* productive of all the generations in their remote-only arrangements.[28] While sheltering-in-place, many Gen Zers were vocal about missing the natural social interaction with coworkers that comes from having regular access to an office or a classroom. According to a study conducted by the National Research Group,

> With Gen Z being digital natives, or growing up in a technological age and thus more familiar with the equipment, it may seem ironic that they are the least productive. However, the office space does provide a sense of structure—a quality that is often critical for young professionals. That sense of accountability and oversight is particularly important for Gen Z employees, most of whom have been probably accustomed to a school structure.[29]

Case in point: While I had initially believed my Gen Z students would seamlessly adjust to the high-tech format of many college classes, I decided to practice what I preach and utilized the Gentelligence practice of Resisting Assumptions instead. I asked all of my students what was working well and what was missing for them in our new remote way of learning. The responses surprised me but reinforced the need for this practice. Most reported being comfortable with the technology but greatly missed the face-to-face interactions and the accountability a physical workspace brought. To apply the practice of Building Trust, I asked them what changes they might make and what strategies were working well for them, and then I altered our class approach accordingly. The result was worth the effort: almost overnight, there was less stress, more engagement, and an improvement in performance (mine and theirs)! I had learned a great deal about what they needed in order to thrive in such a time of chaos, and they felt empowered that they had been asked for input—Expanding the Pie for all of us, in a time when we greatly needed it.

Similar to Gen Zers, Millennials also reported greater struggle with the shift to remote work during the COVID-19 crisis compared to older generations. According to the Society of Human Resource Management, only 60 percent of Millennials reported being "as productive as usual or more so" while working remotely (compared with 67 percent of Generation Xers and 72 percent of Baby Boomers).[30] While these reports are preliminary, they suggest that the narrative about younger generations not wanting or needing an office is incomplete. Instead, it appears younger generations may value both the opportunities associated with working in an office environment and the ability to choose when they may be more productive working elsewhere.

The pandemic also brought assumptions about older generations and how much they would struggle with an abrupt shift to remote work that was highly dependent on technology. Technology has already developed to the point that most employees can view, send, sign, and collaborate on work materials from their phones or laptops, but digital tools like Microsoft Teams, Slack, and Zoom fundamentally transformed "the office" into something that can exist anywhere—and suddenly it needed to do just that. At the start of the pandemic, social media was saturated with mocking memes of Boomers trying to figure out Zoom and tweets questioning whether older faculty would be able to navigate teaching online. While stereotypes about older generations' lack of digital savvy abound, when it comes to the technology aspect of virtual work, recent research has revealed that younger and older workers actually share a similar desire to stay up to date on how to use the latest technology.[31]

While Millennials and Gen Zers share the designation of being labeled "digital natives," exhibiting natural ease while learning new technology, evidence shows that all generations are willing and able to pick up the technical skills needed to be successful in their current working environment. That said, there may be important differences in how quickly or easily they are able to do so. Older workers may be picking up the technical skills later in their careers and may want additional instruction and support to learn tools that younger generations grew up using as second nature. This creates a perfect opportunity to practice Gentelligence by Expanding the Pie, with younger people sharing their skills with older ones interested in learning new tools for the remote working environment (and beyond).

The need to remember and apply Gentelligent practices to people strategy continues as companies begin to recover from the initial shock of the pandemic and develop their "return to work" plans. These practices have already proved vital in understanding what different generations may need to adapt to the changing work environment. As initial data show, younger generations struggled more with remote work than was initially expected, while older generations tended to adjust better than anticipated, providing a cautionary lesson that falling back on generational stereotypes is not a wise management strategy. Moving forward in the months and years to come, companies should continue to Resist Assumptions, Adjust the Lens, and Build Trust by promoting open dialogue with employees across all ages and career stages about what is successful and what isn't when it comes to working remotely. Doing so will allow organizations to Expand the Pie in terms of discovering new ways to approach work, as well as determining which tried-and-true approaches are worth maintaining.

Time Agnostic and Flexible Work Schedules

For better or worse, almost every organization has now had a crash course in experimenting with alternate working arrangements. While remote work focuses on where work is done—allowing employees to do some or all of their job somewhere other than the office—a related question is *when* work can be done. Just as work may not always need to be done within the four set walls in an office, it's also important to consider whether the traditional work schedule is still the best approach.

Flexible work schedules are not new to the workplace. The origins of flextime can be traced back to the late 1960s, credited to a woman named Christel Kammerer and first implemented by West German aerospace firm Messarschmilt-Boklow-Blohm.[32] This concept then gained traction when Gen Xers entered the workplace desiring a better work-life balance. While myriad versions of flextime now exist, all center around allowing employees to work with their companies to determine when they will be in the office. The flexible-time possibilities are almost infinite, as long as the employer and employee agree that the arrangement will allow for work expectations to be met. We've seen this approach referred to as "time agnostic" (which we love), meaning that no single schedule is preferred.[33] All employers should consider whether such a neutral stance would meet their business needs and impact employee satisfaction.

Despite its widespread use, the phrase "flexible work" can take multiple forms: flexible schedules (including compressed workweeks and modified arrival and departure times) and job sharing are just a few of the ways companies can accommodate their employees' needs. Employers continue to explore and innovate how they implement these approaches within their organizational cultures.

While flexible and remote work may be second nature for younger employees, workers who have spent most of their careers logging face time in the office might be less confident about using these options. In some cases, this resistance not only might prevent older workers from taking advantage of flexible work arrangements but also could generate tension and judgment toward younger employees who do. There's even a name for this concept: *flex stigma*.

This bias against taking advantage of alternative work arrangements (including those above, but also things like the Family Medical Leave Act and sabbaticals) is well documented, especially in industries like consulting that are known for long hours and extensive travel. Even when a company provides flexible arrangements, some employees may resist using them for fear of appearing less committed to their work. Therefore, having flexible and remote opportunities will not be enough; companies will also have to work to actively create cultures that Resist Assumptions about taking advantage of such programs and support employees and their ability to embrace new workplace options. There are several strategies to help eliminate flex stigma, including training managers to prioritize outcomes (rather than face time), having leaders utilize flexible arrangements themselves to serve as role models, and highlighting how successful alternative work arrangements benefit both the company and the employee.[34]

Employers report that offering work flexibility allows them to recruit top talent; yet they caution that the need exists for clear communication in workplaces with so many different schedules and arrangements. Coworkers and customers still need to know how and when to reach employees, and companies must ensure that flexible and remote work arrangements won't create bottlenecks in productivity or decision making. It's also vital that managers establish accountability for employees' work done outside of the office. Some organizations evaluate employees exclusively on their work products, whereas other companies still require employees to track their time through apps or software to account for their hours spent elsewhere. When moving toward flexibility, organizations should make sure expectations and communications are clear. Despite its challenges, embracing flexible work approaches seems to be paying off. Employees who control their schedules report reduced stress and burnout, as well as higher levels of job satisfaction.[35]

The abrupt changes brought about by the COVID-19 crisis demonstrated clearly that few people of *any* age want rigid work arrangements. Moving forward, companies that want to attract and keep their top talent will have to be open to flexible work arrangements or risk losing those employees. Research has shown flexibility is nearly twice as important to employees as health benefits, with a third of the employees indicating their willingness to take a pay cut in exchange for greater workplace flexibility. Over a third reported leaving jobs that lacked the flexibility employees needed.[36]

By giving employees of all ages the flexibility to do their work on their own terms, workplaces stand a better chance of recruiting and retaining top talent. It has been said that one should never waste a good crisis—and in many ways, the forced remote work arrangements during the pandemic were the catalyst workplaces needed to leapfrog ahead in how they think about flexibility and what it means to work. We believe this dramatic pivot may, in some ways, be the wakeup call many workplaces needed to become more progressive with their people strategies.

Now more than ever, winning the war for talent in the twenty-first century requires a paradigm shift. Letting go of approaches that no longer make sense, retaining those that have stood the test of time, and remaining open to new strategies are necessary to both attract and retain the best people now and in the future. However, merely embracing change won't be enough. Ultimately, companies must be strategic in the kind of workplace innovations they undertake. Gentelligent answers to difficult questions will enable organizations across industries to formulate a cohesive Gentelligent people strategy adept at tackling the challenges ahead. In the end, thoughtful change programs center around the employee, whose needs and expectations change with the times—a move that shows compassion and also makes good business sense.

WHY WILL THEY WORK?

It is essential to understand why employees do what they do, whether they identify with the mission of their organizations, and if they find their work meaningful. By focusing on *why* employees do what they do instead of *what* they do, employers can better tailor the employee experience to improve engagement and reduce turnover. Today, most employees leave their jobs for preventable reasons. The cost of voluntary turnover is projected to reach levels that could place organizations at "continuous and enormous risk" by 2035.[37] Recognizing that employees seek purpose and care deeply about the image of the company they work for will enable companies to take some necessary and targeted actions to minimize this risk.

Employees Seek Purpose

Employee engagement is a vital part of any business, and the essential ingredient for transforming human and social capital into competitive advantage. Engaged employees are involved and passionate about their work and are actively committed to adding value to their organizations. On the flip side, those who are actively disengaged are the most dangerous employees. These employees actually put energy into taking *away* value from their companies, whether by wasting company resources, bringing a negative attitude to their work, or approaching younger or older coworkers with a fixed-pie mindset. Studies show that almost two-thirds of every generation is either neutral or actively disengaged at work,[38] representing a staggering amount of lost human and social capital.

According to a 2017 Gallup report, "The U.S.—and the world at large—is in the midst of an employee engagement crisis."[39] In a 2017 survey of over two thousand workers across industries, nine out of ten professionals reported that they would sacrifice some of their future earnings for work that is always meaningful.[40] Employees who feel that their work is purposeful and meaningful also report higher job satisfaction, and their employers benefit from increased employee engagement.[41] As discussed in chapter 3, employees across all generations want to feel valued and vital to the organization (shared value: respect). In the last decade, meaningfulness as a job-selection criterion has grown among all job seekers who today increasingly prioritize fulfilling work during their job searches,[42] but generational cohorts may express this desire differently. Research has found that "since individuals spend the majority of life at work, and work often defines a portion of their sense of self, believing that one's job is meaningful should enhance employees' well-being and provide significance to life."[43] But for talent professionals, designing work that is always meaningful is challenging, as what is considered meaningful work is a largely subjective quality. While many employees will accept lower salaries for personally meaningful jobs, an opportunity described as fulfilling to one person could be viewed as meaningless to the next.[44] Organizations facilitating a personalized work experience based on employees' individual priorities can expect their employees to stay in their jobs longer, improving productivity and driving company success, resulting in new ways to Expand the Pie.

While ways to facilitate personalized work experiences can take many forms, one of the first examples of individualized work that comes to mind is the 20 percent time policy at Google. The program was formally recognized in the 2004 Founders' IPO Letter, which includes the following language: "We encourage our employees, in addition to their regular projects, to spend 20% of their time working on what they think will most benefit Google."[45] While the company has since moved away from the management philosophy in favor of a more targeted and focused approach to innovation, some of the company's most successful products came out of the 20 percent time program. According to various news articles, the program was the birthplace for products like Google News, Google Earth, Google's autocompleting system, Gmail, and AdSense (Google's advertising program).[46,47]

Google is not the only company experimenting with ways to make the employee experience more customized. Although more limited than the 20 percent program at Google, Apple announced the "Blue Sky" initiative in 2014 following Google's initial success. Apple's version of the 20 percent time policy awards some select employees two weeks to do work on projects outside their typical job responsibilities.[48] Other companies like Facebook, LinkedIn, and Microsoft have launched their own versions of 20 percent time as well as other programs that encourage employees to work on projects that they are passionate about.[49]

Brand Resonance and Employee Pride

Business strategy today is influenced by employees' sense of pride. The idea of organizations developing strong talent brands has become more important as employees develop closer relationships with their employers, and those bonds become essential to their identity. Ultimately, these bonds have the potential to Strengthen Trust between employees and the organizations they work for. Pride is a powerful human emotion, representing an individual's belief that they are viewed positively and as competent by others. Therefore, as the lines between work and private life become blurred or even disappear altogether, bad press about the company one works for can become increasingly personal. For Gen Zers and Millennials who spend more time on social media than any other generation, the image matters. If one's employer is a bad corporate citizen, it can reflect poorly on the employee. For example, Facebook employees staged a virtual "walkout" during the COVID-19 pandemic in an effort to pressure Facebook executives to take a tougher stand on some of President Trump's Twitter posts and show their support for demonstrators across the United States.[50] The sobering reality for companies is that only about one-third of our Millennials (the largest generation in our workforce) have a strong connection to the work they are doing and the places where they are doing it. Additionally, according to the Gallup Organization, half of Millennial employees don't see a future where they work in their current companies.[51]

In a talent-centric economy, brand resonance (the employees' relationship or psychological connection to the company or brand), a strong company brand, and employee pride built from inside of the organization (driven by things such as the company values and mission) are essential to retaining employees. Although much of how employers build brand resonance, a strong company brand, and employee pride depends on external marketing, internal marketing is crucial to increasing satisfaction and reducing turnover. Internal marketing, also known as internal communications, is a strategy to promote a company's objectives, products, and services to employees within the organization. Organizations can both decrease employee turnover rates and increase satisfaction through internal marketing, as well as facilitate change programs.[52] Proud employees make more dedicated and engaged workers.

The outdoor wear company Patagonia has always been dedicated to environmental causes and embodies what it means to be a purpose-driven organization. The company has donated 1 percent of sales to the preservation and restoration of natural environments since 1986 and received the UN "Champions of the Earth" award in 2019.[53] Recently, the company changed its mission statement from "Build the best product, cause no unnecessary harm, use business to inspire and implement solutions to the environmental crisis" to "Patagonia is in business to save our home planet."[54] The decision to revise its already purpose-oriented mission to one that is narrowly focused on maintaining life on earth is a powerful move, clearly signaling its long-standing and enduring commitment to the environment. The work done by Patagonia has undoubtedly made a positive impact on the environment, as the 1 percent pledge alone has generated over "$100 million to grassroots organizations and helped train thousands of young activists," according to the UN.[55] But the company's strong brand, ongoing recognition in the media, and activist behavior have also had a profound impact on this talent. The company's employee turnover rate in their corporate offices is stunningly, almost unimaginably, low at 4 percent.[56] The turnover in their retail stores is also notably lower than the industry average.[57] Their enduring commitment to the environment may also appeal more to Millennial and Gen Z employees than other generations, setting them up for attracting these employees effectively in the future. Gallup found that these generations are "highly worried about global warming, [and] think it will pose a serious threat in their lifetime, believe it's the result of human activity, and think news reports about it are accurate or underestimate the problem."[58] As such, the causes fought for by Patagonia today may secure them top talent in the future.

HOW WILL THEY WORK?

Who our workers are and how to keep them engaged is changing quickly. While employee wellness programs are more common than they used to be, the twenty-first-century multigenerational workforce also demands that we answer questions about workplace well-being and mental health through a Gentelligent lens. If we don't, the engagement strategies discussed above risk falling on deaf ears.

Embracing Multiple Views on Work-Life Integration

While the need to help employees achieve work-life balance is not new, the presence of multiple generations simultaneously in the workplace necessitates a broader and more inclusive view of *why* people may need more flexible work arrangements. Organizations must also Adjust the Lens to recognize the various ways employees across generations may be impacted by the forces around them and how they define such balance. Think about what the integration of work and life may mean for employees at different stages of life and whether companies' current programs and policies treat these diverse needs as equally valid.

For example, many Gen Xers are currently providing primary care for their aging parents while still supporting their growing children. These pressures suggest that Gen Xers need flexible work arrangements and possibly personal support to manage the stress of these family demands. Elder-care responsibilities alone have been found to cost companies about $5 billion in absenteeism annually.[59] Some organizations are responding to these employee pressures in novel ways. Astellas, a pharmaceutical company, developed a program to help manage the complex needs that come with the demands of caring for aging parents, including providing their employees with access to elder-care managers to identify options and develop plans for their parents' care.[60] Employees with more autonomy to complete their jobs are better able to succeed in them.

Understanding the Socioemotional Needs of Employees

Gen Xers aren't the only employees who need more emotional support. Mental strain is also taking a toll on younger generations. Millennial and Gen Z workers both suffer from higher rates of mental health symptoms, in some cases leading them to leave their jobs. As a result, organizations need to better support their employees' social and emotional needs to foster a healthy, fully engaged workforce. Such concerns are leading companies to expand and update their definitions of *employee wellness*. In the end, today's workforce expects and needs more from their companies than an on-site gym.

A number of options have emerged to help employers support improved mental health in the workplace. EY, one the largest professional services firms in the world, has a mental health program known simply as "r u ok?" that provides tools and resources to encourage employees to both get help and support coworkers who are dealing with mental illness issues.[61] Right Direction, a program developed by the Center for Workplace Mental Health and the Employers Health Coalition, provides user-friendly free materials and tools to help companies address depression in the workplace. This program is already in place in hundreds of companies, including Kent State University and Online Computer Library Center Inc., a nonprofit, membership, computer library service, and research organization. Other workplace programs that facilitate mental health are on the rise, including pet-friendly workplaces (associated with helping owners and coworkers handle stress), meditation and Zen rooms, and access to telehealth (virtual) mental health counseling.[62]

While caregiving demands and mental health concerns are two significant drivers, employees from different generations will also have other reasons for needing work-life balance. To accommodate the wide range of needs associated with all stages of life, more and more employers are beginning to explore the potential of unlimited paid time off (PTO).

Providing Unlimited Paid Time Off

The United States has long had a reputation for offering its workers a limited number of vacation days. It was not unusual that the youngest employees were asked to pay their dues, receiving minimal paid vacation days each year, with only more tenured workers who had earned the right for a more extended vacation each year receiving one. Historically, the average number of days provided for full-time private industry employees has varied significantly depending on how long the employee had worked for the company, and while all workers saw slight increases in the number of vacation days since 1993, the gap between new and long-serving workers remains.[63]

However, recently, organizations have begun experimenting with the idea of unlimited PTO, something that would have been unthinkable just a decade ago. Unlimited PTO is a relatively straightforward concept: Employees are given an unlimited number of days off each year without having to accrue any vacation days, as the traditional model required. For most companies, the only requirement is that the employee ensures his or her work is up to date and that the absence will not negatively impact business operations while they are gone.[64]

But why would a company offer its employees unlimited vacation? Aron Ain, the CEO of Kronos, a workforce-management and human-capital-management cloud provider, instituted an unlimited vacation policy as a recruitment tool. The new program improved employee engagement and increased the number of positive (anonymous) employee comments, with employees taking an average of 2.6 more days off than the prior year. That same year, Kronos had its best financial performance ever. Aron Ain doesn't think that was a coincidence.[65]

In 2015, General Electric began a flexible PTO plan called "permissive time off policy," which was offered to more senior U.S. salaried employees.[66] An employee testimonial on GE's website speaks to the potential impact of such policies:

> I am so grateful I now feel empowered to take the time away that I need, both unplanned and planned, without feeling the stress of always "having to be there." Of course, I always coordinate with my manager. Permissive

> time just adds another tool to the toolkit. It is great knowing that we are not being measured on the amount of time we are at work or not, but rather on delivering on our priorities.[67]

Naturally, the implementation of such a policy raises several questions. Most notably, how would the company know that its employees won't abuse the new program and take multiple weeks in a row off without adequately ensuring that their work is being covered by someone else while they are gone? Rest assured, research has found that employees are unlikely to abuse the policy; instead, in many cases, the practice leads to employees taking *less* time off. Nevertheless, experts recommend that companies looking to offer unlimited vacation days ensure that the program sets clear expectations and adequately defines what is meant by *unlimited*, as no company expects their employees to stop showing up to work.[68]

MOVING FORWARD: EVOLVING TALENT STRATEGIES

Organizations that manage individual talent effectively can acquire a sustained competitive advantage in the labor market. Answering these questions through a Gentelligent lens ensures that the people strategy focuses equally on all age groups and is executed across the employee lifecycle to facilitate a tailored, employee-focused experience, delivering meaningful work in a personalized way. We urge companies to utilize the questions in this chapter to hone their own Gentelligent people strategy:

> Who will your talent be?
>
> What will they need to stay committed?
>
> When and where will they work?
>
> Why will they work?
>
> How will they work?

While the answers to the questions might change with the times, the questions will not. The future of talent acquisition depends on identifying and attracting a diverse spectrum of workers through job redesign or returnship programs, to name a couple of effective strategies. Retaining an organization's workforce, however, focuses more on developing employee pride, offering meaningful work, and responding to the socioemotional needs of a changing workforce. Ultimately, Gentelligence empowers employers to establish a thoughtful employee-centric change program that considers the needs of today's workforce as well as tomorrow's. A Gentelligent people strategy that allows companies to evolve alongside employees' changing needs is vital for success in the twenty-first century. Organizations that adopt this new way of managing talent will stand as winners, with an engaged, devoted, age-diverse workforce by their side.

8

Creating a Gentelligent Work Culture

Diversity is being invited to the party; inclusion is being asked to dance.

—*Verna Myers, vice president of inclusion strategy at Netflix*[1]

In almost every leadership class I teach, I share with my students the famous Peter Drucker line: "Culture eats strategy for breakfast." It's a reminder that even the most carefully constructed approaches to leadership, teams, and talent will fail if they don't align with the values and norms of the existing organizational environment. Culture is the most potent catalyst for every other aspect of our organizations; it is the critical factor in whether strategies help our vision become a reality. As such, this means that true generational inclusion can only occur in the context of a culture that is Gentelligent in what it believes, what it says, and what it does.

Culture consists of the shared beliefs, values, and norms of interaction, establishing what it means to work in an organization. *Culture* is difficult to define, and it's hard to measure, an "invisible glue."[2] Lou Gertsner, the former CEO of IBM, captures the importance of this element: "Culture isn't just one aspect of the game, it is the game. In the end, an organization is no more than the collective capacity of its people to create value."[3] It is in this collective capacity that organizational culture creates a competitive advantage. Research shows that culture significantly impacts almost every people metric, including job performance, satisfaction, employee engagement and motivation, and turnover.[4]

The paradox of culture is that it is vital to understand, yet challenging to define. Even those who work and live in a particular culture may not be fully aware of the many aspects that influence their environment. To help organizations get a more complete sense of the cultural complexities, Edgar H. Schein, professor emeritus at the MIT Sloan School of Management, identifies three levels of organizational culture that must be understood. Starting with the *deepest level* and building to the *most visible,* he refers to these layers as underlying assumptions, espoused ideals, and artifacts.[5]

These levels of culture are evident in a company well known for its strong and somewhat quirky culture: Zappos, the online shoe retailer. When you first walk into a Zappos office, you'll notice its relaxed and personalized nature. Employees are allowed to dress casually, decorate their workspaces in any way they like, and even nap if they wish.[6] All of these visible workplace aspects illustrate Zappos's cultural artifacts. Artifacts can also include company programming and perks. For example, Zappos uses the unique approach of offering new hires $1,000 to quit if they believe that the company is not the right fit for them.[7]

Just like with many other companies, when employees start working for Zappos, they attend a four-week training program that introduces the new hires to the company's beliefs.[8] But what makes Zappos unique is its focus and training on the ten espoused values of the company, including "Create Fun and a Little Weirdness," "Do More with Less," and "Be Humble." Espoused values describe what organizations profess to prioritize, including norms created collectively to guide behavior. However, what an organization *claims* to stand for is one thing; experiencing those values as authentic and deeply embedded in the way the company does business is another matter entirely. Schein refers to these actual norms as *underlying assumptions.*[9]

Underlying assumptions are the foundational thoughts an organization takes for granted that fundamentally impact how it works. If an underlying assumption contradicts the stated values of the company, the culture becomes diluted and inauthentic. Enron was a powerful example of the risk created by this kind of disconnect. Let's look at the stated values of that company:

> *Communication*—We have an obligation to communicate.
>
> *Respect*—We treat others as we would like to be treated.
>
> *Integrity*—We work with customers and prospects openly, honestly, and sincerely.
>
> *Excellence*—We are satisfied with nothing less than the very best in everything we do.[10]

Despite this articulation of Enron's priorities, investigations into the energy and commodities company later revealed common practices of shredding documents, ignoring internal warnings about accounting inaccuracies, and hiding huge losses.[11] While the official values included operating with honesty and integrity, the underlying assumption of the culture of Enron was to profit at any cost. This disconnect between what they claimed to care about and what they actually valued was at the heart of the lack of credibility of the company, and it ultimately contributed to Enron's downfall.

Zappos, by contrast, has established that each and every one of its employees should feel free to be themselves. Their unique traits distinguish them individually, but the collective weirdness unites them. This commitment to authenticity is consistent throughout all levels of Zappos's culture, from the distinctive office decorations to the values themselves. Its value of "Creating Fun and a Little Weirdness" has resulted in Zappos developing a team of "Fungineers," which aims to ensure that the company is living out that value through unique employee experiences across the company. These stated mantras evolved from Zappos's core priority to embrace the unconventional and the unexpected. What one sees and experiences when visiting a Zappos office clearly reflects its espoused values, leading to its reputation as a credible and authentic company.

When talking about changing or creating a culture, it's tempting to start with new programming or renovating workspaces. However, the most crucial part of building an authentic culture involves connecting the visible artifacts to the company's deeper and less visible layers to manifest what the organization fundamentally believes.

THE GENTELLIGENT CULTURE

Most existing efforts to transform organizational cultures to appeal to multiple generations focus exclusively on the layer of artifacts. To catch the attention of the newest and youngest job seekers, for example, organizations tend to invest in surface-level, visible improvements rather than focusing on the more challenging, more in-depth aspects of their corporate cultures. One current trend is the incentive or perk-based culture. Companies have reimagined their offices and their employee benefits by removing cubicles in favor of open floor plans, building new gaming rooms with foosball tables and Nintendo Switches, and adding beer on tap in the employee lounges. While these perks were meant to welcome Millennials and Gen Zers into the workplace, they have partially resulted in the opposite, pushing away the targeted young audiences and other generations as well.

Gallup's article "How Millennials Want to Work and Live" found that only 18 percent of Millennials prioritized having a "fun" place to work, and only 15 percent viewed an informal work environment as important. This highlights a generational assumption that must be resisted—that Millennials are constant fun seekers who are drawn in by surface-level attempts to entertain them. In reality, Millennials, Baby Boomers, and Gen Xers all ranked other factors, such as the quality of their managers and company management, higher across the board.[12] According to Nina McQueen, LinkedIn's vice president of global talent,

> While people generally love the idea of perks like free food and game rooms, our research shows this is actually one of the least enticing factors for keeping professionals at their current companies. Instead, people would much rather see their company focusing on benefits like learning and development programs, philanthropic opportunities, and more.[13]

In a company like Zappos, the quirky artifacts and trendy perks are successful because they align with what the company fundamentally believes. However, focusing solely on the visible elements of culture without exploring what lies beneath can reveal that the generationally inclusive culture exists only superficially.

In our quest to find an organization that has successfully integrated generational inclusion at all levels, we discovered Workday, the HR and financial-management software company. Workday is one of the few organizations to be named by the Great Place to Work Institute as a "Best Workplace for Millennials,"[14] "Best Workplace for Gen X,"[15] and "Best Workplace for Baby Boomers,"[16] as well as "Global Best Workplace."[17] To accomplish this, the company has created a range of programs and experiences that reflect a deeply rooted commitment to making sure the input of all generations is evident in how they do business. By working to understand what matters to employees of different ages and generational identities, Workday has been able to create an environment that authentically includes all levels and layers of culture. Kala Moynihan, an account executive at Workday, enjoys opportunities to work with colleagues across generations. (Moynihan is a member of Gen X but has a Millennial boss and several Gen Z teammates.) She states,

> Our founders have put a premium on the employee experience and our culture. They believe that happy employees create happy customers. They are very intentional about maintaining our culture and investing in programs to keep Workday a "Best Place to Work." Workday also does a good job of career development programs that are valuable to younger generations (in my opinion), but also benefit the entire workforce.[18]

Its Generation Workday program is a powerful example of this commitment. The program aims to develop and engage its newest employees as they begin their journey at the company. By investing in its young employees, the company believes everyone ultimately benefits from the early transfer of organizational wisdom and a strong leadership pipeline. One element of this program, known as Generation Workday Pitch In, harnesses the fresh insight of younger employees to develop ideas for products, technologies, and service opportunities. Older employees mentor participants, lending their organizational experience to troubleshoot new concepts. Senior executives choose the winners, and many of the ideas ultimately influence company decisions and product offerings.[19] Workday reports that Millennial participants in the Generation Workday program average a 90 percent retention rate, and chief human resource officer Ashley Goldsmith states, "We've really listened to what Millennials want from their work environment. . . . Money and advancement will always play a role, but it's also important to this generation that their work is vital to Workday's success. In turn they have shown us their commitment to Workday."[20]

Workday's attention to generational diversity goes beyond its strong focus on Millennials and Gen Zers. The company's commitment to engaging and valuing all generations is apparent in its Opportunity Onramps™ program as well. This initiative includes returnships for parents and caregivers who left the workforce for any duration, allowing employees at mid-career to rejoin and flourish with the necessary support.[21] While these programs are visible artifacts of the culture, they stem from an embedded assumption and foundational belief that employees of all ages and generations are vital to the company's success and connect to the organization's core values of dedication to employees and innovation.[22]

Companies in more traditional industries are also feeling the pressure to reconsider their approach to age and generational diversity. At Huntington Ingalls Industries (HII), the largest military shipbuilding company in the United States, the median age of the workforce is forty-five. Many of its long-time employees are preparing to retire, and the need to transfer institutional knowledge and wisdom is vital. This concentration of older workers in the company has created a Gentelligence opportunity: to Expand the Pie by offering new paths and opportunities for older workers willing to take on new career challenges through an apprenticeship program. While apprenticeships are traditionally thought of as paths for younger workers, HII has eliminated age limits for its apprenticeship program, increasing participation opportunities for older workers. Charlene DeWindt graduated from HII's apprenticeship program in her late fifties, becoming an electrician and significantly increasing her salary, opportunities, and job engagement. DeWindt calls the program life-changing, telling *Forbes* in 2016, "This program has allowed me the opportunity to learn so much, keep my brain and body active, and save more for retirement."[23] By Resisting Assumptions about how to fill its talent pipeline, HII is able to better meet twenty-first-century business challenges.

While employees tend first to experience organizational culture at a surface level, to create meaningful, lasting change, it is important to dive deeper to more substantive levels. By exploring what we *believe*, then connecting what we believe to what we *say*, and finally aligning those with what we *do* and *see*, we can identify ways to transform our cultures into truly Gentelligent workplaces.

Transformation 1: What We Believe

If employees do not recognize and address what is presumed at the very deepest levels of their organizations, their cultures will not genuinely change. To move forward, managers must ask what beliefs their organizations cling to surrounding age diversity and expectations. According to Schein, these kinds of beliefs are hard to identify because they are so deeply ingrained in how business is, often unconsciously, done. Schein says it well: "It is only if we dig beneath the surface of values by observing behavior carefully, noting anomalies, inconsistencies, or phenomena that remain unexplained that we elicit from the insiders their underlying assumptions."[24] In order to discover what an organization believes, its employees have to further explore their own actions.

To see what is hiding in plain sight, managers must examine corporate practices and norms through a critical lens. Bill Taylor, cofounder of *Fast Company*, describes how this is done at the game company Cranium, Inc. On a recent visit, Taylor was struck by the commitment of the company leadership to determine whether its existing practices met the standards of CHIFF—an acronym standing for *clever*, *high-quality*, *innovative*, *friendly*, and *fun*, which are the core values of Cranium, Inc. Every employee at the company can question whether practice aligns with those values. The company even invested in a senior executive who champions the presence of those beliefs throughout the organization.[25]

This practice of reevaluating whether the values match the actions can help create more Gentelligent cultures as well. We suggest encouraging (and incentivizing) leaders and employees to identify existing practices and norms that are not generationally inclusive. Nothing should be sacred, even (or especially) practices that represent company tradition and established protocol. By enlisting people of all ages and career stages in this critical review, companies will likely uncover embedded beliefs that obstruct or limit intergenerational potential. Such roadblocks can be lurking in a company's hiring, decision-making, and ongoing learning processes. A great starting point asks, "What around here *isn't* Gentelligent?"

A growing practice in multigenerational workplaces is to implement reverse mentoring, or pairing of a younger employee with an older one to teach the senior employee new kinds of knowledge or skills. GE is credited with developing the first reverse-mentoring program in 1999 when Jack Welch paired managers with younger employees to accelerate management's learning about the newly formed internet.[26] Today, approximately 14 percent of organizations report having a reverse-mentoring program of some kind, meaning that it is far from a widespread practice.[27] Broadly defined, *reverse mentoring* involves a younger employee sharing perspectives and skills with a more seasoned colleague.[28] Most often, reverse mentoring helps older individuals better understand technology and innovation.

While we applaud the idea of reverse mentoring in practice, we want to highlight an underlying assumption embedded in the term itself. *Reverse mentoring* implies that true mentoring typically occurs only in one direction, with an older employee teaching a younger one. This idea reveals a presumption that learning happening the other way is unexpected and arguably opposite its intended direction. Regardless of which direction the knowledge is flowing, a Gentelligent culture will view multidirectional, intergenerational information exchange and guidance as merely "mentoring." In the case of an exchange of different types of knowledge, we suggest using the term *mutual mentoring* as a more inclusive, precise, and desirable term.

Mutual Mentoring

Mentoring, regardless of the direction of the learning, provides employees across generations a chance to connect on a deeper level and explore their distinct, yet equally important, kinds of knowledge, experience, and perspectives. Mutual mentoring is an intergenerational learning opportunity that both Strengthens Trust and Expands the Pie. Research has established that successful intergenerational learning allows its participants to learn about each other and their respective generations; to better appreciate the world, people, and events that are relevant to them; and to build knowledge or skills.[29]

The concept of intergenerational learning describes any task that asks multiple generations to work together on a shared activity.[30] Research has shown that intergenerational learning benefits its participants, regardless of age, by developing strong positive relationships between the generations and furthering cohesion and social inclusion between the generations.[31] Through intergenerational learning, all participants are given the chance to teach and to learn, growing their skills while impacting wisdom on the other party. The benefits are spread out, allowing each generation to gain without anyone losing. In order to move employees toward a mindset of Expanding the Pie, leaders must create opportunities for these sorts of experiences.

The Fung Fellowship for Wellness & Technology Innovation at UC Berkeley is a great example of an innovative program harnessing the power of intergenerational learning. According to director Joni Rubin, the program aims to train undergraduates as health and tech innovators to address the health and wellness needs of older adults. An integral part of the training is an intergenerational partnership within the design team. While the students work to use their skills to develop technology that will help older adults live healthier and longer lives, the older adults on the teams provide feedback and mentoring—on both the products being designed and professional skills.[32] This relationship benefits all parties by giving the students much-needed feedback on their products from the target audience and giving the older adults the chance to coach and train a student as they are developing.

Kellogg Co. is jumping aboard the intergenerational learning trend as well, hiring a set of "inspiring Gen Z leaders" to help the company design its newest Kashi cereal. Why does such a well-established company need (or want) the input of twelve- to seventeen-year-olds to launch a new kind of cereal? The same reason the students in the Fung Fellowship would want to hear from their elders: if they listen to members of a different generational cohort who happen to be their product user, everyone wins. Kellogg will sell more cereal if it is designed the way the kids want it, and the kids will get a product that is more likely to appeal to them. While marketing to the next generation is not a new concept, leveraging that generation's talent for unique ideas is a great example of Gentelligence in action.

Huntington Ingalls Industries is also meeting this ongoing challenge head on by focusing on both the importance of older workers' expertise and the fresh perspective younger workers bring. While new digital technology is changing the way ships are built, traditional methods endure, and blending the old with the new ways is essential for success.

Brent Woodhouse, a former manager of digital shipbuilding workforce development for the company, says that HII relies on its more experienced workers to mentor and guide its newest ones through challenges and process issues. HII also leans on its younger, more digitally savvy workers to teach less technologically proficient colleagues new skills, creating Gentelligent team collaborations.[33] This is the power of intergenerational learning and collaboration: to build more together, to innovate, and to successfully adapt.

The University of Pittsburgh created a program called "Intergenerational Engineering" that pairs students with retired engineers as mentors. The mentors, who have been retired for between four and ten years, use their career experience to assist these students and explain subjects in a concrete way that makes sense to them. This cross-generational program has improved the retention rate of female and African American students and helped international students to understand American culture as it relates to engineering. This initiative has become a model for other engineering schools in facilitating mentorship programs that benefit both groups. Retirees with decades of experience get to share their expertise with young people soon entering their profession. The college students welcome guidance as they begin their professional journeys and show the retirees that their perspectives are relevant, appreciated, and valued.

For Millennials and Gen Zers, mutual mentoring provides a chance to contribute to their companies in a meaningful way, to be heard, and to demonstrate their leadership abilities early in their careers.[34] Mutual mentoring often has substantial benefits for both the mentor and the mentee, including increased job satisfaction and organizational commitment. Empowering younger employees to mentor also allows the organization to recognize its future leaders, to create a more collaborative culture by building stronger intergenerational relationships, and to minimize generational conflicts. Regardless of age, these experiences bring benefits to all participants, including strong positive relationships across generations, shared learning activities, and increased cohesion and social inclusion between age cohorts.[35] Once leaders have established what the overall organization believes, they can begin to share and demonstrate these beliefs with stakeholders.

Transformation 2: What We Say

The second transformation involves how employees talk about their company cultures. To build Gentelligent workplaces, we suggest building a generationally aligned set of shared values and setting a bold goal for a company's intergenerational collaborations. To inspire action, an organization needs a substantive, aspirational target to envision what is possible. Since so few organizations currently promote a Gentelligent culture, we use the term *aspirational* intentionally to capture the need to work collectively toward a desired future rather than being content with the current reality. For an organization to build this culture, it must set a goal that focuses attention and energy on valuing, appreciating, and leveraging perspectives of all generations.

Aspirational Goal

How can companies ensure that the Gentelligence goals they set will be successfully achieved? Research on goal setting provides several key suggestions to maximize the likelihood of achieving the goal. First, the most motivating goals are specific and challenging, yet realistic.[36] Such goals focus on an organization's collective energy by establishing a clear target without being so ambitious as to seem unattainable. In most studies, these types of goals resulted in greater success than vague "do your best" goals or the absence of any aim whatsoever.[37] In determining the sweet spot for aspirational achievement, we recommend imagining a reality that doesn't presently exist but one that organizational leaders believe is possible with increased effort and energy. Another key strategy for effective goal setting allows all employees to help determine the finish line. Involvement in goal setting has been shown to increase the overall effectiveness of the goal, enabling individuals to take ownership of that shared direction, helping to break down resistance to change, and building commitment, all of which are essential to achieving the desired culture.[38]

For those who previously viewed generational differences merely as frustration, the goal of creating a Gentelligent culture may seem out of reach. Gentelligence itself is an audacious goal and a daunting undertaking. We have found countless instances of companies that moved closer to it by creating training programs, piloting talent strategies to attract and retain younger workers, and developing returnships to more fully engage older workers. Yet if such programs aren't grounded in a shared aspiration for creating a Gentelligent culture, they are likely to lose steam over time, replaced by subsequent trends. As is the case with any kind of diversity initiative, piecemeal programs and one-off efforts often fail to create an authentic "atmosphere of inclusion."[39] Conversely, initiatives that are clearly linked to a broader collective ambition are more likely to be given leadership support and find successful integration within the organization.

The Gentelligent culture is built in the spirit of what management guru Peter Senge famously calls "the learning organization." Senge envisions a learning organization as one "made up of employees skilled at creating, acquiring, and transferring knowledge. These people could help their firms cultivate tolerance, foster open discussion, and think holistically and systemically."[40] Gentelligent entities are true learning organizations, built on an aspirational vision for intergenerational learning and defined by a recognition of shared values across generations. Through the creation of learning opportunities between ages, all workplace perspectives are included.

While the specific goal around Gentelligence should be customized to represent the direction of each organization, it should be rooted in the shared belief that all ages and generations of people have valuable perspectives and insights that enhance the collective experience of employees, customers, and other stakeholders. Textbox 8.1 provides a starting point to developing a Gentelligent aspiration but should be tailored to the unique nature of the organization.

TEXTBOX 8.1

GENTELLIGENT ASPIRATION

To create an organization built on *growth and learning* that can *unlock the potential and power* of a *multigenerational* workforce.

Organizational Values

When it comes to this layer of organizational culture, establishing a shared aspiration to become more Gentelligent means that colleagues must also consider how their current organizational values may be seen differently by those of different ages and career stages. The values of an organization serve as its guideposts in aligning its decisions with what the company prioritizes most. While these beliefs belong to the organization as a whole, every person in the organization also needs to see themselves represented in those values to feel membership. There is a bit of a balancing act involved in simultaneously appreciating generational differences while also building a cohesive culture of shared values. Diversity researchers Nicola Pless and Thomas Maak describe this delicate balance as "recognizing difference while looking for the common bond."[41] How, then, do employees appreciate and support individuality while also building something collectively? They Adjust the Lens to consider how organizational values might be interpreted and expressed differently across generations.

Remember the four values that research has shown all generations to share? The first is *respect*, which includes feeling valued and vital to the organization. The next is *competence* or the perception that one is knowledgeable and skilled. Everyone craves *connection*, or collaborating with colleagues and experiencing mutual trust. Finally, individuals seek *autonomy*, including the freedom and independence to exercise judgment and make sound decisions. While employees of all ages share these values, the way they prioritize those values may differ across different life and career stages. For example, research shows that younger generations tend to focus more on career development and older age cohorts often seek involvement with family and society.[42] When considering organizational values, leaders must recognize these nuances between employees based on their life stages and allow for latitude in how such values are expressed in the workplace.

Returning to the example of a company that talks the talk and walks the walk, Zappos's oath of employment expands its ten core values to include sample behaviors that fit each value. As an example, for the mantra "Create Fun and a Little Weirdness," it suggests that an employee could demonstrate this by "embrac[ing] others' points of view and individuality, [having] an authentic sense of self, and let[ting] their inner quirkiness come out."[43] This description articulates the role of fun in the workplace while acknowledging that employees of different ages and generations may have different ways of interpreting it.

A successful change toward a Gentelligent culture does not require an entirely new organizational vision, nor does it require tossing out old values. Rather, it requires intentionally aiming for generational inclusion, and being willing to consider our current values in potentially new ways.

Transformation 3: What We Do and See

The final transformation necessary to create genuine, lasting culture change in an organization is to consider our artifacts: *what we do* and *see*. Once organizations have become more Gentelligent in what they believe and what they say, they can then invest in artifacts that will make their efforts toward generational inclusion more visible. Developing formal programs that signal the importance of all employees' voices regardless of their positions or career stages can powerfully signal a deeper commitment. When leadership invests time and resources into such opportunities, it closes the gap between theoretically "valuing generational diversity of thought" and the everyday practice of hearing and understanding these perspectives.

Throughout this book, we have addressed ways to approach talent, teams, and leadership in ways that will create Gentelligence in your organization. We now offer two more examples of highly visible programs (artifacts) that demonstrate a clear commitment to generational inclusion and diversity: Employee Resource Groups (ERGs) and Intergenerational Boards. These two programs reflect practical ways to take a Gentelligent approach to talent, teams, *and* leadership.

Employee Resource Groups

One growing strategy to promote all types of diversity within an organization is creating an Employee Resource Group. ERGs are voluntary, employee-led groups that are often built around common demographic factors, such as gender, race, sexual orientation, and age, and are sponsored by the organization.[44] ERGs have long provided members of diverse communities with support within a corporate structure. These groups have found great deals of success at both the individual and the organizational levels. For individual employees, ERGs facilitate professional development, networking, mentoring, and other learning opportunities. Companies that implement ERGs show improved business operations, greater attraction and retention of diverse employees, and more successful change initiatives.[45]

Organizations have begun to explore how ERGs can provide the same benefits for generational diversity as they have for other kinds of differences in the workplace. To date, such ERG efforts have primarily focused on making one generation (usually a younger one) feel more included. In 2010, MasterCard developed an ERG for young professionals known as YoPros for employees with less than ten years of experience. Ryan Beautry, the founder and current global chair of the group, explained the reason for the group: "We realized that Millennials bring a different perspective to MasterCard, one that could help move from a world of cash and plastic to a world integrated across new technologies and platforms."[46] The group regularly holds Youth Summits, in which members consider the interest that young people will have in prospective products.[47] By reviewing products for the company, YoPros can meaningfully contribute to Mastercard using their expertise, and Mastercard is able to collect feedback from the very group to which it is marketing.

While groups aimed at one generation are necessary and helpful, Gentelligent cultures need resource groups that invite members across ages to the same table. Some companies have already begun building such groups. While Aetna currently has three separate ERGs that serve Baby Boomers, Generation Xers, and Millennials, the groups often work together around substantive projects such as onboarding for new employees and, more informally, as cross-generational mentors.

Nielsen developed Nielsen Generation (NGen) to educate and understand generational differences between employees. This group recently launched *GenTalk*, a video series that places two employees of different generations who share a common characteristic, such as demographic similarities, together and asks them to discuss generational differences.[48] For example, two members of PRIDE (Nielsen's ERG for LGBTQ+), one Gen Xer and one Millennial, shared what they wish they could tell members of other generations as well as what they would say to future generations of their group's leaders. PNC Financial Services has developed a group known as iGen, which focuses on intergenerational learning. William Demchak, the CEO and president of PNC, comments, "A diverse and multigenerational workforce better positions PNC to understand and provide for our customer's evolving preferences."[49] By focusing on what employees share, companies can find common ground between their employees. Affinity groups like these allow for cross-generational transfers of knowledge and promote a workplace culture of respect and connection.

Kiyona Miah of the U.S. Census helped form NextGen, an ERG for younger generations to learn from older employees. While NextGen began as a group designed for Millennials, over time, it has removed any generational constraint to welcome all ages. She believes this resource group was essential in allowing employees across generations to Adjust the Lens:

> You can be intimidated by someone's tenure or title, and working in these groups can help people connect on a different level, allowing us to have dialogue and conversations. All of the organizations/affinity groups have executive champions who shepherd the group along—guiding, furthering the mission, and giving support. For NextGen, one of our former leaders wanted to see where our generational differences truly are. Through this, we found department areas where there weren't many people of the younger generations and where we lacked older people who could mentor.[50]

Companies that already have generationally based ERGs in place should consider whether those groups evolved in a way that both supports the unique needs of individual generations and provides opportunities to learn across age cohorts. Entities that have yet to develop such programs should think strategically about the best way to set them up. Some organizations need an individual ERG for every generation; others may construct groups to break down current barriers in different ways. Using resource groups in this way can be a key tool to Resist Assumptions, help employees Adjust the Lens, and Strengthen Trust.

Board Inclusion (and Those "Shadow Boards")

For any culture-building strategy to succeed, company leaders must not only support Gentelligence but also show that support in highly visible ways. In doing so, leadership sends an important signal about what matters. When it comes to what we see and do, one of the most vital considerations is who is allowed a seat at the decision-making table. Traditionally, these seats have been reserved for those with the longest tenure and the highest rank, reflecting an underlying cultural assumption that those at the top know best and that those who are younger, newer, or just entering the hierarchy should have less influence when policies and protocols are being crafted.

Organizational boards are one highly visible place to revisit this assumption. The purpose of a board is to envision the company's future and develop a plan to get there. Boards often comprise older individuals with extensive experience, which remains important, but frequently lack the perspective of the organization's younger employees, who have high stakes in the company's long-term success. Ultimately, a look at current board demographics suggests that a radical shift is needed in who companies invite to the boardroom table. Historically, boards have assumed that the insight needed on the board only comes with age. The time for such assumptions is over, and the time to include diverse perspectives and types of knowledge is now. Boards are tackling issues that younger generations have vital insights on, including social and cultural trends and rapidly changing digital technologies.[51] Furthermore, the future of every company is decided at that table; therefore, room must be made for those with the greatest stake in that future: the youngest members.

While discussions about board diversity have recently increased, they have focused primarily on gender, race, ethnicity, and to some extent, skills. A recent poll by PwC found that directors were over twice as interested in increasing gender diversity as they were in increasing age diversity on boards.[52] Currently, only 6 percent of seats are estimated to be held by individuals under the age of fifty.[53] While boards still largely exclude younger generations from the mix, there are some notable exceptions. Kiran Ariz of EY was elected to the Norwegian Refugee Council at age thirty. She comments,

> I am part of an extremely dedicated board where I probably have more to learn than I have to give, but I do have insights to share. I am a Millennial, like a large number of today's refugees; I am a lawyer; and I am Norwegian-Pakistani. I bring a different perspective to the conversation.[54]

In March 2019, the Tate Modern appointed Anna Lowe, a twenty-eight-year-old digital strategist and trained art educator, to its board as a youth engagement Tate trustee.[55] This appointment, coupled with additional programs the museum had already begun, was a visible step in finding new approaches to attract young people to visit the Tate Modern. As the board builds its vision and shapes the museum's culture, having a Millennial on the board brings another perspective to these meetings. According to Colleen Dilenschneider, chief market engagement officer at IMPACTS Research & Development,

> Neglecting millennial board representations doesn't necessarily mean that there aren't loads of important conversations taking place in these Millennial-bereft boardrooms about how to better engage this valuable cohort. I have found that it's not uncommon at many board meetings for there to be many Baby Boomers and a few members of Generation X waxing poetic about the urgent need to engage Millennials without any input from actual Millennials.[56]

In addition to inviting younger employees to the board, a new concept known as "shadow boards" is starting to emerge. On a shadow board, younger non-executive employees assist senior executives on strategic initiatives and provide their age cohorts' perspectives and insights. Gucci created a shadow board of Millennials in 2015 to make the company more relevant to modern consumers. Composed of some of the organization's top talent, this board of younger employees meets with the senior leadership regularly. Gucci CEO Mario Bizzarri reported to *Harvard Business Review* that the exchanges from its shadow board have "served as a wakeup call for the executives" on how they could run their business more effectively.[57]

While we love the increased role for younger people at the boardroom table, we take issue with the term *shadow board*. This is where our earlier tool for detecting problematic underlying assumptions forces us to ask whether the term itself is truly Gentelligent. Just like the phrase *reverse mentoring*, using the qualifier of *shadow* reflects an underlying assumption that must be addressed. Namely, it implicitly signals that young people, while invited into the boardroom, should stay in the shadow of the older and more experienced "real" board members, providing value that is peripheral to the primary source of executive power.

Despite the questionable semantics, research has found that these groups do help companies redesign business models and processes, transform organizational cultures, and engage all generations in executive decision making.[58] We suggest that if the younger members were taken out of the shadows, they could have an even greater impact. The benefits of including younger people on boards are not limited to the perspective they can add; they also involve the development and learning that board membership provides. Given the importance Millennials place on understanding the purpose of their work, being present for high-level strategy and vision conversations can be a career-changing experience.

These benefits do not come without struggles. Intergenerational boards can encounter issues as seemingly inconsequential as ideal formats and schedules for meetings to more serious conflicts such as time commitments and the meaning of member engagement. For many years, I was a recurring speaker at an annual board chair meeting for a regional cooperative council. While the chairs came from a range of different cooperative industries (such as electrical and agricultural), most were struggling with ways to create age diversity on their boards. The average age of these board chairs was over seventy years, and they were focused on succession planning.

Some chairs reported initial success with a shadow board model; others issued open invitations to younger candidates to sit in on occasional meetings to see how things were done. Other meeting participants reported that many of the younger people they had approached felt they wouldn't be able to make the lengthy regular board meetings (often in the evenings and sometimes requiring travel) due to both work and life commitments. At one point, I asked whether there might be flexibility in meetings to allow for more involvement of younger members, such as allowing board members to use virtual conferencing tools to call in remotely. For most, this suggestion was not seen as a possible solution, as there had been no precedents for alternative ways to schedule or participate in the meetings. A few, however, seemed intrigued by this different approach to their goal, and we spent time brainstorming other options that might allow those with different life-stage demands to have a voice in that board setting. While COVID-19 has undoubtedly forced many organizations—including organizations previously hesitant to use virtual conference calls—to experiment with virtual conferencing tools, it remains to be seen whether this transformative period leads to enduring change. Regardless, a precedent for alternative ways to schedule or participate in meetings has been established.

Just like mutual mentoring, Gentelligent boards facilitate intergenerational learning. They require expertise from both people in senior leadership (who tend to be older) and newer, younger employees who closely connect to rising demographic markets. Such boards bring their participants substantial opportunities to Resist Assumptions, Adjust the Lens, and Strengthen Trust across generations, as well as Expand the Pie by finding ways to work together.

To be genuinely inclusive, organizations must support others who voice diverse perspectives and be open to alternative ways of working.[59] We have highlighted just a few programs that demonstrate how organizations can accomplish this task in highly visible ways, providing a clear signal to everyone engaged in the culture that there is a seat at the table for all generations.

TOWARD GENERATIONALLY INCLUSIVE CULTURES

We are often asked why generational differences are getting so much attention these days. The easy answer is because there are now an unprecedented number of generations in the workplace, with Gen Z reaching adulthood and entering the labor market. Yet simply *having* so many generations in companies will not automatically build Gentelligent cultures. Conversely, so many age cohorts within a workplace might create tensions between generations. Cohesion between these generations will require strategic action and practice. Perceptions of inclusion push beyond the mere presence of diversity to create "an environment that allows people with multiple backgrounds, mindsets, and ways of thinking to work effectively together and perform to their highest potential."[60] An inclusive climate recognizes, values, and engages these generational differences to help solve problems and make decisions.[61] Transformation to an authentically Gentelligent culture is a complex undertaking. It demands thoughtfully considering whether all aspects of what companies believe, say, and do are in alignment. It requires utilizing the Gentelligence principles. Companies must Resist Assumptions that consign them to old patterns and Adjust the Lens to redefine what kinds of knowledge and experience are valuable. Through mutual mentoring and other intergenerational learning opportunities, employees must take the initiative to Strengthen Trust with those who aren't initially seen as likely teachers. Leaders must seek out innovative and forward-thinking approaches to Expand the Pie in visible ways.

While developing inclusive organizational culture requires significant investment, early research suggests that the returns can be substantial. Benefits include increased levels of organizational commitment and job satisfaction, greater well-being, decreased stress, and lower turnover.[62] Pless and Maak state that within inclusive cultures,

> Different voices are understood as being legitimate and as opening up new vistas; they are heard and integrated in decision making and problem-solving processes; they have an active role in shaping culture and fostering creativity and innovation; and eventually in adding value to the company's performance.[63]

Through a Gentelligent culture aligned across the three levels of organizational culture (underlying assumptions, espoused ideals, and artifacts), companies ensure that every generation feels connected and included. Ultimately, a strong and thoughtfully designed culture ensures the lasting success and power of Gentelligent solutions.

9

Gentelligence for the Future of Work

It is not necessary to change. Survival is not mandatory.

—Edward Deming[1]

In early 2020, the phrase "OK Boomer" made it to the U.S. Supreme Court, with Chief Justice John Roberts questioning whether its use represented ageism.[2] To mark this formal case of generation conflict, I wrote an article for *NBC News*, highlighting several troublesome concerns. Ultimately, generational name-calling forced the issue of whether what started as an amusing meme had the potential to violate the U.S. Age Discrimination Act. Our generational tensions have become so evident that they found their way into the federal conversation of the Supreme Court. Do we need formal legislation to ensure that we treat other generations with respect? As I argue in my article, legal protections from generational name-calling aren't going to solve the problem completely.[3] In reality, what is needed is a fundamental shift in how we value people of all ages.

We call for an end to the generation wars. In their place, we challenge business leaders to unlock the talent potential of our diverse, intergenerational workforce by proactively attracting, developing, and engaging employees at every age. The current conversations surrounding generational differences in the news and in everyday life are often full of stereotypes and finger-pointing. Many rely on anecdotes rather than research and do little more than feed the generational bias that restricts our ability to become Gentelligent.

Gentelligence is needed now and needed urgently. Changes to the nature of work, a seismic shift in our demographic makeup, and an increasingly connected world demand thoughtful strategies to attract, develop, and lead our talent. Organizations that attempt to launch change programs and revamp their cultures without holistically considering the views and needs of all generations will fail to survive.

THE CASE FOR CHANGE

A Demographic Urgency

The world is home to almost 7.8 billion people, and workplace age demographics are shifting globally in unprecedented ways. The number of people above the age of seventy is universally *increasing*, while the number of people under the age of twenty-four is *decreasing*. However, when it comes to the age cohorts in between—Millennials, Gen Xers, and the youngest Baby Boomers—the trends shift substantially in different parts of the world. For example, Asia, Africa, and Latin America will experience a spike in the number of people aged twenty-five to sixty-nine between 2020 and 2050, while Europe and Northern America will have a decline of the population in that age group. While the demographic dynamics differ by geographic region, as shown in table 9.1, one thing is clear: generational cooperation will be urgently needed to navigate the changes these shifts will bring.

Moving beyond Current Laws and Policies

The rapid changes in demographic trends and in the workplace paint a clear picture for the need for stronger, more productive generational and age dynamics; yet the way forward to achieve this goal has continued to be elusive. So far, formal attempts to legislate better age and generational relationships in the United States and abroad have had limited impact.

Table 9.1. Age Percentage Trends Around the World (all numbers in percentages [%])

	2020			2050			Change		
Graphic Region	*0–24*	*25–69*	*70+*	*0–24*	*25–69*	*70+*	*0–24*	*25–69*	*70+*
Africa	59.6	38.4	2.0	50.4	46.2	3.5	↓	↑	↑
Asia	38.8	55.8	5.3	30.3	56.9	12.8	↓	↑	↑
Europe	26.3	60.3	13.4	24.5	53.9	21.6	↓	↓	↑
Latin America and the Caribbean	40.3	53.9	5.8	29.4	57.0	13.6	↓	↑	↑
Northern America	31.1	57.6	11.4	27.9	54.7	17.4	↓	↓	↑
Oceania	37.9	53.3	8.8	33.6	53.2	13.3	↓	↔	↑

Source: United Nations, Department of Economic and Social Affairs, Population Division, *World Population Prospects 2019*, United Nations, 2019, https://population.un.org/wpp.

As previously discussed, the United States currently lacks substantial laws or policies to address age or generational challenges in the workplace, relying only on the Age Discrimination in Employment Act as a way to prevent older-age discrimination, and having no current legislation addressing or promoting generational cooperation. While the bar to meet the current U.S. legal requirements on age seems low, there are still far too many instances when companies fail to reach it.

For decades, IBM was known as the darling of integrating diversity within its business strategy. It created programs that focused on the essential differences between diverse groups instead of the widespread practice of sweeping diversity under the rug. While race and gender became a part of IBM's proactive diversity strategy in the early 1990s, age and generational differences did not. This oversight may have cost the company more than anticipated. In 2019, IBM was accused of implementing rolling layoffs for its older workers as a way to appeal more to potential applicants from the youngest generations. According to internal documents, IBM is said to have begun its efforts to "correct [its] seniority mix" in 2014. Based on an in-depth investigation by *ProPublica*, this "correction" involved firing as many as twenty thousand employees over the age of forty in the last five years to compete with employers like Apple and Facebook as "hip" workplaces of choice for Millennial workers.[4] They went so far that they announced, "What's good for Millennials is good for everyone."[5] A class-action age-discrimination lawsuit and several individual civil suits were filed against IBM in 2019.[6]

IBM is not the only company missing this legal mark when it comes to age in the workplace. In 2018, Google settled a similar class-action lawsuit, with more than two hundred job applicants over the age of forty accusing the tech giant of discriminatory hiring practices. While Google denied any wrongdoing, the case settled for $11 million.[7] The settlement also required Google's parent company, Alphabet Inc., to deliver age bias training to all employees and managers, in addition to creating a committee on age diversity in recruiting.[8]

Outside of the United States, greater government-driven efforts to reduce generational conflicts have been seen in Europe, where the scarcity of jobs often creates a strain between older employees wishing to remain in their positions and younger workers who need to secure employment. The French government introduced its *Contrat de Génération* in 2013 to help balance the needs of younger people entering the labor market while remaining aware of older workers' concerns as well. Under this contract, an employer creates an agreement with two employees, one older than fifty-five and one under thirty. The employer agrees to train younger employees with the help of more senior workers, who agree to devote up to a third of their time to mentor and guide the younger coworkers.

In another example, Belgium introduced its Intergenerational Solidarity Pact in 2005. This pact was originally intended to support older workers by helping to reduce their working hours but discourage them from exiting the job market entirely before the legal retirement age. It was subsequently modified to also address increasing job opportunities for younger ones. The most recent assessment of the impact of this act on improving these targeted age relationships has been deemed "minimal."[9]

These examples offer more formal attempts to promote age and intergenerational cooperation than have been seen in the United States, but even these policies to mandate better intergenerational relations in places across the world appear to have been met with mixed results in terms of effectiveness. While additional efforts may be made in these areas as time goes on, it seems unwise to rely solely on legal mandates to improve age and generational dynamics. Instead, the responsibility for finding the way to move forward falls to the leaders and organizations who wish to thrive in the future of work.

THE FUTURE IS NOW

An online search for the phrase "future of work" currently returns 3.9 million results. The attention to the phenomena manifests its importance and anticipated impact. Concerns and speculation about our rapidly changing business environment have led virtually all organizations to actively prepare for the future of work and future workplaces. Yet no one knows exactly what forms that future will take. In the competition for survival, start-ups are creating quick and agile business models, leveraging new technology infrastructure to become nimbler, and implementing fully digital platforms powered by advanced analytics to enhance the employee experience. As discussed in chapter 8, many well-established businesses are also searching for the future without a detailed and contemporary map, attempting to tackle their human-resource tensions with surface-level interventions.

So far, we have seen some early signs of what is to come, from the emerging gig economy and New Collar jobs to increasing preferences for remote and flexible work arrangements. Beyond this, more fundamental changes in who will work, where work happens, and the kind of work that employees produce are inevitable. Based on rapidly changing age demographics, generational intelligence will be essential to successfully navigating this complex landscape.

Over the past few years, we have sought out people and organizations that are thriving through a Gentelligent approach. We have also explored organizations that found new business ideas in the opportunities of generational partnership; such companies recognize the challenges ahead as moments to thrive and deliver value to the people around them, their communities, and the global economy.

Papa is one such organization. Andrew Parker, CEO and founder of Papa, came up with this business idea in response to a need of his own family in finding companionship for his senior family members. Founded in 2016, the company pairs college students (known as "Papa Pals") with senior citizens to arrange "grandkids on demand," providing companionship as well as help with everyday errands and tasks.[10] The Gen Z college students who work there tend to be interested in social issues and helping professions. Their involvement prepares them for success in future careers in the helping professions by teaching them communication skills, teamwork, and compassion. The seniors enjoy the companionship and the opportunity to remain independent for longer than they otherwise would have without help from their "Papa Pals." Parker believes that the benefits for both the students and the seniors have exceeded expectations. He says, "I don't think we fully understood the impact connecting the two generations would have. We just thought of it as connecting the incredible students and seniors. It was just a huge pool of potential resources that was untapped."[11] In 2020, Papa announced an expansion of its original services to now include a "family on demand" model, stating, "We are proud to affect so many lives with this intergenerational innovation positively."[12] According to its website, the new program "pairs older adults and families with motivated college students for companionship and assistance with everyday tasks."[13]

Another innovative intergenerational business idea is 4GenNow, a nonprofit organization that connects and facilitates funding across four generations of entrepreneurs to support intergenerational startups. Cofounder Jim Sugarman started 4GenNow with his daughter Samantha in 2016, creating their very own successful intergenerational partnership. According to Samantha Sugarman,

> A successful collaboration is coming from a place of wanting to understand a different perspective. Being a great communicator—knowing when to listen, when is the appropriate time to speak, and doing one's best to understand another point a view—goes beyond age. But it's especially important when it comes to bringing different generations together and understanding one's strengths and weaknesses.[14]

The father-and-daughter team has brought this wisdom to their business model, which focuses on the idea that "startups with co-founders from different generations bring complementary skills, experiences and perspectives to be successful and attract angel investment."[15]

Yet another intergenerational business model can be seen at Judson Manor, a retirement community in Cleveland, Ohio. In 2010, Judson partnered with the Cleveland Institute of Music to establish its Student Resident Program. Graduate-level students can live free of charge at Judson in exchange for providing cultural programming for the senior residents. The program has been so successful that it recently expanded to include students from the Cleveland Institute of Art as well.[16]

A different twist on this model comes in the form of intergenerational care centers, such as OneGeneration in Van Nuys, California. Intergenerational care centers are a rapidly growing trend among Gen Xers and Millennials. These centers provide solutions to an urgent and growing need for members of these generations: simultaneous care for both their growing children and their aging parents. Organizations like OneGeneration offer preschool, child daycare, adult care, and senior enrichment programs under one roof.[17] This environment allows for several different types of beneficial partnerships, from seniors caring for young children and tutoring school-aged ones to teens coaching older adults on technology, while providing care for multiple family members.

Similarly, the Eisner Foundation (founded by former Disney CEO Michael Eisner) has an exclusive focus on funding projects and research to create intergenerational solutions to society's problems. According to the foundation, "Intergenerational programs help combat age segregation, which is detrimental to our society. Without regular interaction with older or younger generations outside family, ageism creates an us-versus-them mentality that prevents us from uniting around shared goals and an integrated community."[18] To date, the Eisner Foundation has worked with nonprofit organizations such as Generations United, the Stanford Center on Longevity, Milken Institute Center for the Future of Aging, and Encore.org to support intergenerational initiatives.

Undoubtedly, our example organizations have found opportunities in their current multigenerational reality. However, these companies are only beginning to scratch the surface of what is possible. We predict that new, currently unimaginable business models will continue to emerge as a result of intergenerational information sharing and opportunities for knowledge exchange. While some entrepreneurs and small businesses are already reaping the benefits of a Gentelligent mindset, there has been more of a lag among existing, well-established companies. However, these organizations can choose to be fast followers, unlocking the potential of Gentelligence and reinvigorating their workplaces with new energy to harness novel solutions to changing demands. Doing so requires a Gentelligence toolkit.

YOUR GENTELLIGENCE TOOLKIT

Explicitly designed to create and sustain Gentelligent cultures, the four Gentelligence practices of Resisting Assumptions, Adjusting the Lens, Strengthening Trust, and Expanding the Pie are applicable across industries and address current (and future) critical twenty-first-century business challenges. We need these strategies to tap into the new kinds of diversity, not only those brought by the young or offered from the more experienced but also the types of innovation that can occur by blending those talents to create something entirely new.

This kind of collaboration is only possible with a Gentelligence mindset. The first two practices of Gentelligence (Resist Assumptions and Adjust the Lens) focus on breaking down the barriers that may eclipse the possibilities for intergenerational breakthroughs. To face the daunting challenges ahead, it's useful to revisit some of the more common generational myths that contribute to these barriers. Once misperceptions have dissolved, the final Gentelligence practices (Strengthen Trust and Expand the Pie) become the focus, as these practices are specifically designed to unlock the potential of generational diversity. Those organizations that can leverage this positive power will not simply survive; they will thrive. Throughout this book, we have presented different ways to leverage these practices to navigate everyday business challenges. Table 9.2 displays these strategies as a practical toolkit to help identify the correct approach for any Gentelligent concern.

BUILDWITT MEDIA: A CASE STUDY OF GENTELLIGENCE TOOLS IN ACTION

After dozens of interviews and countless hours of research on intergenerational learning, challenges, and opportunities, we discovered an organization that embodies Gentelligence both internally and externally: BuildWitt Media. BuildWitt, founded by twenty-three-year-old Aaron Witt in 2018, is a digital media group focused on using modern technology to tell the stories of its clients in the construction and mining industries and attract the next generation to work in those fields. The company asks, "How can we expect young people to choose to work alongside us when they don't know we exist?"

Witt's team currently contains eight employees, including vice president Dan Briscoe, who is more than twice his boss's age. The company is driven by a vision to help its clients bring Gentelligence to the construction industry, embodying many of the strategies discussed throughout this book in its Gentelligent approach to talent, teaming, and leadership.[19]

A Gentelligent Approach to Talent

Like many skilled trades, the construction field is struggling to attract younger workers. Kristina Mahler, BuildWitt's partner director, explains that in her view, the industry has struggled severely since Baby Boomers started to retire. According to the Bureau for Labor Statistics,

Table 9.2. The Gentelligence Toolkit

	A Gentelligent Approach to Talent	*The Gentelligent Team*	*Gentelligent Leadership*	*A Gentelligent Culture*
Resist Assumptions	Appreciate individual contributions and create new work categories as well as returnship programs	Identify and welcome different types of knowledge	Focus on competence and expertise to overcome typical age and generational leadership stereotypes	Recognize shared values across generations to avoid falling into an "us-versus-them" mentality
Adjust the Lens	Welcome multiple views on meaningful work to provide tailored opportunities	Create opportunities for the team to discover each contributor's strengths, how they add value, and why no team member is replaceable	Integrate diverse viewpoints from all generations to adapt leadership style to the needs of each generation and meet team members where they are	Embrace and integrate age-diverse perspectives in the workplace to develop programs that allow for cross-generational transfers of knowledge
Strengthen Trust	Develop remote work policies and provide unlimited paid time off to allow flexibility	Establish ground rules and norms for communication to foster psychologically safe team environments	Share power to demonstrate the value of individual contributions and believe in the abilities of team members	Give every employee permission to question whether a practice aligns with the company's values
Expand the Pie	Provide continuous learning and career-development opportunities	Implement programs that focus on the benefits of collaboration rather than competition	Practice generativity (regardless of age) by leading to guide and develop others	Enable intergenerational knowledge exchange through programs such as mutual mentoring and intergenerational boards

Table 9.3. Employed Persons by Detailed Industry and Age (numbers in thousands)

Industry	2019							
	16–19	20–24	25–34	35–44	45–54	55–64	65+	Median Age
Construction	193	875	2,502	2,831	2,454	1,909	609	42.6

Source: U.S. Bureau of Labor Statistics, "Labor Force Statistics from the Current Population Survey," accessed March 27, 2020, www.bls.gov/cps/cpsaat18b.htm.

the median age for those working in the construction field in 2020 is 42.6 years, as seen in table 9.3.[20]

The construction field has surpassed all other industries in terms of the workforce age gap.[21] A report from the USG Corporation and the U.S. Chamber of Commerce found that firms are now asking their existing workers to do more work, struggling to meet scheduling requirements, and turning down opportunities.[22]

BuildWitt's mission is to reverse this trend and "to encourage the younger generation to consider construction as a career."[23] In some ways, what BuildWitt is doing to help its clients attract and retain younger workers may not seem unique or unconventional at all. It uses social media to connect with the younger generation and leverages photography and videography, website development, graphic design, and content writing to tell stories. The *way* they do it is what sets them apart.

Many industry frontrunners are struggling in their attempts to appeal to the desire of younger generations. Despite the pressure to change, few are taking the necessary steps to understand those generational needs at a deep level. Dan Briscoe highlights that "most [companies] are using old-school methods to reach a new-school crowd, like creating brochures and presentations or exhibiting at job fairs."[24] Instead of creating paper pamphlets and giving an endless number of presentations, Aaron Witt uses his social media network to connect with younger workers and potential job seekers.

Too often, companies rely on old traditions when they do business while expecting different and novel outcomes. To attract young talent where others have fallen short, BuildWitt has adjusted its lens to consider how and where young Millennials and Gen Zers get their information. Thanks to its ongoing commitment to better understand the younger generations as a means to help clients attract potential new colleagues, BuildWitt has discovered meaningful demographic insights. It has learned that young people are less influenced by a company's sales pitch or having a bunch of marketing materials thrown at them. Instead, BuildWitt understands that Millennials and Gen Zers respond better to behind-the-scenes footage via YouTube or an Instagram post.

This insight is critical to drawing younger generations to the construction field, but it also creates another hurdle. In construction, the fear of giving away trade secrets or posting something that might not be considered safe leaves companies reluctant to use social media. Construction firms often opt to heavily control what posts appear on various platforms (if they use social media at all). Consequently, their output tends to be generic, lacking the transparency and in-depth content that younger generations crave. This misplaced strategy lacks Gentelligence and often backfires, failing to attract new employees. But BuildWitt's success and genuine social media presence (including an impressive combined following of over 425,000 people) is proof that striking the right balance is possible.

Witt views what his company does as merely shifting the perspective people have on the construction industry:

> While people say we're making construction "cool again," I argue that it's already cool. We just need to get the word out about it and educate people about the extremely fulfilling career opportunities available for people either about to graduate high school or who are older but miserable in their current career.[25]

While building an active social media campaign is a powerful tool to promote an organization, most job candidates don't apply using the same channel. Once initial interest sparks, posting a job ad that appeals to potential workers is the next step.

Just as younger generations want authenticity in a brand, they also look for meaning in the work they do. BuildWitt's website reveals that the company is always looking for people with passion and experience in construction or mining as well as an interest in storytelling. It clearly outlines its fundamental principles and mission to change construction for the better on the landing page. As we would expect from a forward-thinking company, to win the war for talent, it also displays an ongoing commitment to continuous, holistic career development on its website: "BuildWitt will invest in its employees from day one—there aren't any secrets and we don't withhold our trust for months like most."[26] BuildWitt explains on its website that it is a place where employees are expected to push themselves to meet their potential and that it gives its workers the tools they need to be not only better coworkers and clients but also better parents, friends, and leaders.[27]

While there are many ways to attract young workers, BuildWitt shows that it doesn't have to be a complex undertaking. It just requires a willingness to Resist Assumptions and Adjust the Lens. Witt has found that many of his company's clients start out assuming that younger generations aren't willing to work hard, an assumption he pushes back on. He explains, "They lean on this stereotype as an excuse for their own inability to attract the next generation rather than learning how they can better communicate with young people."[28]

Working to really understand the people a company hopes to recruit is vital, and utilizing firsthand sources who belong to the desired recruiting cohort is ideal. Companies that want to hire Gen Zers or Millennials should place a member of those generations (or a few!) in charge of developing the hiring strategy. At a minimum, representatives of the sought-after demographic should have seats at the table and voices in the process.

The Gentelligent Team

At BuildWitt, a deep understanding that the company's success stems from leveraging various generational perspectives in senior leadership keeps the team together. The team members appreciate the different skills and knowledge they bring to the table and are willing to invite additional views when necessary. Briscoe believes the company and his partnership with Witt benefit from their age difference:

> Aaron is technically my boss, but we form a team trying to reach our mission. He often listens to me when my experience is helpful, and I often listen to him when his younger vision is needed. As the oldest person on our team, I have thirty years of experience with leadership, sales, and marketing. But the world has changed. In the first ten years of my career, the internet was just starting to spread. In the second decade, the mobile phone became popular. And just in the last 10 years, we've seen the power of social media. So my experience is sometimes helpful, but often, I'm behind the curve because I didn't grow up with this technology. So, I have to be careful of when to talk and share my advice based on my experience, and when I need to shut up and learn from the experts.[29]

Managing multiple generations in the workplace can seem like a challenging task. Strong individual performances are often recognized and rewarded, while the collective efforts of teams are less likely to receive praise. This recognition gap has the unintended result of undercutting teams and preventing coworkers from developing an Expand the Pie mindset. As we saw in chapter 6, believing our individual contributions are impactful and understanding how our teamwork matters to the organization helps us build significance.

By looking beyond generational stereotypes and intentionally avoiding common pitfalls, team members at BuildWitt have opened up the possibility for everyone to contribute and be seen as valuable team members. On the topic of age-based expertise, Briscoe notes,

> In general, the younger generation is likely more tech-savvy and better with smartphones, social media, and apps. And older generations are typically more well rounded as people leaders and business leaders. But not always. Aaron is constantly learning about business and leadership,

> and he teaches me new things every week in those areas. And there are some areas where I'm much stronger in technology.[30]

Intergenerational teams are a paradox. They can be an utter disaster, or they can be a transformational breakthrough in the diversity of thought (or somewhere in between) depending on how these teams are led and managed. BuildWitt's initial success comes from defining a team structure, enabling everyone to feel valued and respected, and ensuring that people feel supported. Both Briscoe and Witt recognize the benefits they've received from the Gentelligent teaming structure:

> *Briscoe:* Aaron and I, and the rest of BuildWitt, make a good team because we are very different, and both of us are willing to learn from the other. He started the company, and he's the boss, but he also knows he can't be as successful without me. I couldn't create my own company that would work as well as the one that Aaron created. So, we both value each other.[31]
>
> *Witt*: While generational diversity has never been a deliberate goal of ours, I've known it's crucial to our long-term success from the beginning. Being in only my mid-twenties, I don't know what I don't know. I need to surround myself with others who are older and have much more life experience to guide our company in decision making. I'm not concerned much with professional experience, but I am with life experience. Dan, for example, has kept me from imploding many times over. I'm a young bull ready to charge, whereas he's more patient and thoughtful thanks to his decades more life experience that I have.[32]

Gentelligent Leadership

Witt's interest in the construction industry was born at an early age while doing manual labor at a ranch owned by a friend's dad. His next job in the industry was with a storm-drain construction crew in his own upper-class Phoenix neighborhood. Witt's love for getting his hands dirty was what led him to take the relatively unusual (for kids who grow up in affluent families) summer job. While he enjoyed the work itself, his early experiences in construction led him to develop an appreciation for those who work in the industry. "Construction workers don't complain," Witt says. "They just get it done, and they have a ton of fun doing it."[33] It was during this summer internship that he decided that he wanted to spend the rest of his life making a difference in the construction industry.

Rather than starting his own construction business, Witt decided to launch a media group, leveraging his social media platform to connect with people. Undoubtedly, his social media status was a powerful tool and foundation for his business, but to gain respect from his clients and employees, he also had to work hard, listen, and put himself out there. Witt's journey is one about passion, hard work, and continuously meeting new people to innovate driving change. But it is also a story about how Gentelligent leadership rests less on a person's age and more on one's particular idea and willingness to work hard to create the necessary progress.

Gentelligent leadership occurs when age doesn't equate to position or rank, and when expertise, passion, and the ability to build trust and establish respect determine who our leaders are. For young leaders like Witt, negative perceptions and biases can make it challenging to earn workplace respect and credibility from his generationally diverse coworkers or clients.

As such, to unlock the potential of Gentelligent leadership, the team must share a Gentelligent mindset by Resisting Assumptions and Adjusting the Lens. Witt and Briscoe initially worked together at another marketing agency, and Briscoe recalls knowing within the first ten minutes of speaking with Witt that he was going to make a big difference in the construction industry. When Witt opened his own media group in 2018, Briscoe was inspired to go work for him. By Resisting Assumptions about traditional ages and titles, the two have developed a strong relationship. When asked how they would advise others working through a similar dynamic, they responded:

Briscoe: My advice would be to get over yourself and get rid of your ego, to both age groups. Teams have a mission, and someone has to be in

> charge. If you're working for a younger boss, listen and learn in areas where you might not be strong, like technology and communicating with younger workers. And then lend your experience in situations where that is helpful.[34]
>
> *Witt*: Frankly, I ignore the age difference. People ask me what it's like to lead people older than myself, and I have to sit there and think about it because I don't ever give it thought. It's a non-issue. If you have confidence in your vision and ability to drive change and show everyone on your team respect while you do it, you won't have any issues.[35]

While Witt himself has much of the expertise to deliver the competencies his clients need, he also knows that the experience and knowledge of older colleagues helps to build the credibility of BuildWitt to their clients. To do so, Witt sees his older employees as vital partners rather than followers, sharing leadership with his team members. Briscoe adds, "He listens often to me when my experience is helpful, and I listen often to him when his younger vision is needed. That's because both of us put our egos below accomplishing the mission of our company."[36] Witt describes his personal conundrum with clients who have not yet grown a Gentelligent mindset:

> If it were only me running around trying to sell older people on our company, I'd be screwed. I'm a twenty-five-year-old kid who can't grow facial hair. Thanks to leaning on others who are older and more experienced like Dan, we've had a ton of success becoming parts of organizations we'd otherwise have no business being a part of. While people appreciate my drive and vision, they also like to do business with those who are peers.[37]

Ultimately, sharing leadership has made the intergenerational dynamics at BuildWitt the company's secret weapon.

A Gentelligent Culture

To unlock the potential of a multigenerational workforce, organizations need to create a Gentelligent culture. Starting with the *deepest level* and building to the *most visible* connections between underlying assumptions, espoused ideals, and artifacts are prerequisites for creating and sustaining a positive and strong corporate environment. Ultimately, when these elements are evident and connected throughout the entire organization, they substantially impact corporate culture.

In our quest to understand the cultural dynamics at BuildWitt, we started with what we were able to see, then explored what its employees said, and finally pinpointed what the organization believes. We uncovered strong connections between all layers of culture at BuildWitt, pointing to a highly aligned Gentelligent environment. Witt states,

> It's not hard if you have defined and well thought out your values, are vocal about them, and hire based on them. I believe values are universal, regardless of age. Frankly, I could care less what age someone is coming into our organization. I think about things like, "Do they fit with our values?" "Would they enjoy working here?" "Would we enjoy working with them?"[38]

What They Do

BuildWitt has invested in artifacts that reflect what it believes and values. Every email from BuildWitt ends with the signature logo that carries its bright yellow tagline: "Making the dirt world a better place." A visit to its website also clearly signals the company's passion for dirt and the construction industry; the photo gallery is titled "You Won't Find Dirt Photos Like This Anywhere Else." Another click takes you to BuildWitt's "People" page, which depicts construction professionals from all generations—a visual representation of its belief that the industry needs all ages to thrive. These artifacts illustrate BuildWitt's commitment to inspire the next generation of builders and also sets an example for its clients. Witt is on a mission to change the industry: "I'm changing marketing and will soon be changing hiring and training, yes, but I want to ultimately change mindsets—mindsets of both our clients and everyone who views my work."[39]

But the most telling artifact is BuildWitt's own team: Witt (otherwise known as its chief dirt nerd) began the company when he was twenty-three years old (a Millennial, but just barely!), while its vice president (Briscoe) was fifty (a Gen Xer). Krista Mahler, BuildWitt's partnership director, looks at the team at BuildWitt as a living artifact of the change its employees want to bring: "Just by showing up on a job site, our team is challenging the industry norm. Not only do we arrive with a clean-cut twenty-four-year-old and a mom from the suburbs, but we arrive with cameras and drones. All with the intention of improving the outward-facing image and company cultures of our clients and the industry as a whole."[40]

Shortly after joining BuildWitt in 2018, Briscoe wrote an article for LinkedIn titled "My 24-Year-Old Millennial Boss," telling his story of how much he was enjoying working for a boss half his age. The article went viral, with over two million views, twenty-eight thousand likes, and five hundred comments. The written testimonial manifests how BuildWitt is disrupting conventions in construction and generational norms.

What They Say

The middle layer of culture involves what the company says when it talks about its culture. At this level, a Gentelligent organization sets a bold goal for where it wants to be and builds a generationally aligned set of shared values. At BuildWitt, the intergenerational aspiration is to inspire generations of young workers who love dirt to join the industry. When BuildWitt establishes a challenging yet realistic goal, it motivates and inspires its clients to do the same.

At this layer of organizational culture, it's important to also consider how organizational values may be viewed differently across generations. While established at a corporate level, all employees need to see themselves represented in those values to feel like they belong. Thus, it's essential that the guiding principles are flexible enough to speak to everyone at the organization. Take a look at the stated principles at BuildWitt[41]:

Develop 3X people.

Excellence is a habit.

Transparency wins.

Do what's right.

Make decisions!

Be a friend.

Stay humble or be humbled.

Be the example.

KISS (Keep It Simple, Stupid).

BuildWitt's principles serve as its guideposts, laying the groundwork for decisions that align with what the company proclaims to most care about. They also allow individuals to interpret the principles in slightly different ways to make them their own. Unlike some other companies we have found throughout this process, BuildWitt unequivocally asserts the principles' importance. Potential new workers are met with a clear message—an expectation that they already live the organizational values and principles—when searching for new opportunities on BuildWitt's Career page[42]:

Are you the right fit?

You work effectively without someone constantly telling you what to do.
You don't mind long hours, especially while traveling.
You have blue-collar work experience (not required, but a plus).
You're obsessed with getting better, faster, and stronger.
You already live our values.
You aren't afraid of change.

As an organization works to attract employees of all ages and career stages, using their values and mission as a filter in deciding who the organization hires is essential to keep it from accidentally diluting their culture. BuildWitt does this by stressing the importance of its organizational principles and sending a blunt message to potential job seekers who don't share these values: please don't apply.

What They Believe

While underlying assumptions are challenging to uncover, a culture as transparent as BuildWitt's makes the task easier. Briscoe emphasizes that employees must know that the mission of the company comes first. The most potent and efficient way to effectively create a culture is to walk the talk and establish the norms and practices that demonstrate the company's integrity. At BuildWitt, the aspirational goals are to change construction for the better, inspire its future generations, and bring members from all age cohorts to the table. These aims also represent BuildWitt's foundational thoughts and fundamentally impact how the company operates. When BuildWitt's leaders make decisions that align with what the organization values, it shows their deep commitment to those articulated aims. Subsequently, employees recognize the company's stated principles concretely in the way the company does business. Take a look at one such example from one of Briscoe's LinkedIn posts:

> The other day, our team was sitting around the kitchen table in an Airbnb working after a long day in the field. I had an important email to send to a client that mattered to our future. As I finished the email, I looked across at Aaron and asked if he would like to review it before I hit send. He paused for a few seconds, stared at me, and then said: "No, just send it if you like it." I read the message a few more times and then sent it. A few minutes later, Aaron shared that he really wanted to read the message. But he was worried about setting a precedent where our team felt like they needed his approval before we could act. One of our core principles at BuildWitt Media Group is "Decision making is expected." It's simple and refreshing.[43]

This story illustrates a value in action: not only is decision making expected, but it also belongs to everyone.

What the company believes at the deepest level of its organizational culture is the foundation of BuildWitt's culture. Briscoe says that core to its mission and business is the company's desire to show that young people can greatly impact the construction industry. Because the underlying assumptions are congruent with its stated values, the culture at BuildWitt is perceived as authentic and credible.

BuildWitt emerged as one of the most thoroughly Gentelligent organizations we found while writing this book. While its internal intergenerational approach to talent, teams, leadership, and culture is impressive on its own, the company is bringing Gentelligence to an industry that needs it to survive. Using their generational insight, BuildWitt's employees are disrupting how their clients market and communicate, consequently allowing these companies to reach an entirely new (and younger audience). This is a powerful illustration of what is possible when we see and ultimately unlock the potential of generational diversity.

COMING SOON . . . GENERATION ALPHA?

Author Margaret Oliphant once wrote, "I suppose every generation has a conceit of itself which elevates it, in its own opinion, above that which comes after it."[44] This is the nature of generations. They grow up together, facing the challenges of their times with the tools given to them, whether those tools are the GI Bill or smartphones. When it becomes apparent that the times have changed, generations collectively begin to change themselves, creating new ways of thinking and behaving that they believe will help them to survive and thrive. In this way, age cohorts develop a fondness for their particular ways of seeing the world, feeling connected to those who have navigated it with them through the same window of time. Yet people forget, or perhaps fail to consider, that the preceding generation before them did the same, and the one that follows will keep the pattern going. The beliefs and behaviors that spark generational success will not be sufficient or static forever.

The world is nothing if not dynamic; yet each generation feels confusion and disbelief when others do not share their ways of seeing and surviving in a changing environment. At a recent workshop, one participant commented, "I don't know about kids these days. How do they expect to survive?" The answer is that those kids are facing an entirely different world than the one in which the skeptical participant grew up—one that likely will require the "kids these days" to hone a set of new skills he has never needed. Those kids undoubtedly have much to learn from older colleagues that will secure their survival as well. Yet younger generations also have much to teach those they work with and will replace, and much to teach those who will ultimately replace them.

We began this book wanting to change the way people were thinking about generations and age in the workplace. Everywhere we looked, the conversation was negative. We aspired to narrate the story of generations in a way that saw their collective potential as a powerful kind of diversity.

We've talked extensively about the five generations currently in today's workplace: the Silent generation, Boomers, Gen Xers, Millennials, Gen Zers. With the Traditional generation largely moved into retirement, it is mentioned less as time goes by. The newest generations get the most attention and media buzz. Who are they? What do they care about? How did they turn out this way? What forms of change will they bring? How can the whole of a dynamic intergenerational workplace be more than the sum of its parts?

Before the oldest of Gen Z was even out of high school, I was fielding inquiries from journalists asking what was known about this generation. Clearly, there is something about generations so many find fascinating. Regardless of how many headlines proclaim otherwise, there is substantial research supporting that generational identity impacts who people are in meaningful ways. Individuals share core similarities with all people, regardless of their generation, but also differ substantially from those who moved through the world before and will move through after them. Generational identity is not everything, but it's also not nothing.

I read an article in *The Atlantic* titled "Oh No, They've Come Up with Another Generation Label."[45] It announced that a name had been declared for the generation that will follow Gen Z; in other words, there's a new kid on the block. An official birth year for this new generation has yet to be determined. However, given that the typical length of a generation is between sixteen and twenty years long, we can estimate it will begin somewhere between 2013 and 2018, depending on the critical life events that are determined to be most relevant for this new cohort. That means the first members of "Generation Alpha" (if the name holds) are currently no older than seven years old and possibly as young as two.

Speculation already abounds about how things happening at this very moment are shaping who these kids will become. The COVID-19 pandemic of 2020, for example, sparked an immediate firestorm of speculation about the role it would play in defining the next generation. Economist Tyler Cowen of George Mason University predicted in March 2020, only a few months into the global health disaster, "I think there's a good chance . . . that this becomes like this generation's World War II, a totally formative event that shapes how people see the world."[46] Indeed, it seems likely that both Generation Alpha and Generation Z will have futures shaped to some degree by the COVID pandemic—with Gen Z having memories of a school year cut abruptly short by the coronavirus, and both generations having their future paths altered by the pandemic's economic, cultural, and social aftermath.

Why the urgency to put a box around this new generation, especially given that they have barely started elementary school? We share the fascination but suggest caution—rushing to create stereotypes and make quick assumptions is not productive, while understanding what matters to this next generation and exploring its shared narrative is critical to Gentelligence.

Generation Alpha will not be the last one. There will be a generation right behind them, questioning their decisions and blazing a new path. Colleagues, mentors, relatives, neighbors, and citizens need to meet each generation with not just fascination but also appreciation. People need to respect that each generation's success requires them to create their own set of tools and remember that one generation's achievement does not come at the expense of another's. Instead, older generations should lend younger ones whatever wisdom they have gained on their paths and be open to learning lessons from them as well. With Gentelligence, every generation is both a teacher and a student.

Notes

INTRODUCTION

1. Megan Gerhardt, "Today's Managers 'Blew It' with Millennials, College Professor Says, and Here's How We Can Avoid Doing It Again with Generation Z," *Business Insider*, March 11, 2019, www.businessinsider.com/managers-blew-it-with-millennials-generation-z-megan-gerhardt-2019-3.

CHAPTER 1. BLAME *60 MINUTES*: HOW MORLEY SAFER FUELED THE GENERATION WARS

1. "The 'Millennials' Are Coming," *CBS News*, November 8, 2007, www.cbsnews.com/news/the-millennials-are-coming.
2. Ibid.
3. "What Is Wrong with Young People Today?—A View from the Past," *Proto-Knowledge* (blog), https://proto-knowledge.blogspot.com/2010/11/what-is-wrong-with-young-people-today.html.
4. "Auguste Comte on the Natural Progress of Human Society," *Population and Development Review* 37, no. 2 (2011): 389–94, www.jstor.org/stable/23043288.
5. Sapna Maheshwari and Erin Griffith, "How Outdoor Voices, a Start-Up Darling, Imploded," *New York Times*, March 10, 2020, www.nytimes.com/2020/03/10/business/outdoor-voices-ty-haney-mickey-drexler.html.
6. Patricia Barnes, "Proposed Settlement of Age Discrimination Case Hardly Onerous for PricewaterhouseCoopers," *Forbes*, March 18, 2020, www.forbes.com/sites/patriciagbarnes/2020/03/16/proposed-settlement-of-age-discrimination-case-hardly-onerous-for-pricewaterhousecoopers/#30d1dea75d7f.

7. Katie Clarey, "IKEA Hit with 5th Lawsuit Alleging Age Discrimination," *HR Dive*, February 27, 2019, www.hrdive.com/news/ikea-hit-with-5th-lawsuit-alleging-age-discrimination/549155.

8. Sheila Callaham, "Citibank, IBM, IKEA: Age Discrimination Lawsuits on the Rise," *Forbes*, March 28, 2019, www.forbes.com/sites/sheilacallaham/2019/03/27/citibank-ibm-ikea-age-discrimination-lawsuits-on-the-rise/#4bc3bbfc4654.

9. Quentin Fottrell, "Step Aside, Generation X—the Millennials Are Coming," *MarketWatch*, May 30, 2015, www.marketwatch.com/story/step-aside-generation-x-the-millennials-are-coming-2015-05-11.

10. Caitlin Fisher, "The Gaslighting of the Millennial Generation," *Caitlin Fisher: Run Like Hell toward Happy* (blog), October 17, 2016, https://bornagainminimalist.com/2016/10/17/the-gaslighting-of-millennials.

11. Linzrinzz, "Lin on TikTok," TikTok, July 17, 2019, www.tiktok.com/@linzrinzz/video/6714782003637521670.

12. Lisa Nagele-Piazza, "Beware of Workplace Ageism Claims Stemming from 'OK, Boomer,'" SHRM, November 20, 2019, www.shrm.org/resourcesandtools/legal-and-compliance/employment-law/pages/ok-boomer-age-discrimination.aspx.

13. Taylor Lorenz, "'OK Boomer' Marks the End of Friendly Generational Relations," *New York Times*, October 29, 2019, www.nytimes.com/2019/10/29/style/ok-boomer.html.

14. Elizabeth C. Tippett, "Why Saying 'OK, Boomer' at Work Can Be Age Discrimination," *CBS News*, November 21, 2019, www.cbsnews.com/news/why-saying-ok-boomer-at-work-can-be-age-discrimination.

15. Nicole Spector, "'OK Boomer' Is Dividing Generations. What Does It Mean?" *NBC News*, November 6, 2019, www.nbcnews.com/better/lifestyle/ok-boomer-diving-generation-what-does-it-mean-ncna1077261#anchor-Boomerhasbecomeacatchallphraseforsomeoneolderwhoisclosemindedandresistanttochange.

16. Megan Gerhardt, "The 'OK, Boomer' Meme Hurts Gen Z More Than the Older Generation It's Aimed At," *NBC News*, November 18, 2019, www.nbcnews.com/think/opinion/ok-boomer-meme-hurts-gen-z-more-older-generation-it-ncna1079276.

17. "Why Diversity and Inclusion Matter: Quick Take," Catalyst, June 4, 2020, www.catalyst.org/research/why-diversity-and-inclusion-matter.

18. Vijay Eswaran and QI Group, "The Business Case for Diversity Is Now Overwhelming. Here's Why," *World Economic Forum*, April 29, 2019, www.weforum.org/agenda/2019/04/business-case-for-diversity-in-the-workplace.

19. T. H. Cox and S. Blake, "Managing Cultural Diversity: Implications for Organizational Competitiveness," *The Executive* 5 (1991): 45–56.

20. Eswaran and QI Group, "The Business Case for Diversity Is Now Overwhelming."

21. Josh Bersin, "Google for Jobs: Potential to Disrupt the $200 Billion Recruiting Industry," *Forbes*, May 26, 2017, https://www.forbes.com/sites/joshbersin/2017/05/26/google-for-jobs-potential-to-disrupt-the-200-billion-recruiting-industry/#602058954d1f.

22. Kate Rockwood, "Hiring in the Age of Ageism," SHRM, August 16, 2019, www.shrm.org/hr-today/news/hr-magazine/0218/pages/hiring-in-the-age-of-ageism.aspx.

23. Chip Conley, *Wisdom @ Work: The Making of a Modern Elder* (New York: Currency, 2018), 10.

24. Lori Trawinski, *Disrupting Aging in the Workplace: Profiles in Intergenerational Diversity Leadership* (AARP Public Policy Institute, 2017), www.aarp.org/content/dam/aarp/ppi/2017/08/disrupt-aging-in-the-workforce.pdf.

25. David A. Thomas and Robin J. Ely, "Making Differences Matter: A New Paradigm for Managing Diversity," *Harvard Business Review*, April 29, 2016, https://hbr.org/1996/09/making-differences-matter-a-new-paradigm-for-managing-diversity.

26. Ibid.

27. Jürgen Wegge, F. Jungmann, S. Liebermann, M. Shemla, B. C. Ries, S. Diestel, and K. H. Schmidt, "What Makes Age Diverse Teams Effective? Results from a Six-Year Research Program," *Work* 41, supplement 1 (2012): 5145–51.

CHAPTER 2. OUR GENERATIONAL IDENTITIES

1. Rich Cohen, "Why Generation X Might Be Our Last, Best Hope," *Vanity Fair*, August 10, 2017, www.vanityfair.com/style/2017/08/why-generation-x-might-be-our-last-best-hope.

2. Oliver Holmes, "José Ortega y Gasset," *Stanford Encyclopedia of Philosophy*, November 20, 2017, https://plato.stanford.edu/entries/gasset/#ConcGeneTempHistReasCritPhilHist.

3. Karl Mannheim, "The Problem of Generations," in *Essays on the Sociology of Knowledge* (London: Routledge and Kegan Paul, 1928/1952), 276–320.

4. "The Whys and Hows of Generations Research," Pew Research Center for the People and the Press, December 31, 2019, www.people-press.org/2015/09/03/the-whys-and-hows-of-generations-research.

5. Emma Parry, *Generational Diversity at Work: New Research Perspectives* (London: Routledge, 2014), 41.

6. Michael Dimock, "Defining Generations: Where Millennials End and Generation Z Begins," Pew Research Center, January 17, 2019, www.pewresearch.org/fact-tank/2019/01/17/where-millennials-end-and-generation-z-begins/.

7. William Strauss and Neil Howe, *Generations: The History of America's Future, 1584 to 2069* (New York: William Morrow, 1991).

8. Kimberly A. Wade-Benzoni, "A Golden Rule over Time: Reciprocity in Intergenerational Allocation Decisions," *Academy of Management Journal* 45, no. 5 (2002): 1011–28.

9. José Ortega y Gasset, *The Origin of Philosophy*, trans. Toby Talbot (Champaign: University of Illinois Press, 2000), 15.

10. Michael J. Urick, Elaine C. Hollensbe, Suzanne S. Masterson, and Sean T. Lyons, "Understanding and Managing Intergenerational Conflict: An Examination of Influences and Strategies," *Work, Aging and Retirement* 3, no. 2 (2016): 167.

11. "Generations and Age," Pew Research Center, January 17, 2019, www.pewresearch.org/topics/generations-and-age.

12. Michael Dimock, "Defining Generations: Where Millennials End and Generation Z Begins," Pew Research Center, January 17, 2019, www.pewresearch.org/fact-tank/2019/01/17/where-millennials-end-and-generation-z-begins.

13. Ron Zemke, Claire Raines, and Bob Filipczak, *Generations at Work: Managing the Clash of Boomers, Gen Xers, and Gen Yers in the Workplace* (New York: Amacom, 2013).

14. Ibid., 64.

15. Ibid.

16. "The Whys and Hows of Generations Research."

17. Alex Williams, "Actually, Gen X Did Sell Out, Invent All Things Millennial, and Cause Everything Else That's Great and Awful," *New York Times*, May 14, 2019, www.nytimes.com/2019/05/14/style/gen-x-millenials.html.

18. "Breaking Down Divorce by Generation: Goldberg Jones: PDX," Goldberg Jones, May 16, 2019, www.goldbergjones-or.com/divorce/divorce-by-generation.

19. Mary Donahue, *The Marcia Moment: The Death of the Manage-Me Workplace* (Donahue Learning, 2017), www.donohuelearning.com/wp-content/uploads/2017/04/Final-White-Paper-Marcia-Moment-Copyright-Donohue-Learning-1.pdf.

20. Stephanie Neal, Kabir Sehgal, Priscilla Claman, and Rebecca Knight, "Are Companies about to Have a Gen X Retention Problem?" *Harvard Business Review*, July 29, 2019, https://hbr.org/2019/07/are-companies-about-to-have-a-gen-x-retention-problem.

21. Jean M. Twenge, *iGen: Why Today's Super-Connected Kids Are Growing Up Less Rebellious, More Tolerant, Less Happy—and Completely Unprepared for Adulthood—and What That Means for the Rest of Us* (New York: Simon and Schuster, 2017), 193.

22. Ibid.

23. Ibid.

24. C. Seemiller and M. Grace, *Generation Z Goes to College Study* (San Francisco: Jossey-Bass, 2016).

25. Megan Gerhardt, "Coronavirus and Zoom Have Marked a Generation. Let's Call Them Zoomers," *NBC News*, June 7, 2020, www.nbcnews.com/think/opinion/coronavirus-zoom-have-marked-generation-let-s-call-them-zoomers-ncna1226241.

26. "The Rising Cost of College," *College Choice*, accessed March 25, 2020, www.collegechoice.net/the-rising-cost-of-college.

27. Patrick, "Charli D'Amelio Net Worth Reveal: Income Sources, Instagram & TikTok Earnings, Meet and Greet, Sister Dixie D'Amelio, Age 15," Celebs Fortune, March 17, 2020, https://celebsfortune.com/charli-damelio-net-worth.

28. Jonah Engel Bromwich, "The Evolution of Emma Chamberlain," *New York Times*, July 9, 2019, www.nytimes.com/2019/07/09/style/emma-chamberlain-youtube.html.

29. Salvatore Babones, "Hao, Boomer!" *Foreign Policy*, November 25, 2019, https://foreignpolicy.com/2019/11/25/ok-boomer-millennials-resent-ruining-world-generational-politics-mainland-china-hong-kong.

30. Tammy Erickson, "Generations around the Globe," *Harvard Business Review*, July 23, 2014, https://hbr.org/2011/04/generations-around-the-globe-1.

31. Johanna Nordin and Catharina Rengensjö, "Guldklockan Klämtar—En Studie Om Kompetensbevaring I Samband Med Generationsskifte," University of Borås, Institute of Data and Business, 2010, https://hb.diva-portal.org/smash/get/diva2:1311928/FULLTEXT01.

32. "1968 in Germany: A Generation with Two Phases and Faces," *Eurozine*, June 22, 2018, www.eurozine.com/1968-germany-generation-two-phases-faces.

33. "South Africa's Born Free Generation," *BJP Online*, June 7, 2019, https://1854.studio/communities/south-africas-born-free-generation.

34. "Uhuru Generation: Over 3 Million Will Retire into Poverty," *The East African*, May 24, 2009, www.theeastafrican.co.ke/news/2558-602434-view-printVersion-3082pxz/index.html.

35. "Generation Ni/Ni: Latin America's Lost Youth," *Americas Quarterly* (Spring 2012), www.americasquarterly.org/salazar.

36. "Generation Next: Meet Gen Z and the Alphas," McCrindle, February 15, 2020, https://mccrindle.com.au/insights/blog/generation-next-meet-gen-z-alphas.

37. Mei Fong, "China's Lost Little Emperors . . . How the 'One-Child Policy' Will Haunt the Country for Decades," *Guardian*, September 2, 2018, www.theguardian.com/commentisfree/2018/sep/02/chinas-lost-little-emperors-how-the-one-child-policy-will-haunt-the-nation-for-decades.

38. Malcolm Moore, "China: The Rise of the 'Precious Snowflakes,'" *The Telegraph*, January 8, 2012, www.telegraph.co.uk/news/worldnews/asia/china/8997627/China-The-rise-of-the-Precious-Snowflakes.html.

39. Eddy Ng, Sean T. Lyons, and Linda Schweitzer, eds., *Managing the New Workforce: International Perspectives on the Millennial Generation* (Cheltenham, UK: Edward Elgar Publishing, 2012), xxii.

40. Mannheim, "The Problem of Generations."

CHAPTER 3. MIND THE GAP: ROADBLOCKS TO CLOSING THE GENERATIONAL DIVIDE

1. Ryan Jenkins, "Why Generational Diversity Is the Ultimate Competitive Advantage," *Inc.*, May 15, 2017, www.inc.com/ryan-jenkins/why-generational-diversity-is-the-ultimate-competitive-advantage.html.

2. *Leveraging the Value of an Age Diverse Workforce* (Society of Human Resource Management, 2020), www.shrm.org/foundation/ourwork/initiatives/the-aging-workforce/Documents/Age-Diverse%20Workforce%20Executive%20Briefing.pdf.

3. Nancy Miller, "The *Wall Street Journal* Says It's Done Being Snarky AF about Millennials," *Quartz*, December 12, 2017, https://qz.com/1154304/the-wall-street-journal-says-it-is-done-stereotyping-millennials.

4. *Harnessing the Power of a Multigenerational Workforce* (SHRM Foundation, 2017), www.shrm.org/foundation/ourwork/initiatives/the-aging-workforce/Lists/Curated%20source%20for%20page%20The%20Aging%20Workforce/Attachments/17/2017%20TL%20Executive%20Summary-FINAL.pdf.

5. Karen A. Jehn, Clint Chadwick, and Sherry M. B. Thatcher, "To Agree or Not to Agree: The Effects of Value Congruence, Individual Demographic Dissimilarity, and Conflict on Workgroup Outcomes," *International Journal of Conflict Management* 8, no. 4 (1997): 287–305.

6. John McDermott, "Why Gen X Is So Pissed at Millennials," *MEL Magazine*, January 30, 2019, https://melmagazine.com/en-us/story/why-gen-x-is-so-pissed-at-millennials-2.

7. Libby DeLana, "Are We There Yet? How Ageism Is Holding Back Our Industry," Campaign, June 11, 2019, www.campaignlive.com/article/yet-ageism-holding-back-industry/1581531.

8. *Stress in America™: The Impact of Discrimination* (American Psychological Association, 2016), www.apa.org/news/press/releases/stress/2015/impact-of-discrimination.pdf.

9. "Frequently Asked Questions," Project Implicit, accessed March 29, 2020, https://implicit.harvard.edu/implicit/faqs.html#faq1.

10. Kate Rockwood, "Hiring in the Age of Ageism," SHRM, August 16, 2019, www.shrm.org/hr-today/news/hr-magazine/0218/pages/hiring-in-the-age-of-ageism.aspx.

11. "CompTIA: Managing the Multigenerational Workforce 2018," CompTIA, accessed March 27, 2020, www.comptia.org/resources/managing-the-multigenerational-workforce-2018.

12. Lisa M. Finkelstein and Michael J. Burke, "Age Stereotyping at Work: The Role of Rater and Contextual Factors on Evaluations of Job Applicants," *Journal of General Psychology* 125, no. 4 (1998): 317–45, https://doi.org/10.1080/00221309809595341.

13. Peter Cappelli and Bill Novelli, *Managing the Older Worker: How to Prepare for the New Organizational Order* (Boston: Harvard Business Press, 2010).

14. Monica Anderson and Andrew Perrin, "Barriers to Adoption and Attitudes towards Tech among Older Americans," Pew Research Center, December 31, 2019, www.pewresearch.org/internet/2017/05/17/barriers-to-adoption-and-attitudes-towards-technology.

15. Cody B. Cox, Friederike K. Young, Adrian B. Guardia, and Amy K. Bohmann, "The Baby Boomer Bias: The Negative Impact of Generational Labels on Older Workers," *Journal of Applied Social Psychology* 48, no. 2 (2018): 71–79.

16. "Ageism in America Is Hurting Us All," Senior Planning Services, August 10, 2017, www.seniorplanningservices.com/2017/08/21/ageism-america-hurting-us.

17. Ed Snape and Tom Redman, "Too Old or Too Young? The Impact of Perceived Age Discrimination," *Human Resource Management Journal* 13, no. 1 (2003): 78–89.

18. "CompTIA: Managing the Multigenerational Workforce 2018."

19. Hillary Collyer, "Can Employers Discriminate against Younger Workers?" HR Daily Advisor, October 23, 2009, https://hrdailyadvisor.blr.com/2009/10/23/can-employers-discriminate-against-younger-workers.

20. "General Dynamics Land Systems, Inc. v. Cline," Legal Information Institute, February 24, 2004, www.law.cornell.edu/supct/html/02-1080.ZO.html.

21. Collyer, "Can Employers Discriminate Against Younger Workers?"

22. Patrick J. Kiger, "Older and Younger Workers See Each Other Negatively," AARP, September 18, 2018, www.aarp.org/work/working-at-50-plus/info-2018/older-younger-workers-opinions.html.

23. Jamie Chamberlin, "Overgeneralizing the Generations," *Monitor on Psychology* 40, no. 6 (2009), www.apa.org/monitor/2009/06/workplaces.

24. Lisa Nagele-Piazza, "Beware of Workplace Ageism Claims Stemming from 'OK, Boomer,'" SHRM, February 28, 2020, www.shrm.org/resourcesandtools/legal-and-compliance/employment-law/pages/ok-boomer-age-discrimination.aspx.

25. Chris Blauth, Jack McDaniel, Craig Perrin, and Paul Perrin, *Age-Based Stereotypes: Silent Killer of Collaboration and Productivity* (AchieveGlobal, 2010), www.aarp.org/content/dam/aarp/ppi/2017/08/disrupt-aging-in-the-workforce.pdf.

26. Jean M. Twenge, "A Review of the Empirical Evidence on Generational Differences in Work Attitudes," *Journal of Business and Psychology* 25, no. 2 (2010): 201–10.

27. Sarah Green Carmichael, "Millennials Are Actually Workaholics, According to Research," *Harvard Business Review*, August 17, 2016, https://hbr.org/2016/08/millennials-are-actually-workaholics-according-to-research.

28. Lawrence Samuel, "Young People Are Just Smarter," *Psychology Today*, October 2, 2017, www.psychologytoday.com/us/blog/boomers-30/201710/young-people-are-just-smarter.

29. Tad Friend, "Why Ageism Never Gets Old," *New Yorker*, July 9, 2019, www.newyorker.com/magazine/2017/11/20/why-ageism-never-gets-old.

30. Sophie Nachemson-Ekwall, interview by authors, July 14, 2018.

31. Ariane Berthoin Antal, "Types of Knowledge Gained by Expatriate Managers," *Journal of General Management* 26, no. 2 (2000): 32–51.

32. Ibid.

33. Simon Sinek, "Why Good Leaders Make You Feel Safe," filmed March 2014, TED video, 11:47, www.ted.com/talks/simon_sinek_why_good_leaders_make_you_feel_safe?language=en.

34. Adam M. Grant, *Originals: How Non-Conformists Move the World* (New York: Penguin, 2017).

CHAPTER 4. THE GENTELLIGENCE SOLUTION: FOUR KEY PRACTICES

1. Richard Fry, "Millennials Expected to Outnumber Boomers in 2019," Pew Research Center, March 1, 2018, www.pewresearch.org/fact-tank/2018/03/01/millennials-overtake-baby-boomers.

2. Jib Fowles, "On Chronocentrism," *Futures* 6, no. 1 (1974): 65.

3. Tom Standage, *The Victorian Internet: The Remarkable Story of the Telegraph and the Nineteenth Century's On-Line Pioneers* (New York: Bloomsbury Publishing, 2009), 213.

4. Aparna Joshi, John C. Dencker, Gentz Franz, and Joseph J. Martocchio, "Unpacking Generational Identities in Organizations," *Academy of Management Review* 35, no. 3 (2010): 392–414.

5. Becca R. Levy and Mahzarian R. Banaji, "Implicit Ageism," *Ageism: Stereotyping and Prejudice against Older Persons* 2004 (2002): 49–75.

6. Chimamanda Ngozi Adichie, "The Danger of a Single Story," filmed October 7, 2009, TED video, 19:16, www.ted.com/talks/chimamanda_ngozi_adichie_the_danger_of_a_single_story.

7. Lisa M. Finkelstein, Donald M. Truxillo, Franco Fraccaroli, and Ruth Kanfer, *Facing the Challenges of a Multi-Age Workforce* (New York: Routledge, 2015).

8. Jeff Atkins, "Scientists Who Selfie: Building Public Trust through Social Media," *PLOS Blogs*, May 10, 2019, https://theplosblog.plos.org/2019/05/scientists-who-selfie-building-public-trust-through-social-media.

9. Tom Koulopoulos and Dan Keldsen, *Gen Z Effect: The Six Forces Shaping the Future of Business* (New York: Routledge, 2016), 36.

10. P. Christopher Earley and Elaine Mosakowski, "Cultural Intelligence," *Harvard Business Review*, April 20, 2016, https://hbr.org/2004/10/cultural-intelligence.

11. P. Christopher Earley, Soon Ang, and Joo-Seng Tan, *CQ: Developing Cultural Intelligence at Work* (Stanford: Stanford University Press, 2006).

12. Lynne C. Lancaster and David Stillman, *When Generations Collide: Who They Are, Why They Clash, How to Solve the Generational Puzzle at Work* (New York: HarperBusiness, 2003).

13. Earley, Ang, and Tan, *CQ*.

14. J. Bennett, Milton Bennett, and Kathryn Stillings, "DIE (Describe, Interpret, and Evaluate) Model Handout" (unpublished, 1979).

15. Joshi, Dencker, Franz, and Martocchio, "Unpacking Generational Identities in Organizations."

16. Lynda Gratton, Andreas Voigt, and Tamara J. Erickson, "Bridging Faultlines in Diverse Teams," *MIT Sloan Management Review* 48, no. 4 (2007): 22.

17. Michele Williams, "Being Trusted: How Team Generational Age Diversity Promotes and Undermines Trust in Cross-Boundary Relationships," *Journal of Organizational Behavior* 37, no. 3 (September 1, 2015): 349.

18. Ana Cristina Costa, Robert A. Roe, and Tharsi Taillieu, "Trust within Teams: The Relation with Performance Effectiveness," *European Journal of Work and Organizational Psychology* 10, no. 3 (2001): 225–44.

19. Gratton, Voigt, and Erickson, "Bridging Faultlines in Diverse Teams," 22.

20. Jake Herway, "How to Create a Culture of Psychological Safety," Gallup, March 5, 2020, www.gallup.com/workplace/236198/create-culture-psychological-safety.aspx.

21. "Re:Work—Guide: Understand Team Effectiveness," Google, accessed March 27, 2020, https://rework.withgoogle.com/guides/understanding-team-effectiveness/steps/foster-psychological-safety.

22. Herway, "How to Create a Culture of Psychological Safety."

23. Ibid.

24. "Creating Value in Integrative Negotiations: Myth of the Fixed-Pie of Resources," Program on Negotiation, Harvard Law School, March 5, 2020, www.pon.harvard.edu/daily/negotiation-skills-daily/when-the-pie-seems-too-small.

25. "Integrative Negotiation Examples: MESOs and Expanding the Pie," Program on Negotiation, Harvard Law School, May 18, 2017, www.pon.harvard.edu/daily/dealmaking-daily/limit-their-options%E2%80%94and-expand-the-pie.

26. "2016–17: Healthy Workplaces for All Ages," European Agency for Safety and Health at Work, accessed October 14, 2020, https://healthy-workplaces.eu/previous/all-ages-2016/en.

27. Ksenija Ramovš, "Medgeneracijsko sožitje in solidarnost (Intergenerational Cohesion and Solidarity)," in *Staranje v Sloveniji* (*Ageing in Slovenia*), ed. J. Ramovš (Ljubljana: Inštitut Antona Trstenjaka, 2013), 63–97.

CHAPTER 5. FILLING THE PIPELINE: LEADING UP (AND DOWN)

1. John F. Kennedy, "Remarks Prepared for Delivery at the Trade Mart in Dallas, TX, November 22, 1963 [Undelivered]," JFK Library, n.d., www.jfklibrary.org/archives/other-resources/john-f-kennedy-speeches/dallas-tx-trade-mart-undelivered-19631122.

2. Oliver Staley, "How the Average Age of CEOs and CFOs Has Changed since 2012," *Quartz*, September 11, 2017, https://qz.com/1074326/how-the-average-age-of-ceos-and-cfos-has-changed-since-2012.

3. Brian R. Spisak, Allen E. Grabo, Richard D. Arvey, and Mark van Vugt, "The Age of Exploration and Exploitation: Younger-Looking Leaders Endorsed for Change, and Older-Looking Leaders Endorsed for Stability," *Leadership Quarterly* 25, no. 5 (2014).

4. Ibid.

5. Ibid.

6. Ibid.

7. Joanne Kaufman, "When the Boss Is Half Your Age," *New York Times*, March 17, 2017, www.nytimes.com/2017/03/17/your-money/retiring-older-workers-younger-bosses.html.

8. Richard Fry, "Millennials Are Largest Generation in the U.S. Labor Force," Pew Research Center, April 11, 2018, www.pewresearch.org/fact-tank/2018/04/11/millennials-largest-generation-us-labor-force.

9. Andrew Van Dam, "Baby Boomers Upend the Workforce One Last Time," *Washington Post*, March 1, 2019, www.washingtonpost.com/us-policy/2019/03/01/baby-boomers-parting-gift-workforce-one-last-mess.

10. Stephanie Neal, Kabir Sehgal, Priscilla Claman, and Rebecca Knight, "Are Companies about to Have a Gen X Retention Problem?" *Harvard Business Review*, July 29, 2019, https://hbr.org/2019/07/are-companies-about-to-have-a-gen-x-retention-problem.

11. Lisa M. Finkelstein, Donald M. Truxillo, Franco Fraccaroli, and Ruth Kanfer, *Facing the Challenges of a Multi-Age Workforce* (New York: Routledge, 2015), 253.

12. Peter Cappelli and Bill Novelli, *Managing the Older Worker: How to Prepare for the New Organizational Order* (Boston: Harvard Business Press, 2010).

13. Florian Kunze and Jochen I. Menges, "Younger Supervisors, Older Subordinates: An Organizational-Level Study of Age Differences, Emotions, and Performance," *Journal of Organizational Behavior* 38, no. 4 (2017): 461–86.

14. Mary Hair Collins, Joseph F. Hair Jr., and Tonette S. Rocco, "The Older-Worker-Younger-Supervisor Dyad: A Test of the Reverse Pygmalion Effect," *Human Resource Development Quarterly* 20, no. 1 (2009): 253.

15. Karen K. Myers and Kamyab Sadaghiani, "Millennials in the Workplace: A Communication Perspective on Millennials' Organizational Relationships and Performance," *Journal of Business and Psychology* 25, no. 2 (2010): 225–38.

16. Anne S. Tsui, Katherine R. Xin, and Terri D. Egan, "Relational Demography: The Missing Link in Vertical Dyad Linkage," in *Diversity in Work Teams: Research Paradigms for a Changing Workplace*, ed. S. E. Jackson and M. N. Ruderman, 97–129 (Washington, DC: American Psychological Association, 1995), https://doi.org/10.1037/10189-004.

17. Jack Zenger and Joseph Folkman, "What Younger Managers Should Know about How They Are Perceived," *Harvard Business Review*, September 29, 2015, https://hbr.org/2015/09/what-younger-managers-should-know-about-how-theyre-perceived.

18. Ibid.

19. Ibid.

20. Brené Brown, *Daring Greatly: How the Courage to Be Vulnerable Transforms the Way We Live, Love, Parent, and Lead* (New York: Penguin, 2015).

21. Tobias Lütke, interview with Guy Raz, *How I Built This with Guy Raz* (Podcast), August 5, 2019, www.npr.org/2019/08/02/747660923/shopify-tobias-l-tke.

22. Rachel Emma Silverman, "Young Boss May Make Older Workers Less Productive," *Wall Street Journal*, December 20, 2016, www.wsj.com/articles/young-boss-may-make-older-workers-less-productive-1482246384.

23. Collins et al., "The Older-Worker-Younger-Supervisor Dyad," 25.

24. John Boitnott, "How to Partner Successfully with a Younger Boss," *Entrepreneur*, April 24, 2018, www.entrepreneur.com/article/312343.

25. Spisak et al., "The Age of Exploration and Exploitation."

26. Jena McGregor, "Fewer Companies Are Forcing CEOs to Retire When They Hit Their Golden Years," *Washington Post*, September 27, 2018, www.washingtonpost.com/business/2018/09/27/fewer-companies-are-forcing-ceos-retire-when-they-hit-their-golden-years.

27. Holly Valovick, "CEOs & Mandatory Retirement Age," Quick Leonard Kieffer, July 2, 2018, www.qlksearch.com/blog/ceo-mandatory-retirement-age.

28. Megan W. Gerhardt, "The Importance of Being . . . Social? Instructor Credibility and the Millennials," *Studies in Higher Education* 41, no. 9 (2016): 1533–47.

29. Azhdar Karami, Farhad Analoui, and Nada Korak Kakabadse, "The CEOs' Characteristics and Their Strategy Development in the UK SME Sector," *Journal of Management Development* (2006).

30. Hannes Zacher, Kathrin Rosing, Thomas Henning, and Michael Frese, "Establishing the Next Generation at Work: Leader Generativity as a Moderator of the Relationships between Leader Age, Leader-Member Exchange, and Leadership Success," *Psychology and Aging* 26, no. 1 (2011): 241–52.

31. Dan McAdams, interview with authors, August 14, 2019.

32. Marc Freedman, *How to Live Forever: The Enduring Power of Connecting the Generations* (New York: Ingram Publisher Services US, 2019), 123.

CHAPTER 6. THE SECRETS OF GENTELLIGENT TEAMS

1. Kenneth H. Blanchard and Spencer Johnson, *The One Minute Manager* (New York: William Morrow, 2015), 15.

2. Vivian Hunt, Lareina Yee, Sara Prince, and Sundiatu Dixon-Fyle, "Delivering through Diversity," McKinsey & Company, January 18, 2018, www.mckinsey.com/business-functions/organization/our-insights/delivering-through-diversity.

3. "The Missing Perspective in the Boardroom: Millennials," *Wall Street Journal*, February 9, 2015, https://deloitte.wsj.com/riskandcompliance/2015/02/09/the-missing-perspective-in-the-boardroom-millennials.

4. Jake Herway, "How to Create a Culture of Psychological Safety," Gallup, March 5, 2020, www.gallup.com/workplace/236198/create-culture-psychological-safety.aspx.

5. Charles Duhigg, "What Google Learned from Its Quest to Build the Perfect Team," *New York Times*, February 25, 2016, www.nytimes.com/2016/02/28/magazine/what-google-learned-from-its-quest-to-build-the-perfect-team.html.

6. Melissa Dittman, "Generational Differences at Work," *Monitor on Psychology*, June 2005, www.apa.org/monitor/jun05/generational.

7. Jeffrey T. Polzer, "Making Diverse Teams Click," *Harvard Business Review*, July/August 2008, https://hbr.org/2008/07/making-diverse-teams-click.

8. Florian Kunze, Stephan A. Boehm, and Heike Bruch, "Age Diversity, Age Discrimination Climate and Performance Consequences—a Cross-Organizational Study," *Journal of Organizational Behavior* 32, no. 2 (2011): 264–90.

9. Julie Christian, Lyman W. Porter, and Graham Moffitt, "Workplace Diversity and Group Relations: An Overview," *Group Processes & Intergroup Relations* 9, no. 4 (2006): 459–66.

10. Dr. Elizabeth Lokon, interview with authors, June 28, 2018.

11. "Generational Conflict: A Matter of Clout," Center for Creative Leadership (Podcast), www.ccl.org/multimedia/podcast/generational-conflict-a-matter-of-clout.

12. Ibid.

13. Aaron Hornbrook, interview with authors, July 17, 2019.

14. Jean M. Twenge, *Generation Me: Why Today's Young Americans Are More Confident, Assertive, Entitled—and More Miserable Than Ever Before* (New York: Free Press, 2006).

15. Jean M. Twenge, *iGen: Why Today's Super-Connected Kids Are Growing up Less Rebellious, More Tolerant, Less Happy—and Completely Unprepared for*

Adulthood—and What That Means for the Rest of Us (New York: Simon and Schuster, 2017).

16. "Generational Conflict: A Matter of Clout."

17. "Gaining Consensus among Stakeholders through the Nominal Group Technique," Centers for Disease Control, 2018, www.cdc.gov/healthyyouth/evaluation/pdf/brief7.pdf.

18. Steven G. Rogelberg, Janet L. Barnes-Farrell, and Charles A. Lowe, "The Stepladder Technique: An Alternative Group Structure Facilitating Effective Group Decision Making," *Journal of Applied Psychology* 77, no. 5 (1992): 730.

19. Stephanie Korey, "Bringing the Ideal Suitcase to Market with Slack," Slack, accessed March 27, 2020, https://slack.com/customer-stories/away.

20. Susan Hoffman, interview with authors, May 13, 2019.

21. Ibid.

22. Ariane Berthoin Antal, "Types of Knowledge Gained by Expatriate Managers," *Journal of General Management* 26, no. 2 (2000): 32–51.

23. Alaina G. Levine, "From Selfies to Selfless: Managing Multigenerational Teams," *Science*, December 8, 2017, www.sciencemag.org/features/2017/09/selfies-selfless-managing-multigenerational-teams.

24. Dr. Joshua Pearce, interview with authors, February 11, 2020.

25. Ibid.

26. Lora Berg, Elandre Dedrick, Elisabeth Winter, Corinna Blutguth, Maria Elena Gutierrez, Maria Florea, Mihnea-Mihail Florea, and Hana Kovhan, "Window on GMF's Diverse Workplace: Building Successful Multi-Generational Teams," German Marshall Fund of the United States, October 7, 2019, www.gmfus.org/blog/2019/10/07/window-gmfs-diverse-workplace-building-successful-multi-generational-teams.

CHAPTER 7. A GENTELLIGENT PEOPLE STRATEGY

1. James C. Collins, *Good to Great* (London: Random House Business, 2001), 13.

2. U.S. Census Bureau, "Older People Projected to Outnumber Children for First Time in U.S. History," 2018, www.census.gov/newsroom/press-releases/2018/cb18-41-population-projections.htmlV.

3. D'vera Cohn and Paul Taylor, "Baby Boomers Approach 65—Glumly," Pew Research Center, 2010, www.pewsocialtrends.org/2010/12/20/baby-boomers-approach-65-glumly.

4. "2019 Global Human Capital Trends," Deloitte Insights, 2019, www2.deloitte.com/us/en/insights/focus/human-capital-trends.html.

5. Ibid.

6. "2021 Virtual Returnship Program," Goldman Sachs, accessed October 16, 2020, www.goldmansachs.com/careers/professionals/returnship.

7. Maxine Boersma, "Schemes to Hire People after Career Breaks Are Proving Popular," *Financial Times*, November 11, 2015, www.ft.com/content/18f7870a-8227-11e5-a01c-8650859a4767.

8. Lisa Eadicicco, "Apple CEO Tim Cook Explains Why You Don't Need a College Degree to Be Successful," *Business Insider*, March 7, 2019, www.businessinsider.com/apple-ceo-tim-cook-why-college-degree-isnt-necessary-2019-3.

9. Thiel Institute, "The Thiel Fellowship," accessed March 27, 2020, https://thielfellowship.org.

10. Justin Bariso, "It Took Elon Musk Exactly 5 Words to Reveal What He Looks for in Every New Hire (and It's Not a College Degree)," *Inc.*, November 18, 2019, www.inc.com/justin-bariso/it-took-elon-musk-exactly-5-words-to-reveal-what-he-looks-for-in-every-new-hire-and-its-not-a-college-degree.html.

11. "Gallup's Perspective on the Gig Economy and Alternative Work Arrangements," Gallup, 2018, www.gallup.com/workplace.

12. *The State of Independence in America* (MBO Partners, 2019), www.mbopartners.com/wp-content/uploads/2019/02/State_of_Independence_2018.pdf.

13. *The Gig Economy: Opportunities, Challenges, and Employer Strategies* (MetLife, 2019), www.metlife.com/content/dam/metlifecom/us/ebts/pdf/MetLife_EBTS-GigReport_2019.pdf.

14. *2019 Retention Report* (Work Institute, 2019), https://info.workinstitute.com/hubfs/2019%20Retention%20Report/Work%20Institute%202019%20Retention%20Report%20final-1.pdf.

15. Roy Maurer, "Millennials Expect Raises, Promotions More Often Than Older Generations," Society for Human Resource Management, February 26, 2015, www.shrm.org/resourcesandtools/hr-topics/talent-acquisition/pages/millennials-raises-promotions-generations.aspx.

16. Amy Adkins, "Millennials: The Job-Hopping Generation," Gallup, accessed October 16, 2020, www.gallup.com/workplace/231587/millennials-job-hopping-generation.aspx.

17. Kristen Bialik and Richard Fry, "How Millennials Compare with Prior Generations," Pew Research Center's Social & Demographic Trends Project, February 14, 2019, www.pewsocialtrends.org/essay/millennial-life-how-young-adulthood-today-compares-with-prior-generations.

18. Eddy Ng, Linda Schweitzer, and Sean T. Lyons, "New Generation, Great Expectations: A Field Study of the Millennial Generation," *Journal of Business and Psychology* 25, no. 2 (2010): 281–92.

19. *2019 Retention Report.*

20. Bailey Nelson, "How to Get the Best out of Baby Boomers," Gallup, February 28, 2020, www.gallup.com/workplace/246443/best-baby-boomers.aspx.

21. "Third Annual 'Future Workforce Report' Sheds Light on How Younger Generations Are Reshaping the Future of Work," Upwork, March 5, 2019, www.upwork.com/press/2019/03/05/third-annual-future-workforce-report.

22. Dennis B. Arnett, Debra A. Laverie, and Charlie McLane, "Using Job Satisfaction and Pride as Internal-Marketing Tools," *Cornell Hotel and Restaurant Administration Quarterly* (2002).

23. "PwC's Talent Exchange: Find Exciting Opportunities with PwC," PwC Talent Exchange, accessed March 27, 2020, https://talentexchange.pwc.com.

24. Ben McLannahan, "PwC Launches Online Market Place to Tap into 'Gig Economy,'" *Financial Times*, March 7, 2016, www.ft.com/content/9c0f5248-e25e-11e5-96b7-9f778349aba2.

25. "Why Top Companies Are Ditching the 9-to-5 for Flexible Working Arrangements," Upwork, August 16, 2019, www.upwork.com/hiring/enterprise/top-companies-ditching-9-5-flexible-working-arrangements.

26. *Nextgen: A Global Generational Study* (PwC, 2013), www.pwc.com/gx/en/hr-management-services/pdf/pwc-nextgen-study-2013.pdf.

27. Claire Cain Miller and Sanam Yar, "Young People Are Going to Save Us All from Office Life," *New York Times*, September 17, 2019, www.nytimes.com/2019/09/17/style/generation-z-millennials-work-life-balance.html.

28. Macy Bayern, "The Generational Divide: Telecommuting during the Coronavirus Pandemic," TechRepublic, March 23, 2020, www.techrepublic.com/article/the-generational-divide-telecommuting-during-the-coronavirus-pandemic.

29. Ibid.

30. Theresa Agovino, "Millennials Say They Are Struggling More to Work from Home," SHRM, May 18, 2020, www.shrm.org/resourcesandtools/hr-topics/employee-relations/pages/millennials-say-they-are-struggling-more-to-work-from-home.aspx.

31. D2L, "New Survey Reveals That Workers Rank Human Interaction and On-Demand Video Highest among Workplace Learning Methods," *GlobeNewswire*, February 13, 2018, www.globenewswire.com/news-release/2018/02/13/1485064/0/en/New-Survey-Reveals-That-Workers-Rank-Human-Interaction-and-On-Demand-Video-Highest-Among-Workplace-Learning-Methods.html.

32. Alvin Toffler, "Riding the Third Wave," *The Rotarian*, July 1980.

33. Rich Bellis, "5 Flexible Work Strategies and the Companies That Use Them," Fast Company, April 6, 2016, www.fastcompany.com/3058344/5-flexible-work-strategies-and-the-companies-who-use-them.

34. "Supporting Flexible Work: 6 Tips for Executives," *FlexJobs Employer Blog*, September 13, 2016, www.flexjobs.com/employer-blog/supporting-flexible-work-tips-for-executives.

35. Rebecca Greenfield, "How to Make Flexible Work Schedules a Reality," Bloomberg, January 21, 2016, www.bloomberg.com/news/articles/2016-01-21/how-to-make-flexible-work-schedules-a-reality.

36. "Millennials Say Flexibility Is More Important than Salary," The Predictive Index, July 31, 2019, www.predictiveindex.com/blog/why-flexibility-is-a-better-perk-than-salary.

37. *2019 Retention Report*, 7.

38. Adkins, "Millennials."

39. Gallup, *State of the American Workplace* (Washington, DC: Gallup, Inc., 2017), www.gallup.com/workplace/238085/state-american-workplace-report-2017.aspx.

40. Brian O'Connell, "The Search for Meaning," Society for Human Resource Management, March 23, 2019, www.shrm.org/hr-today/news/all-things-work/pages/the-search-for-meaning.aspx.

41. Andrew Reece, Gabriella Kellerman, and Alexi Robichaux, "Meaning and Purpose at Work," BetterUp, 2017, https://get.betterup.co/rs/600-WTC-654/images/betterup-meaning-purpose-at-work.pdf.

42. Shawn Achor, Andrew Reece, Gabriella Rosen Kellerman, and Alexi Robichaux, "9 Out of 10 People Are Willing to Earn Less Money to Do More Meaningful Work," *Harvard Business Review*, November 6, 2018, https://hbr.org/2018/11/9-out-of-10-people-are-willing-to-earn-less-money-to-do-more-meaningful-work.

43. Kelly Weeks, "Generational Differences in Definitions of Meaningful Work: A Mixed Methods Study," *Journal of Business Ethics* 156, no. 4 (2019): 2.

44. Jing Hu and Jacob B. Hirsh, "Accepting Lower Salaries for Meaningful Work," *Frontiers in Psychology* 8 (September 2017).

45. "2004 Founders' IPO Letter," Alphabet Investor Relations, accessed October 16, 2020, https://abc.xyz/investor/founders-letters/2004-ipo-letter.

46. Ryan Tate, "Google Couldn't Kill 20 Percent Time Even if It Wanted To," *Wired*, June 3, 2017, www.wired.com/2013/08/20-percent-time-will-never-die.

47. Kaomi Goetz, "How 3M Gave Everyone Days Off and Created an Innovation Dynamo," Fast Company, July 9, 2018, www.fastcompany.com/1663137/how-3m-gave-everyone-days-off-and-created-an-innovation-dynamo.

48. Jay Yarow, "Tim Cook Is Giving Apple Employees Two-Week Breaks to Work on Special Projects," *Business Insider*i, November 12, 2012, www.businessinsider.com/apple-tries-20-time-2012-11.

49. Tate, "Google Couldn't Kill 20 Percent Time Even if It Wanted To."

50. Sheera Frenkel, Mike Isaac, Cecilia Kang, and Gabriel J. X., "Facebook Employees Stage Virtual Walkout to Protest Trump Posts," *New York Times*, June 1, 2020, www.nytimes.com/2020/06/01/technology/facebook-employee-protest-trump.html.

51. *How Millennials Want to Work and Live* (Washington, DC: Gallup, Inc., 2016), www.gallup.com/workplace/238073/millennials-work-live.aspx.

52. Arnett et al., "Using Job Satisfaction and Pride as Internal Marketing Tools."

53. "US Outdoor Clothing Brand Patagonia Wins UN Champions of the Earth Award," UNEP—UN Environment Programme, accessed March 27, 2020, www.unenvironment.org/news-and-stories/press-release/us-outdoor-clothing-brand-patagonia-wins-un-champions-earth-award.

54. Veronika Sonsev, "Patagonia's Focus on Its Brand Purpose Is Great for Business," *Forbes*, November 27, 2019, www.forbes.com/sites/veronika

sonsev/2019/11/27/patagonias-focus-on-its-brand-purpose-is-great-for-business/#1d13fea054cb.

55. "US Outdoor Clothing Brand Patagonia Wins UN Champions of the Earth Award."

56. Scott Mautz, "Patagonia Has Only 4 Percent Employee Turnover Because They Value This 1 Thing So Much," *Inc.*, March 30, 2019, www.inc.com/scott-mautz/how-can-patagonia-have-only-4-percent-worker-turnover-hint-they-pay-activist-employees-bail.html.

57. Patagonia Works, "Annual Benefit Corporation Report: Fiscal Year 2017," accessed October 16, 2020, www.patagonia.com/static/on/demandware.static/-/Library-Sites-PatagoniaShared/default/dw824fac0f/PDF-US/2017-BCORP-pages_022218.pdf.

58. Jennifer Robison, "Millennials Worry about the Environment—Should Your Company?" Gallup, May 29, 2020, www.gallup.com/workplace/257786/millennials-worry-environment-company.aspx.

59. Kathy Gurchiek, "More Workers Than You Realize Are Caregivers," SHRM, August 16, 2019, www.shrm.org/resourcesandtools/hr-topics/behavioral-competencies/global-and-cultural-effectiveness/pages/more-workers-than-you-realize-are-caregivers-.aspx.

60. Sherri Snelling, "A New Era: Companies Supporting Caregivers," *Forbes*, April 14, 2015, www.forbes.com/sites/nextavenue/2015/04/14/a-new-era-companies-supporting-caregivers/#72f17937b136.

61. Heather R. Huhman, "These 8 Companies Know the Impact of Supporting Mental Health in the Workplace," *Entrepreneur*, May 15, 2017, www.entrepreneur.com/article/294143.

62. Naz Beheshti, "Pet-Friendly Workplaces Are a Win-Win for Employee Wellbeing and for Business," *Forbes*, September 28, 2019, www.forbes.com/sites/nazbeheshti/2019/05/22/pet-friendly-workplaces-are-a-win-win-for-employee-wellbeing-and-for-business/#7af6862d5dbc.

63. U.S. Bureau of Labor Statistics, "Employer Costs for Employee Compensation," accessed March 27, 2020, www.bls.gov/opub/btn/volume-2/paid-leave-in-private-industry-over-the-past-20-years.htm.

64. Joanne Sammer, "Unlimited Paid Time Off: A Good or Bad Idea?" SHRM, August 16, 2019, www.shrm.org/resourcesandtools/hr-topics/benefits/pages/unlimited-pto.aspx.

65. Inc. Staff, "Free Tools, Resources, and Financial Help for Business Owners Hit by Covid-19," *Inc.*, last updated May 5, 2020, www.inc.com/inc-staff/free-tools-grants-video-conferencing-ad-credits-gift-certificates-cloud-storage-cyber-security.html.

66. Jena McGregor, "Why Unlimited Vacation Is Basically a No-Brainer for Employers," *Washington Post*, October 8, 2015, www.washingtonpost.com/news/on-leadership/wp/2015/10/08/what-your-company-gains-when-it-gives-you-unlimited-vacation.

67. "The US GE Permissive Approach to Paid Time-Off Is Peace-of-Mind for My Family, My Team and Me: GE Careers," GE, accessed March 27, 2020, www.ge.com/careers/culture/the-us-ge-permissive-approach-to-paid-time-off-is-peace-of-mind-for-my-family-my-team-and-me.

68. "More Companies Offering Unlimited Time Off," SAGE Business Researcher, accessed March 27, 2020, http://businessresearcher.sagepub.com/sbr-1863-102641-2779724/20170508/short-article-more-companies-offering-unlimited-time-off.

CHAPTER 8. CREATING A GENTELLIGENT WORK CULTURE

1. Laura Sherbin, "Diversity Doesn't Stick Without Inclusion," *Harvard Business Review*, February 1, 2017, https://hbr.org/2017/02/diversity-doesnt-stick-without-inclusion.

2. Nilofer Merchant, "Culture Trumps Strategy, Every Time," *Harvard Business Review*, March 22, 2011, https://hbr.org/2011/03/culture-trumps-strategy-every.

3. Louis V. Gerstner, *Who Says Elephants Can't Dance? Inside IBM's Historic Turnaround* (New York: HarperInformation, 2002), 182.

4. D. D. Warrick, "What Leaders Need to Know about Organizational Culture," *Business Horizons* 60, no. 3 (2017): 395–404.

5. Edgar H. Schein, "Defining Organizational Culture," *Classics of Organization Theory* 3, no. 1 (1985): 490–502.

6. Julianna Young, "7 Zappos Amenities That Boost Employee Happiness," Zappos, June 12, 2019, www.zappos.com/about/stories/employee-happiness-amenities.

7. Bill Taylor, "Why Zappos Pays New Employees to Quit—and You Should Too," *Harvard Business Review*, February 21, 2018, https://hbr.org/2008/05/why-zappos-pays-new-employees.

8. Ibid.

9. Schein, "Defining Organizational Culture."

10. Enron, "Enron Annual Report 2000," University of Chicago, 2000, https://picker.uchicago.edu/Enron/EnronAnnualReport2000.pdf.

11. "The Fall of Enron," *NPR*, February 12, 2002, www.npr.org/templates/story/story.php?storyId=1137940.

12. *How Millennials Want to Work and Live* (Washington, DC: Gallup, Inc., 2016), www.gallup.com/workplace/238073/millennials-work-live.aspx.

13. Nina McQueen, "Workplace Culture Trends: The Key to Hiring (and Keeping) Top Talent in 2018," *LinkedIn Official Blog*, June 26, 2018, https://blog.linkedin.com/2018/june/26/workplace-culture-trends-the-key-to-hiring-and-keeping-top-talent.

14. "100 Best Workplaces for Millennials," *Fortune*, accessed October 25, 2020, https://fortune.com/best-workplaces-millennials/2016.

15. "20 Best Workplaces for Gen X'ers," *Fortune*, accessed October 25, 2020, https://fortune.com/best-workplaces-gen-x.

16. "20 Best Workplaces for Baby Boomers," *Fortune*, accessed October 25, 2020, https://fortune.com/best-workplaces-baby-boomers.

17. "100 Best Companies to Work For," *Fortune*, accessed October 25, 2020, https://fortune.com/best-companies.

18. Kala Moynihan, interview with authors, February 17, 2019.

19. Mary Hayes Weier, "Generation Workday: A Look at Workday's Future Leaders," *Workday Blog*, October 18, 2019, https://blog.workday.com/en-us/2015/generation-workday-a-look-at-workdays-future-leaders.html.

20. Ibid.

21. Carrie Varoquiers, "Five Ways We're Building Opportunity Onramps in the Workday Community," *Workday Blog*, December 27, 2018, https://blog.workday.com/en-us/2018/five-ways-were-building-opportunity-onramps-in-the-workday-community.html.

22. "Our Core Values," Workday, accessed March 27, 2020, www.workday.com/en-us/company/about-workday/core-values.html.

23. Kerry Hannon, "5 Workplaces That Embrace Older Workers," *Forbes*, November 18, 2016, www.forbes.com/sites/nextavenue/2016/11/18/5-workplaces-that-embrace-older-workers/#719bfe965914.

24. Edgar H. Schein, *Organizational Culture* (Cambridge, MA: MIT, 1988), 9, https://dspace.mit.edu/bitstream/handle/1721.1/2224/SWP-2088-24854366.pdf?sequenc.

25. Bill Taylor, "To Build a Strong Culture, Create Rules That Are Unique to Your Company," *Harvard Business Review*, December 16, 2019, https://hbr.org/2019/12/to-build-a-strong-culture-create-rules-that-are-unique-to-your-company.

26. S. Greengard, "Moving Forward with Reverse Mentoring," *Workforce* 81, no. 3 (2002): 15.

27. Thomas M. Koulopoulos and Dan Keldsen, *The Gen Z Effect: The Six Forces Shaping the Future of Business* (Brookline, MA: Bibliomotion, Books Media, 2014).

28. W. M. Murphy, "Reverse Mentoring at Work: Fostering Cross-Generational Learning and Developing Millennial Leaders," *Human Resource Management* 51, no. 4 (July–August 2012): 549–74.

29. Sally Newman and Alan Hatton-Yeo, "Intergenerational Learning and the Contributions of Older People," *Aging Horizons*, no. 8 (2008): 31–39.

30. Ibid.

31. Ibid.

32. Joni Rubin, interview with authors, April 23, 2019.

33. Brent Woodhouse, interview with authors, May 24, 2019.

34. Greengard, "Moving Forward with Reverse Mentoring."

35. Newman and Hatton-Yeo, "Intergenerational Learning and the Contributions of Older People."

36. Edwin A. Locke, Karyll N. Shaw, Lise M. Saari, and Gary P. Latham, "Goal Setting and Task Performance: 1969–1980," *Psychological Bulletin* 90, no. 1 (1981): 125.

37. Ibid.

38. Miriam Erez and Revital Arad, "Participative Goal-Setting: Social, Motivational, and Cognitive Factors," *Journal of Applied Psychology* 71, no. 4 (1986): 591.

39. Barbara Mazur, "Building Diverse and Inclusive Organizational Culture-Best Practices: A Case Study of Cisco Co," *Journal of Intercultural Management* 6, no. 4 (December 2014): 169–79, https://doi.org/10.2478/joim-2014-0043.

40. David A. Garvin, Amy C. Edmondson, and Francesca Gino, "Is Yours a Learning Organization?" *Harvard Business Review*, March 2008, https://hbr.org/2008/03/is-yours-a-learning-organization.

41. Nicola Pless and Thomas Maak, "Building an Inclusive Diversity Culture: Principles, Processes and Practice," *Journal of Business Ethics* 54, no. 2 (2004): 131.

42. Xi Chen, Alim J. Beveridge, and Ping Ping Fu, "Put Yourself in Others' Age: How Age Simulation Facilitates Intergenerational Cooperation," *Academy of Management Proceedings* 2018, no. 1 (2018): 16250.

43. "Zappos 10 Core Values," Zappos Insights, accessed October 17, 2020, www.zapposinsights.com/about/core-values?utm_campaign=newsroom&utm_medium=about-us&utm_source=what-we-live-by&utm_content=our-core-values.

44. Shelton Goode and Isaac Dixon, "Are Employee Resource Groups Good for Business?" SHRM, August 25, 2016, www.shrm.org/hr-today/news/hr-magazine/0916/pages/are-employee-resource-groups-good-for-business.aspx.

45. Theresa M. Welbourne, Skylar Rolf, and Steven Schlachter, "Employee Resource Groups: An Introduction, Review and Research Agenda," *Academy of Management Proceedings* 2015, no. 1 (August 2015).

46. Ryan Beaudry, "#YoPro, Shaping the Future of Commerce," Master Card Social Newsroom, July 27, 2012, https://newsroom.mastercard.com/2012/07/27/yopro-shaping-the-future-of-commerce.

47. Ibid.

48. "New Video Series 'GenTalk' Sparks Conversations on Diversity and Inclusion—News Center," Nielsen, May 21, 2018, http://sites.nielsen.com/news center/new-video-series-gentalk-sparks-conversations-diversity-inclusion.

49. "Driving Momentum: 2015 Diversity & Inclusion Annual Report," PNC Bank, 2015, www.pnc.com/content/dam/pnc-com/pdf/aboutpnc/2015-diversity-annual-report.pdf.

50. Kiyona Miah, interview with authors, June 13, 2019.

51. Kiran Aziz, "This Is Why Boards of Directors Need Younger Members," World Economic Forum, December 19, 2018, www.weforum.org/agenda/2018/12/boards-of-directors-need-youngsters-millennials.

52. "Age Diversity in the Boardroom," PwC, 2018, www.pwc.com/us/en/services/governance-insights-center/library/younger-directors-bring-boardroom-age-diversity.html.

53. April Hall, "Age Diversity on Boards a Top Priority. But Where Are They?" Directors & Boards, April 23, 2018, www.directorsandboards.com/news/age-diversity-boards-top-priority-where-are-they.

54. Aziz, "This Is Why Boards of Directors Need Younger Members."

55. "Tate Appoints Youth Engagement Trustee," Tate Modern, March 11, 2019, www.tate.org.uk/press/press-releases/tate-appoints-youth-engagement-trustee.

56. Colleen Dilenschneider, "Six Urgent Reasons to Add Millennials to Your Nonprofit Board of Directors," November 19, 2014, www.colleendilen.com/2014/11/19/six-urgent-reasons-to-add-millennials-to-your-nonprofit-board-of-directors.

57. Jennifer Jordan and Michael Sorell, "Why You Should Create a 'Shadow Board' of Younger Employees," *Harvard Business Review*, June 5, 2019, https://hbr.org/2019/06/why-you-should-create-a-shadow-board-of-younger-employees.

58. Ibid.

59. Pless and Maak, "Building an Inclusive Diversity Culture."

60. Barbara Mazur, "Building Diverse and Inclusive Organizational Culture-Best Practices: A Case Study of Cisco Co," *Journal of Intercultural Management* 6, no. 4-1 (2014): 169–79.

61. Pless and Maak, "Building an Inclusive Diversity Culture."

62. Jeongha Hwang and Karen M. Hopkins, "A Structural Equation Model of the Effects of Diversity Characteristics and Inclusion on Organizational Outcomes in the Child Welfare Workforce," *Children and Youth Services Review* 50 (January 19, 2015): 44–52, https://doi.org/10.1016/j.childyouth.2015.01.012.

63. Pless and Maak, "Building an Inclusive Diversity Culture," 130.

CHAPTER 9. GENTELLIGENCE FOR THE FUTURE OF WORK

1. W. Edwards Deming Institute, accessed October 23, 2020, https://deming.org/quotes/10083.

2. Madeleine Carlisle, "Supreme Court Justice Roberts Asks If 'OK Boomer' Is Ageist," *Time*, January 16, 2020, https://time.com/5766438/john-roberts-ok-boomer-scotus.

3. Megan Gerhardt, "Is 'OK, Boomer' Ageist? John Roberts Is Mulling It, but Laws Won't Fix Generational Shaming," *NBC News*, January 17, 2020, www

.nbcnews.com/think/opinion/ok-boomer-ageist-maybe-supreme-court-case-won-t-fix-ncna1117496.

4. Olivia Carville, "IBM Fired as Many as 100,000 in Recent Years, Lawsuit Shows," *Bloomberg*, July 31, 2019, www.bloomberg.com/news/articles/2019-07-31/ibm-fired-as-many-as-100-000-in-recent-years-court-case-shows.

5. Peter Gosselin and Ariana Tobin, "Inside IBM's Purge of Thousands of Workers Who Have One Thing in Common," *Mother Jones*, March 24, 2018, www.motherjones.com/crime-justice/2018/03/ibm-propublica-gray-hairs-old-heads.

6. Andrew R. McIlvaine, "IBM Is Being Accused of Widespread Age Discrimination," HR Executive, September 18, 2019, https://hrexecutive.com/ibm-is-being-accused-of-widespread-age-discrimination.

7. Jack Kelly, "Google Settles Age Discrimination Lawsuit, Highlighting the Proliferation of Ageism in Hiring," *Forbes*, July 24, 2019, www.forbes.com/sites/jackkelly/2019/07/23/google-settles-age-discrimination-lawsuit-highlighting-the-proliferation-of-ageism-in-hiring/#21cb743c5c67.

8. Kathy Gurchiek, "Google Ends Age-Discrimination Suit with $11 Million Settlement," SHRM, July 24, 2019, www.shrm.org/resourcesandtools/hr-topics/behavioral-competencies/global-and-cultural-effectiveness/pages/google-ends-age-discrimination-suit-with-11-million-settlement.aspx.

9. *OECD Employment Outlook 2013* (Paris: Organization for Economic Development, 2013).

10. "Family On-Demand," Papa, accessed October 17, 2020, www.joinpapa.com.

11. Andrew Parker, interview with authors, July 25, 2018.

12. "Papa Evolves to 'Family On-Demand,'" Papa, February 3, 2020, www.joinpapa.com/press-releases/papa-new-brand.

13. "Family On-Demand."

14. Kerry Hannon, "The Family Business Matching Older and Younger Entrepreneurs," Next Avenue, March 28, 2019, www.nextavenue.org/family-business-matching-entrepreneurs.

15. Jim Sugarman, "Jim Sugarman's LinkedIn Profile," LinkedIn, accessed October 17, 2020, www.linkedin.com/in/jimsugarman4gennow.

16. "About—Intergenerational Programs: Student Residents," Judson Senior Living, accessed October 17, 2020, www.judsonsmartliving.org/about/intergenerational-programs/student-residents.

17. Susan Brink, "Good for Each Other," *Los Angeles Times*, December 5, 2005, www.onegeneration.org/wp-content/uploads/2016/02/latimes-onegen.pdf.

18. "Our Focus," Eisner Foundation, accessed October 17, 2020, https://eisnerfoundation.org/our-focus.

19. "About BuildWitt Media Construction Marketing," BuildWitt, accessed October 17, 2020, https://buildwitt.com/about.

20. U.S. Bureau of Labor Statistics, "Labor Force Statistics from the Current Population Survey," accessed March 27, 2020, www.bls.gov/cps/cpsaat18b.htm.

21. Adam Quiñones, "Bridging the Gap Between Old and New Schools of Construction," Construction Executive, June 14, 2019, www.constructionexec.com/article/bridging-the-gap-between-old-and-new-schools-of-construction.

22. "Commercial Construction Index," U.S. Chamber of Commerce, 2019, www.uschamber.com/sites/default/files/cci_q1_2019_3-12-2019_for_release_0.pdf.

23. Dan Briscoe, interview with authors, June 29, 2019.

24. Ibid.

25. Aaron Witt and Dan Briscoe, interview with authors, February 24, 2020.

26. "Careers in Construction Marketing," BuildWitt, accessed October 17, 2020, https://buildwitt.com/careers.

27. Ibid.

28. Aaron Witt and Dan Briscoe, interview with authors, February 24, 2020.

29. Dan Briscoe, interview with authors, June 29, 2019.

30. Ibid.

31. Ibid.

32. Aaron Witt and Dan Briscoe, interview with authors, February 24, 2020.

33. "Aaron Witt's Story," BuildWitt, accessed March 27, 2020, https://buildwitt.com/about/aarons-story.

34. Dan Briscoe, interview with authors, June 29, 2019.

35. Aaron Witt and Dan Briscoe, interview with authors, February 24, 2020.

36. Dan Briscoe, interview with authors, June 29, 2019.

37. Aaron Witt and Dan Briscoe, interview with authors, February 24, 2020.

38. Ibid.

39. Aaron Witt, "Aaron's Travels: A Journey with Anxiety," BuildWitt, June 7, 2019, https://buildwitt.com/aaron-talks-anxiety.

40. Krista Mahler, interview with authors, February 24, 2020.

41. "What We Stand for as People and as a Company," BuildWitt, accessed October 25, 2020, https://buildwitt.com/about-us.

42. "We're on a Mission to Change the Dirt World. Ready to Join?" BuildWitt, accessed October 25, 2020, https://buildwitt.com/careers.

43. Dan Briscoe, "My 24-Year-Old Millennial Boss . . . Part 2," LinkedIn, May 2019, www.linkedin.com/posts/dfbriscoe_my-24-year-old-millennial-boss-part-2-activity-6545326475111915521-uYdB.

44. Margaret Oliphant, *The Open Door, and the Portrait. Stories of the Seen and the Unseen* (n.p.: Hard Press, 2006), 2.

45. Joe Pinsker, "Oh No, They've Come Up with Another Generation Label," *The Atlantic*, February 21, 2020, www.theatlantic.com/family/archive/2020/02/generation-after-gen-z-named-alpha/606862.

46. Peter Suderman, "Tyler Cowen Thinks Coronavirus Could Be This Generation's World War II," *Reason*, March 18, 2020, https://reason.com/2020/03/18/tyler-cowen-thinks-coronavirus-could-be-this-generations-world-war-ii.

Recommended Resources

Brown, Brené. *Daring Greatly: How the Courage to Be Vulnerable Transforms the Way We Live, Love, Parent, and Lead.* New York: Penguin, 2015.

Cappelli, Peter, and Bill Novelli. *Managing the Older Worker: How to Prepare for the New Organizational Order.* Boston: Harvard Business Press, 2010.

Conley, Chip. *Wisdom at Work: The Making of a Modern Elder.* London: Penguin, 2018.

Earley, P. Christopher, Soon Ang, and Joo-Seng Tan. *CQ: Developing Cultural Intelligence at Work.* Stanford: Stanford Business, 2006.

Finkelstein, Lisa M., Donald M. Truxillo, Franco Fraccaroli, and Ruth Kanfer. *Facing the Challenges of a Multi-Age Workforce.* New York: Routledge, 2015.

Freedman, Marc. *How to Live Forever: The Enduring Power of Connecting the Generations.* New York: Ingram Publisher Services US, 2019.

Grant, Adam M. *Originals: How Non-Conformists Move the World.* New York: Penguin, 2017.

Koulopoulos, Tom, and Dan Keldsen. *Gen Z Effect: The Six Forces Shaping the Future of Business.* New York: Routledge, 2016.

Lancaster, Lynne C., and David Stillman. *When Generations Collide: Who They Are, Why They Clash, How to Solve the Generational Puzzle at Work.* New York: HarperBusiness, 2003.

Ng, Eddy, Sean T. Lyons, and Linda Schweitzer, eds. *Managing the New Workforce: International Perspectives on the Millennial Generation.* Cheltenham, UK: Edward Elgar Publishing, 2012.

Stillman, David, and Jonah Stillman. *Gen Z Work: How the Next Generation Is Transforming the Workplace.* New York: HarperCollins, 2017.

Strauss, William, and Neil Howe. *Generations: The History of America's Future, 1584 to 2069.* New York: William Morrow, 1991.

Twenge, Jean M. *Generation Me: Why Today's Young Americans Are More Confident, Assertive, Entitled, and More Miserable Than Ever Before.* New York: Free Press, 2006.

———. *iGen: Why Today's Super-Connected Kids Are Growing Up Less Rebellious, More Tolerant, Less Happy—and Completely Unprepared for Adulthood—and What That Means for the Rest of Us.* New York: Simon and Schuster, 2017.

Zemke, Ron, Claire Raines, and Bob Filipczak. *Generations at Work: Managing the Clash of Veterans, Boomers, Xers, and Nexters in Your Workplace.* New York: Amacom, 1999.

RECOMMENDED ARTICLES

Atkins, Jeff. "Scientists Who Selfie: Building Public Trust through Social Media." *PLOS Blogs*, May 10, 2019. https://theplosblog.plos.org/2019/05/scientists-who-selfie-building-public-trust-through-social-media.

Bialik, Kristen, and Richard Fry. "How Millennials Compare with Prior Generations." Pew Research Center's Social & Demographic Trends Project, February 14, 2019. www.pewsocialtrends.org/essay/millennial-life-how-young-adulthood-today-compares-with-prior-generations.

Dimock, Michael. "Defining Generations: Where Millennials End and Generation Z Begins." Pew Research Center, January 17, 2019. www.pewresearch.org/fact-tank/2019/01/17/where-millennials-end-and-generation-z-begins.

Duhigg, Charles. "What Google Learned from Its Quest to Build the Perfect Team." *New York Times*, February 25, 2016. www.nytimes.com/2016/02/28/magazine/what-google-learned-from-its-quest-to-build-the-perfect-team.html.

Earley, P. Christopher, and Elaine Mosakowski. "Cultural Intelligence." *Harvard Business Review*, April 20, 2016. https://hbr.org/2004/10/cultural-intelligence.

Eswaran, Vijay, and QI Group. "The Business Case for Diversity Is Now Overwhelming. Here's Why." *World Economic Forum*, April 29, 2019. www.weforum.org/agenda/2019/04/business-case-for-diversity-in-the-workplace.

Gallup, Inc. "How Millennials Want to Work and Live." *Gallup*, December 12, 2019. www.gallup.com/workplace/238073/millennials-work-live.aspx.

Gerhardt, Megan. "Today's Managers 'Blew It' with Millennials, College Professor Says, and Here's How We Can Avoid Doing It Again with Generation Z." *Business Insider*, March 11, 2019. www.businessinsider.com/managers-blew-it-with-millennials-generation-z-megan-gerhardt-2019-3.

———. "The 'OK, Boomer' Meme Hurts Gen Z More Than the Older Generation It's Aimed At." *NBC News*, November 18, 2019. www.nbcnews.com/think/opinion/ok-boomer-meme-hurts-gen-z-more-older-generation-it-ncna1079276.

Herway, Jake. "How to Create a Culture of Psychological Safety." *Gallup*, March 5, 2020. www.gallup.com/workplace/236198/create-culture-psychological-safety.aspx.

Jordan, Jennifer, and Michael Sorell. "Why You Should Create a 'Shadow Board' of Younger Employees." *Harvard Business Review*, June 5, 2019. https://hbr.org/2019/06/why-you-should-create-a-shadow-board-of-younger-employees.

Joshi, Aparna, John C. Dencker, Gentz Franz, and Joseph J. Martocchio. "Unpacking Generational Identities in Organizations." *Academy of Management Review* 35, no. 3 (2010): 392–414.

Lorenz, Taylor. "'OK Boomer' Marks the End of Friendly Generational Relations." *New York Times*, October 29, 2019. www.nytimes.com/2019/10/29/style/ok-boomer.html.

Miller, Claire Cain, and Sanam Yar. "Young People Are Going to Save Us All from Office Life." *New York Times*, September 17, 2019. www.nytimes.com/2019/09/17/style/generation-z-millennials-work-life-balance.html.

Neal, Stephanie, Kabir Sehgal, Priscilla Claman, and Rebecca Knight. "Are Companies about to Have a Gen X Retention Problem?" *Harvard Business Review*, July 29, 2019. https://hbr.org/2019/07/are-companies-about-to-have-a-gen-x-retention-problem.

Rockwood, Kate. "Hiring in the Age of Ageism." SHRM, August 16, 2019. www.shrm.org/hr-today/news/hr-magazine/0218/pages/hiring-in-the-age-of-ageism.aspx.

Thomas, David A., and Robin J. Ely. "Making Differences Matter: A New Paradigm for Managing Diversity." *Harvard Business Review*, April 29, 2016.

https://hbr.org/1996/09/making-differences-matter-a-new-paradigm-for-managing-diversity.

"The Whys and Hows of Generations Research." Pew Research Center for the People and the Press, December 31, 2019. www.people-press.org/2015/09/03/the-whys-and-hows-of-generations-research.

Zenger, Jack, and Joseph Folkman. "What Younger Managers Should Know about How They Are Perceived." *Harvard Business Review*, September 29, 2015. https://hbr.org/2015/09/what-younger-managers-should-know-about-how-theyre-perceived.

OTHER USEFUL RESOURCES

"Generational Conflict: A Matter of Clout." Center for Creative Leadership (Podcast). www.ccl.org/multimedia/podcast/generational-conflict-a-matter-of-clout.

Project Implicit. Harvard University. https://implicit.harvard.edu/implicit.

"Tool: Foster Psychological Safety." Re:Work with Google. Accessed October 9, 2020. https://rework.withgoogle.com/guides/understanding-team-effectiveness/steps/foster-psychological-safety.

TED TALKS

Adichie, Chimamanda Ngozi. "The Danger of a Single Story." Filmed July 2009. TED video, 18:34. www.ted.com/talks/chimamanda_ngozi_adichie_the_danger_of_a_single_story.

Conley, Chip. "What Baby Boomers Can Learn from Millennials at Work—and Vice Versa." Filmed September 2018. TED video, 12:14. www.ted.com/talks/chip_conley_what_baby_boomers_can_learn_from_millennials_at_work_and_vice_versa?language=en.

Edmondson, Amy. "Building a Psychologically Safe Workplace." Filmed May 2014 at Harvard Graduate School. TEDx video, 11:26. www.youtube.com/watch?v=LhoLuui9gX8.

Gerhardt, Megan. "Why I Love Millennials (and You Should Too)." Filmed August 2017 at Miami University. TEDx video, 8:14. www.youtube.com/watch?v=pQMt343pMak.

Mentink, Jurriën. "Intergenerational Learning: Exchanges between Young & Old." Filmed April 21, 2016, in Amsterdam. TED video, 8:35. www.youtube.com/watch?v=Pt58fu-TjWc&t=40s.

Bibliography

"100 Best Companies to Work For." *Fortune*. Accessed October 25, 2020. https://fortune.com/best-companies.

"100 Best Workplaces for Millennials." *Fortune*. Accessed October 25, 2020. https://fortune.com/best-workplaces-millennials/2016.

"1968 in Germany: A Generation with Two Phases and Faces." *Eurozine*, June 22, 2018. www.eurozine.com/1968-germany-generation-two-phases-faces.

"20 Best Workplaces for Baby Boomers." *Fortune*. Accessed October 25, 2020. https://fortune.com/best-workplaces-baby-boomers.

"20 Best Workplaces for Gen X'ers." *Fortune*. Accessed October 25, 2020. https://fortune.com/best-workplaces-gen-x.

"2004 Founders' IPO Letter." Alphabet Investor Relations. Accessed October 16, 2020. https://abc.xyz/investor/founders-letters/2004-ipo-letter.

"2016–17: Healthy Workplaces for All Ages." European Agency for Safety and Health at Work. Accessed October 14, 2020. https://healthy-workplaces.eu/previous/all-ages-2016/en.

"2019 Global Human Capital Trends." Deloitte Insights, 2019. www2.deloitte.com/us/en/insights/focus/human-capital-trends.html.

2019 Retention Report. Work Institute, 2019. https://info.workinstitute.com/hubfs/2019%20Retention%20Report/Work%20Institute%202019%20Retention%20Report%20final-1.pdf.

"2021 Virtual Returnship Program." Goldman Sachs. Accessed October 16, 2020. www.goldmansachs.com/careers/professionals/returnship.

"Aaron Witt's Story." BuildWitt. Accessed March 27, 2020. https://buildwitt.com/about/aarons-story.

"About BuildWitt Media Construction Marketing." BuildWitt. Accessed October 17, 2020. https://buildwitt.com/about.

"About—Intergenerational Programs: Student Residents." Judson Senior Living. Accessed October 17, 2020. www.judsonsmartliving.org/about/intergenerational-programs/student-residents.

Achor, Shawn, Andrew Reece, Gabriella Rosen Kellerman, and Alexi Robichaux. "9 Out of 10 People Are Willing to Earn Less Money to Do More Meaningful Work." *Harvard Business Review*, November 6, 2018. https://hbr.org/2018/11/9-out-of-10-people-are-willing-to-earn-less-money-to-do-more-meaningful-work.

Adichie, Chimamanda Ngozi. "The Danger of a Single Story." Filmed October 7, 2009. TED video, 19:16. www.ted.com/talks/chimamanda_ngozi_adichie_the_danger_of_a_single_story.

Adkins, Amy. "Millennials: The Job-Hopping Generation." Gallup. Accessed October 16, 2020. www.gallup.com/workplace/231587/millennials-job-hopping-generation.aspx.

"Age Diversity in the Boardroom." PwC, 2018. www.pwc.com/us/en/services/governance-insights-center/library/younger-directors-bring-boardroom-age-diversity.html.

"Ageism in America Is Hurting Us All." Senior Planning Services, August 10, 2017. www.seniorplanningservices.com/2017/08/21/ageism-america-hurting-us.

Agovino, Theresa. "Millennials Say They Are Struggling More to Work from Home." SHRM, May 18, 2020. www.shrm.org/resourcesandtools/hr-topics/employee-relations/pages/millennials-say-they-are-struggling-more-to-work-from-home.aspx.

Anderson, Monica, and Andrew Perrin. "Barriers to Adoption and Attitudes towards Tech among Older Americans." Pew Research Center, December 31, 2019. www.pewresearch.org/internet/2017/05/17/barriers-to-adoption-and-attitudes-towards-technology.

Antal, Ariane Berthoin. "Types of Knowledge Gained by Expatriate Managers." *Journal of General Management* 26, no. 2 (2000): 32–51.

Arnett, Dennis B., Debra A. Laverie, and Charlie McLane. "Using Job Satisfaction and Pride as Internal-Marketing Tools." *Cornell Hotel and Restaurant Administration Quarterly* (2002).

Atkins, Jeff. "Scientists Who Selfie: Building Public Trust through Social Media." *PLOS Blogs*, May 10, 2019. https://theplosblog.plos.org/2019/05/scientists-who-selfie-building-public-trust-through-social-media.

"Auguste Comte on the Natural Progress of Human Society." *Population and Development Review* 37, no. 2 (2011): 389–94. www.jstor.org/stable/23043288.

Aziz, Kiran. "This Is Why Boards of Directors Need Younger Members." World Economic Forum, December 19, 2018. www.weforum.org/agenda/2018/12/boards-of-directors-need-youngsters-millennials.

Babones, Salvatore. "Hao, Boomer!" *Foreign Policy*, November 25, 2019. https://foreignpolicy.com/2019/11/25/ok-boomer-millennials-resent-ruin ing-world-generational-politics-mainland-china-hong-kong.

Bariso, Justin. "It Took Elon Musk Exactly 5 Words to Reveal What He Looks for in Every New Hire (and It's Not a College Degree)." *Inc.*, November 18, 2019. www.inc.com/justin-bariso/it-took-elon-musk-exactly-5-words-to-re veal-what-he-looks-for-in-every-new-hire-and-its-not-a-college-degree.html.

Barnes, Patricia. "Proposed Settlement of Age Discrimination Case Hardly Onerous for PricewaterhouseCoopers." *Forbes*, March 18, 2020. www.forbes .com/sites/patriciagbarnes/2020/03/16/proposed-settlement-of-age-discrimi nation-case-hardly-onerous-for-pricewaterhousecoopers/#30d1dea75d7f.

Bayern, Macy. "The Generational Divide: Telecommuting during the Coronavirus Pandemic." TechRepublic, March 23, 2020. www.techrepublic.com/article/the-generational-divide-telecommuting-during-the-coronavirus-pandemic.

Beaudry, Ryan. "#YoPro, Shaping the Future of Commerce." MasterCard Social Newsroom, July 27, 2012. https://newsroom.mastercard.com/2012/07/27/yopro-shaping-the-future-of-commerce.

Beheshti, Naz. "Pet-Friendly Workplaces Are a Win-Win for Employee Well-being and for Business." *Forbes*, September 28, 2019. www.forbes.com/sites/nazbeheshti/2019/05/22/pet-friendly-workplaces-are-a-win-win-for-em ployee-wellbeing-and-for-business/#7af6862d5dbc.

Bellis, Rich. "5 Flexible Work Strategies and the Companies That Use Them." Fast Company, April 6, 2016. www.fastcompany.com/3058344/5-flexible -work-strategies-and-the-companies-who-use-them.

Bennett, J., Milton Bennett, and Kathryn Stillings. "DIE (Describe, Interpret, and Evaluate) Model Handout." Unpublished, 1979.

Berg, Lora, Elandre Dedrick, Elisabeth Winter, Corinna Blutguth, Maria Elena Gutierrez, Maria Florea, Mihnea-Mihail Florea, and Hana Kovhan. "Window on GMF's Diverse Workplace: Building Successful Multi-Generational Teams." German Marshall Fund of the United States, October 7, 2019. www.gmfus.org/blog/2019/10/07/window-gmfs-diverse-workplace-building-successful-multi-generational-teams.

Bersin, Josh. "Google for Jobs: Potential to Disrupt the $200 Billion Recruiting Industry." *Forbes*, May 26, 2017. https://www.forbes.com/sites/joshbersin/2017/05/26/google-for-jobs-potential-to-disrupt-the-200-billion-recruiting-industry/#602058954d1f.

Bialik, Kristen, and Richard Fry. "How Millennials Compare with Prior Generations." Pew Research Center's Social & Demographic Trends Project, February 14, 2019. www.pewsocialtrends.org/essay/millennial-life-how-young-adulthood-today-compares-with-prior-generations.

Blanchard, Kenneth H., and Spencer Johnson. *The One Minute Manager*. New York: William Morrow, 2015.

Blauth, Chris, Jack McDaniel, Craig Perrin, and Paul Perrin. *Age-Based Stereotypes: Silent Killer of Collaboration and Productivity*. AchieveGlobal, 2010. www.aarp.org/content/dam/aarp/ppi/2017/08/disrupt-aging-in-the-workforce.pdf.

Boersma, Maxine. "Schemes to Hire People after Career Breaks Are Proving Popular." *Financial Times*, November 11, 2015. www.ft.com/content/18f7870a-8227-11e5-a01c-8650859a4767.

Boitnott, John. "How to Partner Successfully with a Younger Boss." *Entrepreneur*, April 24, 2018. www.entrepreneur.com/article/312343.

"Breaking Down Divorce by Generation: Goldberg Jones: PDX." Goldberg Jones, May 16, 2019. www.goldbergjones-or.com/divorce/divorce-by-generation.

Brink, Susan. "Good for Each Other." *Los Angeles Times*, December 5, 2005. www.onegeneration.org/wp-content/uploads/2016/02/latimes-onegen.pdf.

Briscoe, Dan. Interview with authors. June 29, 2019.

———. "My 24-Year-Old Millennial Boss . . . Part 2." LinkedIn, May 2019. www.linkedin.com/posts/dfbriscoe_my-24-year-old-millennial-boss-part-2-activity-6545326475111915521-uYdB.

Bromwich, Jonah Engel. "The Evolution of Emma Chamberlain." *New York Times*, July 9, 2019. www.nytimes.com/2019/07/09/style/emma-chamberlain-youtube.html.

Brown, Brené. *Daring Greatly: How the Courage to Be Vulnerable Transforms the Way We Live, Love, Parent, and Lead.* New York: Penguin, 2015.

Callaham, Sheila. "Citibank, IBM, IKEA: Age Discrimination Lawsuits on the Rise." *Forbes*, March 28, 2019. www.forbes.com/sites/sheilacallaham/2019/03/27/citibank-ibm-ikea-age-discrimination-lawsuits-on-the-rise/#4bc3bbfc4654.

Cappelli, Peter, and Bill Novelli. *Managing the Older Worker: How to Prepare for the New Organizational Order.* Boston: Harvard Business Press, 2010.

"Careers in Construction Marketing." BuildWitt. Accessed October 17, 2020. https://buildwitt.com/careers.

Carlisle, Madeleine. "Supreme Court Justice Roberts Asks If 'OK Boomer' Is Ageist." *Time*, January 16, 2020. https://time.com/5766438/john-roberts-ok-boomer-scotus.

Carmichael, Sarah Green. "Millennials Are Actually Workaholics, According to Research." *Harvard Business Review*, August 17, 2016. https://hbr.org/2016/08/millennials-are-actually-workaholics-according-to-research.

Carville, Olivia. "IBM Fired as Many as 100,000 in Recent Years, Lawsuit Shows." *Bloomberg*, July 31, 2019. www.bloomberg.com/news/articles/2019-07-31/ibm-fired-as-many-as-100-000-in-recent-years-court-case-shows.

Chamberlin, Jamie. "Overgeneralizing the Generations." *Monitor on Psychology* 40, no. 6 (2009). www.apa.org/monitor/2009/06/workplaces.

Chen, Xi, Alim J. Beveridge, and Ping Ping Fu. "Put Yourself in Others' Age: How Age Simulation Facilitates Intergenerational Cooperation." *Academy of Management Proceedings* 2018, no. 1 (2018): 16250.

Christian, Julie, Lyman W. Porter, and Graham Moffitt. "Workplace Diversity and Group Relations: An Overview." *Group Processes & Intergroup Relations* 9, no. 4 (2006): 459–66.

Clarey, Katie. "IKEA Hit with 5th Lawsuit Alleging Age Discrimination." *HR Dive*, February 27, 2019. www.hrdive.com/news/ikea-hit-with-5th-lawsuit-alleging-age-discrimination/549155.

Cohen, Rich. "Why Generation X Might Be Our Last, Best Hope." *Vanity Fair*, August 10, 2017. www.vanityfair.com/style/2017/08/why-generation-x-might-be-our-last-best-hope.

Cohn, D'vera, and Paul Taylor. "Baby Boomers Approach 65—Glumly." Pew Research Center, 2010. www.pewsocialtrends.org/2010/12/20/baby-boomers-approach-65-glumly.

Collins, James C. *Good to Great*. London: Random House Business, 2001.

Collins, Mary Hair, Joseph F. Hair Jr., and Tonette S. Rocco. "The Older-Worker-Younger-Supervisor Dyad: A Test of the Reverse Pygmalion Effect." *Human Resource Development Quarterly* 20, no. 1 (2009): 21–41.

Collyer, Hillary. "Can Employers Discriminate against Younger Workers?" HR Daily Advisor, October 23, 2009. https://hrdailyadvisor.blr.com/2009/10/23/can-employers-discriminate-against-younger-workers.

"Commercial Construction Index." U.S. Chamber of Commerce, 2019. www.uschamber.com/sites/default/files/cci_q1_2019_3-12-2019_for_release_0.pdf.

"CompTIA: Managing the Multigenerational Workforce 2018." CompTIA. Accessed March 27, 2020. www.comptia.org/resources/managing-the-multigenerational-workforce-2018.

Conley, Chip. *Wisdom @ Work: The Making of a Modern Elder*. New York: Currency, 2018.

Costa, Ana Cristina, Robert A. Roe, and Tharsi Taillieu. "Trust within Teams: The Relation with Performance Effectiveness." *European Journal of Work and Organizational Psychology* 10, no. 3 (2001): 225–44.

Cox, Cody B., Friederike K. Young, Adrian B. Guardia, and Amy K. Bohmann. "The Baby Boomer Bias: The Negative Impact of Generational Labels on Older Workers." *Journal of Applied Social Psychology* 48, no. 2 (2018): 71–79.

Cox, T. H., and S. Blake. "Managing Cultural Diversity: Implications for Organizational Competitiveness." *The Executive* 5 (1991): 45–56.

"Creating Value in Integrative Negotiations: Myth of the Fixed-Pie of Resources." Program on Negotiation, Harvard Law School, March 5, 2020. www.pon.harvard.edu/daily/negotiation-skills-daily/when-the-pie-seems-too-small.

D2L. "New Survey Reveals That Workers Rank Human Interaction and On-Demand Video Highest among Workplace Learning Methods." *GlobeNewswire*, February 13, 2018. www.globenewswire.com/news-release/2018/02/13/1485064/0/en/New-Survey-Reveals-That-Workers-Rank-Human-Interaction-and-On-Demand-Video-Highest-Among-Workplace-Learning-Methods.html.

DeLana, Libby. "Are We There Yet? How Ageism Is Holding Back Our Industry." Campaign, June 11, 2019. www.campaignlive.com/article/yet-ageism-holding-back-industry/1581531.

Dilenschneider, Colleen. "Six Urgent Reasons to Add Millennials to Your Nonprofit Board of Directors." November 19, 2014. www.colleendilen.com/

2014/11/19/six-urgent-reasons-to-add-millennials-to-your-nonprofit-board-of-directors.

Dimock, Michael. "Defining Generations: Where Millennials End and Generation Z Begins." Pew Research Center, January 17, 2019. www.pewresearch.org/fact-tank/2019/01/17/where-millennials-end-and-generation-z-begins.

Dittman, Melissa. "Generational Differences at Work." *Monitor on Psychology*, June 2005. www.apa.org/monitor/jun05/generational.

Donahue, Mary. *The Marcia Moment: The Death of the Manage-Me Workplace.* Donahue Learning, 2017. www.donohuelearning.com/wp-content/uploads/2017/04/Final-White-Paper-Marcia-Moment-Copyright-Donohue-Learning-1.pdf.

"Driving Momentum: 2015 Diversity & Inclusion Annual Report." PNC Bank, 2015. www.pnc.com/content/dam/pnc-com/pdf/aboutpnc/2015-diversity-annual-report.pdf.

Duhigg, Charles. "What Google Learned from Its Quest to Build the Perfect Team." *New York Times*, February 25, 2016. www.nytimes.com/2016/02/28/magazine/what-google-learned-from-its-quest-to-build-the-perfect-team.html.

Eadicicco, Lisa. "Apple CEO Tim Cook Explains Why You Don't Need a College Degree to Be Successful." *Business Insider*, March 7, 2019. www.businessinsider.com/apple-ceo-tim-cook-why-college-degree-isnt-necessary-2019-3.

Earley, P. Christopher, and Elaine Mosakowski. "Cultural Intelligence." *Harvard Business Review*, April 20, 2016. https://hbr.org/2004/10/cultural-intelligence.

Earley, P. Christopher, Soon Ang, and Joo-Seng Tan. *CQ: Developing Cultural Intelligence at Work.* Stanford: Stanford University Press, 2006.

Enron. "Enron Annual Report 2000." University of Chicago, 2000. https://picker.uchicago.edu/Enron/EnronAnnualReport2000.pdf.

Erez, Miriam, and Revital Arad. "Participative Goal-Setting: Social, Motivational, and Cognitive Factors." *Journal of Applied Psychology* 71, no. 4 (1986): 591.

Erickson, Tammy. "Generations around the Globe." *Harvard Business Review*, July 23, 2014. https://hbr.org/2011/04/generations-around-the-globe-1.

Eswaran, Vijay, and QI Group. "The Business Case for Diversity Is Now Overwhelming. Here's Why." *World Economic Forum*, April 29, 2019. www.weforum.org/agenda/2019/04/business-case-for-diversity-in-the-workplace.

"The Fall of Enron." *NPR*, February 12, 2002. www.npr.org/templates/story/story.php?storyId=1137940.

"Family On-Demand." Papa. Accessed October 17, 2020. www.joinpapa.com.

Finkelstein, Lisa M., and Michael J. Burke. "Age Stereotyping at Work: The Role of Rater and Contextual Factors on Evaluations of Job Applicants." *Journal of General Psychology* 125, no. 4 (1998): 317–45. https://doi.org/10.1080/00221309809595341.

Finkelstein, Lisa M., Donald M. Truxillo, Franco Fraccaroli, and Ruth Kanfer. *Facing the Challenges of a Multi-Age Workforce*. New York: Routledge, 2015.

Fisher, Caitlin. "The Gaslighting of the Millennial Generation." *Caitlin Fisher: Run Like Hell toward Happy* (blog), October 17, 2016. https://bornagainminimalist.com/2016/10/17/the-gaslighting-of-millennials.

Fong, Mei. "China's Lost Little Emperors . . . How the 'One-Child Policy' Will Haunt the Country for Decades." *Guardian*, September 2, 2018. www.theguardian.com/commentisfree/2018/sep/02/chinas-lost-little-emperors-how-the-one-child-policy-will-haunt-the-nation-for-decades.

Fottrell, Quentin. "Step Aside, Generation X—the Millennials Are Coming." *MarketWatch*, May 30, 2015. www.marketwatch.com/story/step-aside-generation-x-the-millennials-are-coming-2015-05-11.

Fowles, Jib. "On Chronocentrism." *Futures* 6, no. 1 (1974): 65–68.

Freedman, Marc. *How to Live Forever: The Enduring Power of Connecting the Generations*. New York: Ingram Publisher Services US, 2019.

Frenkel, Sheera, Mike Isaac, Cecilia Kang, and Gabriel J. X. "Facebook Employees Stage Virtual Walkout to Protest Trump Posts." *New York Times*, June 1, 2020. www.nytimes.com/2020/06/01/technology/facebook-employee-protest-trump.html.

"Frequently Asked Questions." Project Implicit. Accessed March 29, 2020. https://implicit.harvard.edu/implicit/faqs.html#faq1.

Friend, Tad. "Why Ageism Never Gets Old." *New Yorker*, July 9, 2019. www.newyorker.com/magazine/2017/11/20/why-ageism-never-gets-old.

Fry, Richard. "Millennials Are Largest Generation in the U.S. Labor Force." Pew Research Center, April 11, 2018. www.pewresearch.org/fact-tank/2018/04/11/millennials-largest-generation-us-labor-force.

———. "Millennials Expected to Outnumber Boomers in 2019." Pew Research Center, March 1, 2018. www.pewresearch.org/fact-tank/2018/03/01/millennials-overtake-baby-boomers.

"Gaining Consensus among Stakeholders through the Nominal Group Technique." Centers for Disease Control, 2018. www.cdc.gov/healthyyouth/evaluation/pdf/brief7.pdf.

Gallup. *State of the American Workplace*. Washington, DC: Gallup, Inc., 2017. www.gallup.com/workplace/238085/state-american-workplace-report-2017.aspx.

"Gallup's Perspective on the Gig Economy and Alternative Work Arrangements." Gallup, 2018. www.gallup.com/workplace.

Garvin, David A., Amy C. Edmondson, and Francesca Gino. "Is Yours a Learning Organization?" *Harvard Business Review*, March 2008. https://hbr.org/2008/03/is-yours-a-learning-organization.

"General Dynamics Land Systems, Inc. v. Cline." Legal Information Institute, February 24, 2004. www.law.cornell.edu/supct/html/02-1080.ZO.html.

"Generational Conflict: A Matter of Clout." Center for Creative Leadership (Podcast). www.ccl.org/multimedia/podcast/generational-conflict-a-matter-of-clout.

"Generation Next: Meet Gen Z and the Alphas." McCrindle, February 15, 2020. https://mccrindle.com.au/insights/blog/generation-next-meet-gen-z-alphas.

"Generation Ni/Ni: Latin America's Lost Youth." *Americas Quarterly* (Spring 2012). www.americasquarterly.org/salazar.

"Generations and Age." Pew Research Center, January 17, 2019. www.pewresearch.org/topics/generations-and-age.

Gerhardt, Megan. "Coronavirus and Zoom Have Marked a Generation. Let's Call Them Zoomers." *NBC News*, June 7, 2020. www.nbcnews.com/think/opinion/coronavirus-zoom-have-marked-generation-let-s-call-them-zoomers-ncna1226241.

———. "The Importance of Being . . . Social? Instructor Credibility and the Millennials." *Studies in Higher Education* 41, no. 9 (2016): 1533–47.

———. "Is 'OK, Boomer' Ageist? John Roberts Is Mulling It, but Laws Won't Fix Generational Shaming." *NBC News*, January 17, 2020. www.nbcnews.com/think/opinion/ok-boomer-ageist-maybe-supreme-court-case-won-t-fix-ncna1117496.

———. "The 'OK, Boomer' Meme Hurts Gen Z More Than the Older Generation It's Aimed At." *NBC News*, November 18, 2019. www.nbcnews.com/think/opinion/ok-boomer-meme-hurts-gen-z-more-older-generation-it-ncna1079276.

———. "Today's Managers 'Blew It' with Millennials, College Professor Says, and Here's How We Can Avoid Doing It Again with Generation Z." *Business Insider*, March 11, 2019. www.businessinsider.com/managers-blew-it-with-millennials-generation-z-megan-gerhardt-2019-3.

Gerstner, Louis V. *Who Says Elephants Can't Dance? Inside IBM's Historic Turnaround.* New York: HarperInformation, 2002.

The Gig Economy: Opportunities, Challenges, and Employer Strategies. MetLife, 2019. www.metlife.com/content/dam/metlifecom/us/ebts/pdf/MetLife_EBTS-GigReport_2019.pdf.

Goetz, Kaomi. "How 3M Gave Everyone Days Off and Created an Innovation Dynamo." Fast Company, July 9, 2018. www.fastcompany.com/1663137/how-3m-gave-everyone-days-off-and-created-an-innovation-dynamo.

Goode, Shelton, and Isaac Dixon. "Are Employee Resource Groups Good for Business?" SHRM, August 25, 2016. www.shrm.org/hr-today/news/hr-magazine/0916/pages/are-employee-resource-groups-good-for-business.aspx.

Gosselin, Peter, and Ariana Tobin. "Inside IBM's Purge of Thousands of Workers Who Have One Thing in Common." *Mother Jones*, March 24, 2018. www.motherjones.com/crime-justice/2018/03/ibm-propublica-gray-hairs-old-heads.

Grant, Adam M. *Originals: How Non-Conformists Move the World.* New York: Penguin, 2017.

Gratton, Lynda, Andreas Voigt, and Tamara J. Erickson. "Bridging Faultlines in Diverse Teams." *MIT Sloan Management Review* 48, no. 4 (2007): 22.

Greenfield, Rebecca. "How to Make Flexible Work Schedules a Reality." Bloomberg, January 21, 2016. www.bloomberg.com/news/articles/2016-01-21/how-to-make-flexible-work-schedules-a-reality.

Greengard, S. "Moving Forward with Reverse Mentoring." *Workforce* 81, no. 3 (2002): 15.

Gurchiek, Kathy. "Google Ends Age-Discrimination Suit with $11 Million Settlement." SHRM, July 24, 2019. www.shrm.org/resourcesandtools/hr-topics/behavioral-competencies/global-and-cultural-effectiveness/pages/google-ends-age-discrimination-suit-with-11-million-settlement.aspx.

———. "More Workers Than You Realize Are Caregivers." SHRM, August 16, 2019. www.shrm.org/resourcesandtools/hr-topics/behavioral-competencies/global-and-cultural-effectiveness/pages/more-workers-than-you-realize-are-caregivers-.aspx.

Hall, April. "Age Diversity on Boards a Top Priority. But Where Are They?" Directors & Boards, April 23, 2018. www.directorsandboards.com/news/age-diversity-boards-top-priority-where-are-they.

Hannon, Kerry. "5 Workplaces That Embrace Older Workers." *Forbes*, November 18, 2016. www.forbes.com/sites/nextavenue/2016/11/18/5-workplaces-that-embrace-older-workers/#719bfe965914.

———. "The Family Business Matching Older and Younger Entrepreneurs." Next Avenue, March 28, 2019. www.nextavenue.org/family-business-matching-entrepreneurs.

Harnessing the Power of a Multigenerational Workforce. SHRM Foundation, 2017. www.shrm.org/foundation/ourwork/initiatives/the-aging-workforce/Lists/Curated%20source%20for%20page%20The%20Aging%20Workforce/Attachments/17/2017%20TL%20Executive%20Summary-FINAL.pdf.

Herway, Jake. "How to Create a Culture of Psychological Safety." Gallup, March 5, 2020. www.gallup.com/workplace/236198/create-culture-psychological-safety.aspx.

Hoffman, Susan. Interview with authors. May 13, 2019.

Holmes, Oliver. "José Ortega y Gasset." *Stanford Encyclopedia of Philosophy*, November 20, 2017. https://plato.stanford.edu/entries/gasset/#ConcGeneTempHistReasCritPhilHist.

Hornbrook, Aaron. Interview with authors. July 17, 2019.

How Millennials Want to Work and Live. Washington, DC: Gallup, Inc., 2016. www.gallup.com/workplace/238073/millennials-work-live.aspx.

Hu, Jing, and Jacob B. Hirsh. "Accepting Lower Salaries for Meaningful Work." *Frontiers in Psychology* 8 (September 2017).

Huhman, Heather R. "These 8 Companies Know the Impact of Supporting Mental Health in the Workplace." *Entrepreneur*, May 15, 2017. www.entrepreneur.com/article/294143.

Hunt, Vivian, Lareina Yee, Sara Prince, and Sundiatu Dixon-Fyle. "Delivering through Diversity." McKinsey & Company, January 18, 2018. www.mckinsey.com/business-functions/organization/our-insights/delivering-through-diversity.

Hwang, Jeongha, and Karen M. Hopkins. "A Structural Equation Model of the Effects of Diversity Characteristics and Inclusion on Organizational Outcomes in the Child Welfare Workforce." *Children and Youth Services Review* 50 (January 19, 2015): 44–52. https://doi.org/10.1016/j.childyouth.2015.01.012.

Inc. Staff. "Free Tools, Resources, and Financial Help for Business Owners Hit by Covid-19." *Inc.*, last updated May 5, 2020. www.inc.com/inc-staff/free-tools-grants-video-conferencing-ad-credits-gift-certificates-cloud-storage-cyber-security.html.

"Integrative Negotiation Examples: MESOs and Expanding the Pie." Program on Negotiation, Harvard Law School, May 18, 2017. www.pon.harvard.edu/daily/dealmaking-daily/limit-their-options%E2%80%94and-expand-the-pie.

Jehn, Karen A., Clint Chadwick, and Sherry M. B. Thatcher. "To Agree or Not to Agree: The Effects of Value Congruence, Individual Demographic Dissimilarity, and Conflict on Workgroup Outcomes." *International Journal of Conflict Management* 8, no. 4 (1997): 287–305.

Jenkins, Ryan. "Why Generational Diversity Is the Ultimate Competitive Advantage." *Inc.*, May 15, 2017. www.inc.com/ryan-jenkins/why-generational-diversity-is-the-ultimate-competitive-advantage.html.

Jordan, Jennifer, and Michael Sorell. "Why You Should Create a 'Shadow Board' of Younger Employees." *Harvard Business Review*, June 5, 2019. https://hbr.org/2019/06/why-you-should-create-a-shadow-board-of-younger-employees.

Joshi, Aparna, John C. Dencker, Gentz Franz, and Joseph J. Martocchio. "Unpacking Generational Identities in Organizations." *Academy of Management Review* 35, no. 3 (2010): 392–414.

Karami, Azhdar, Farhad Analoui, and Nada Korak Kakabadse. "The CEOs' Characteristics and Their Strategy Development in the UK SME Sector." *Journal of Management Development* (2006).

Kaufman, Joanne. "When the Boss Is Half Your Age." *New York Times*, March 17, 2017. www.nytimes.com/2017/03/17/your-money/retiring-older-workers-younger-bosses.html.

Kelly, Jack. "Google Settles Age Discrimination Lawsuit, Highlighting the Proliferation of Ageism in Hiring." *Forbes*, July 24, 2019. www.forbes.com/sites/jackkelly/2019/07/23/google-settles-age-discrimination-lawsuit-highlighting-the-proliferation-of-ageism-in-hiring/#21cb743c5c67.

Kennedy, John F. "Remarks Prepared for Delivery at the Trade Mart in Dallas, TX, November 22, 1963 [Undelivered]." JFK Library, n.d. www.jfklibrary

.org/archives/other-resources/john-f-kennedy-speeches/dallas-tx-trade-mart-undelivered-19631122.

Kiger, Patrick J. "Older and Younger Workers See Each Other Negatively." AARP, September 18, 2018. www.aarp.org/work/working-at-50-plus/info-2018/older-younger-workers-opinions.html.

Korey, Stephanie. "Bringing the Ideal Suitcase to Market with Slack." Slack. Accessed March 27, 2020. https://slack.com/customer-stories/away.

Koulopoulos, Thomas M., and Dan Keldsen. *The Gen Z Effect: The Six Forces Shaping the Future of Business*. Brookline, MA: Bibliomotion, Books Media, 2014.

———. *Gen Z Effect: The Six Forces Shaping the Future of Business*. New York: Routledge, 2016.

Kunze, Florian, and Jochen I. Menges. "Younger Supervisors, Older Subordinates: An Organizational-Level Study of Age Differences, Emotions, and Performance." *Journal of Organizational Behavior* 38, no. 4 (2017): 461–86.

Kunze, Florian, Stephan A. Boehm, and Heike Bruch. "Age Diversity, Age Discrimination Climate and Performance Consequences—a Cross-Organizational Study." *Journal of Organizational Behavior* 32, no. 2 (2011): 264–90.

Lancaster, Lynne C., and David Stillman. *When Generations Collide: Who They Are, Why They Clash, How to Solve the Generational Puzzle at Work*. New York: HarperBusiness, 2003.

Leveraging the Value of an Age Diverse Workforce. Society of Human Resource Management, 2020. www.shrm.org/foundation/ourwork/initiatives/the-aging-workforce/Documents/Age-Diverse%20Workforce%20Executive%20Briefing.pdf.

Levine, Alaina G. "From Selfies to Selfless: Managing Multigenerational Teams." *Science*, December 8, 2017. www.sciencemag.org/features/2017/09/selfies-selfless-managing-multigenerational-teams.

Levy, Becca R., and Mahzarian R. Banaji. "Implicit Ageism." *Ageism: Stereotyping and Prejudice against Older Persons* 2004 (2002): 49–75.

Linzrinzz. "Lin on TikTok." TikTok, July 17, 2019. www.tiktok.com/@linzrinzz/video/6714782003637521670.

Locke, Edwin A., Karyll N. Shaw, Lise M. Saari, and Gary P. Latham. "Goal Setting and Task Performance: 1969–1980." *Psychological Bulletin* 90, no. 1 (1981): 125.

Lokon, Dr. Elizabeth. Interview with authors. June 28, 2018.

Lorenz, Taylor. "'OK Boomer' Marks the End of Friendly Generational Relations." *New York Times*, October 29, 2019. www.nytimes.com/2019/10/29/style/ok-boomer.html.

Lütke, Tobias. Interview with Guy Raz. *How I Built This with Guy Raz* (Podcast), August 5, 2019. www.npr.org/2019/08/02/747660923/shopify-tobias-l-tke.

Maheshwari, Sapna, and Erin Griffith. "How Outdoor Voices, a Start-Up Darling, Imploded." *New York Times*, March 10, 2020. www.nytimes.com/2020/03/10/business/outdoor-voices-ty-haney-mickey-drexler.html.

Mahler, Krista. Interview with authors. February 24, 2020.

Mannheim, Karl. "The Problem of Generations." In *Essays on the Sociology of Knowledge*, 276–320. London: Routledge and Kegan Paul, 1928/1952.

Maurer, Roy. "Millennials Expect Raises, Promotions More Often Than Older Generations." Society for Human Resource Management, February 26, 2015. www.shrm.org/resourcesandtools/hr-topics/talent-acquisition/pages/millennials-raises-promotions-generations.aspx.

Mautz, Scott. "Patagonia Has Only 4 Percent Employee Turnover Because They Value This 1 Thing So Much." *Inc.*, March 30, 2019. www.inc.com/scott-mautz/how-can-patagonia-have-only-4-percent-worker-turnover-hint-they-pay-activist-employees-bail.html.

Mazur, Barbara. "Building Diverse and Inclusive Organizational Culture-Best Practices: A Case Study of Cisco Co." *Journal of Intercultural Management* 6, no. 4 (December 2014): 169–79. https://doi.org/10.2478/joim-2014-0043.

McAdams, Dan. Interview with authors. August 14, 2019.

McDermott, John. "Why Gen X Is So Pissed at Millennials." *MEL Magazine*, January 30, 2019. https://melmagazine.com/en-us/story/why-gen-x-is-so-pissed-at-millennials-2.

McGregor, Jena. "Fewer Companies Are Forcing CEOs to Retire When They Hit Their Golden Years." *Washington Post*, September 27, 2018. www.washingtonpost.com/business/2018/09/27/fewer-companies-are-forcing-ceos-retire-when-they-hit-their-golden-years.

———. "Why Unlimited Vacation Is Basically a No-Brainer for Employers." *Washington Post*, October 8, 2015. www.washingtonpost.com/news/on-leadership/wp/2015/10/08/what-your-company-gains-when-it-gives-you-unlimited-vacation.

McIlvaine, Andrew R. "IBM Is Being Accused of Widespread Age Discrimination." HR Executive, September 18, 2019. https://hrexecutive.com/ibm-is-being-accused-of-widespread-age-discrimination.

McLannahan, Ben. "PwC Launches Online Market Place to Tap into 'Gig Economy.'" *Financial Times*, March 7, 2016. www.ft.com/content/9c0f5248-e25e-11e5-96b7-9f778349aba2.

McQueen, Nina. "Workplace Culture Trends: The Key to Hiring (and Keeping) Top Talent in 2018." *LinkedIn Official Blog*, June 26, 2018. https://blog.linkedin.com/2018/june/26/workplace-culture-trends-the-key-to-hiring-and-keeping-top-talent.

Merchant, Nilofer. "Culture Trumps Strategy, Every Time." *Harvard Business Review*, March 22, 2011. https://hbr.org/2011/03/culture-trumps-strategy-every.

Miah, Kiyona. Interview with authors. June 13, 2019.

"The 'Millennials' Are Coming." *CBS News*, November 8, 2007. www.cbsnews.com/news/the-millennials-are-coming.

"Millennials Say Flexibility Is More Important Than Salary." The Predictive Index, July 31, 2019. www.predictiveindex.com/blog/why-flexibility-is-a-better-perk-than-salary.

Miller, Claire Cain, and Sanam Yar. "Young People Are Going to Save Us All from Office Life." *New York Times*, September 17, 2019. www.nytimes.com/2019/09/17/style/generation-z-millennials-work-life-balance.html.

Miller, Nancy. "The *Wall Street Journal* Says It's Done Being Snarky AF about Millennials." *Quartz*, December 12, 2017. https://qz.com/1154304/the-wall-street-journal-says-it-is-done-stereotyping-millennials.

"The Missing Perspective in the Boardroom: Millennials." *Wall Street Journal*, February 9, 2015. https://deloitte.wsj.com/riskandcompliance/2015/02/09/the-missing-perspective-in-the-boardroom-millennials.

Moore, Malcolm. "China: The Rise of the 'Precious Snowflakes.'" *The Telegraph*, January 8, 2012. www.telegraph.co.uk/news/worldnews/asia/china/8997627/China-The-rise-of-the-Precious-Snowflakes.html.

"More Companies Offering Unlimited Time Off." SAGE Business Researcher. Accessed March 27, 2020. http://businessresearcher.sagepub.com/sbr-1863-102641-2779724/20170508/short-article-more-companies-offering-unlimited-time-off.

Moynihan, Kala. Interview with authors. February 17, 2019.

Murphy, W. M. "Reverse Mentoring at Work: Fostering Cross-Generational Learning and Developing Millennial Leaders." *Human Resource Management* 51, no. 4 (July–August 2012): 549–74.

Myers, Karen K., and Kamyab Sadaghiani. "Millennials in the Workplace: A Communication Perspective on Millennials' Organizational Relationships and Performance." *Journal of Business and Psychology* 25, no. 2 (2010): 225–38.

Nachemson-Ekwall, Sophie. Interview with authors. July 14, 2018.

Nagele-Piazza, Lisa. "Beware of Workplace Ageism Claims Stemming from 'OK, Boomer.'" SHRM, November 20, 2019. www.shrm.org/resourcesandtools/legal-and-compliance/employment-law/pages/ok-boomer-age-discrimination.aspx.

Neal, Stephanie, Kabir Sehgal, Priscilla Claman, and Rebecca Knight. "Are Companies about to Have a Gen X Retention Problem?" *Harvard Business Review*, July 29, 2019. https://hbr.org/2019/07/are-companies-about-to-have-a-gen-x-retention-problem.

Nelson, Bailey. "How to Get the Best out of Baby Boomers." Gallup, February 28, 2020. www.gallup.com/workplace/246443/best-baby-boomers.aspx.

Newman, Sally, and Alan Hatton-Yeo. "Intergenerational Learning and the Contributions of Older People." *Aging Horizons*, no. 8 (2008): 31–39.

"New Video Series 'GenTalk' Sparks Conversations on Diversity and Inclusion—News Center." Nielsen, May 21, 2018. http://sites.nielsen.com/newscenter/new-video-series-gentalk-sparks-conversations-diversity-inclusion.

Nextgen: A Global Generational Study. PwC, 2013. www.pwc.com/gx/en/hr-management-services/pdf/pwc-nextgen-study-2013.pdf.

Ng, Eddy, Sean T. Lyons, and Linda Schweitzer, eds., *Managing the New Workforce: International Perspectives on the Millennial Generation*. Cheltenham, UK: Edward Elgar Publishing, 2012.

Ng, Eddy, Linda Schweitzer, and Sean T. Lyons. "New Generation, Great Expectations: A Field Study of the Millennial Generation." *Journal of Business and Psychology* 25, no. 2 (2010): 281–92.

Nordin, Johanna, and Catharina Rengensjö. "Guldklockan Klämtar—En Studie Om Kompetensbevaring I Samband Med Generationsskifte." University of Borås, Institute of Data and Business, 2010. https://hb.diva-portal.org/smash/get/diva2:1311928/FULLTEXT01.

O'Connell, Brian. "The Search for Meaning." Society for Human Resource Management, March 23, 2019. www.shrm.org/hr-today/news/all-things-work/pages/the-search-for-meaning.aspx.

OECD Employment Outlook 2013. Paris: Organization for Economic Development, 2013.

Oliphant, Margaret. *The Open Door, and the Portrait. Stories of the Seen and the Unseen*. N.p.: Hard Press, 2006.

Ortega y Gasset, José. *The Origin of Philosophy*. Trans. Toby Talbot. Champaign: University of Illinois Press, 2000.

"Our Core Values." Workday. Accessed March 27, 2020. www.workday.com/en-us/company/about-workday/core-values.html.

"Our Focus." Eisner Foundation. Accessed October 17, 2020. https://eisnerfoundation.org/our-focus.

"Papa Evolves to 'Family On-Demand.'" Papa, February 3, 2020. www.joinpapa.com/press-releases/papa-new-brand.

Parker, Andrew. Interview with authors. July 25, 2018.

Parry, Emma. *Generational Diversity at Work: New Research Perspectives*. London: Routledge, 2014.

Patagonia Works. "Annual Benefit Corporation Report: Fiscal Year 2017." Accessed October 16, 2020. www.patagonia.com/static/on/demandware.static/-/Library-Sites-PatagoniaShared/default/dw824fac0f/PDF-US/2017-BCORP-pages_022218.pdf.

Patrick. "Charli D'Amelio Net Worth Reveal: Income Sources, Instagram & TikTok Earnings, Meet and Greet, Sister Dixie D'Amelio, Age 15." Celebs Fortune, March 17, 2020. https://celebsfortune.com/charli-damelio-net-worth.

Pearce, Dr. Joshua. Interview with authors. February 11, 2020.

Pinsker, Joe. "Oh No, They've Come Up with Another Generation Label." *The Atlantic*, February 21, 2020. www.theatlantic.com/family/archive/2020/02/generation-after-gen-z-named-alpha/606862.

Pless, Nicola, and Thomas Maak. "Building an Inclusive Diversity Culture: Principles, Processes and Practice." *Journal of Business Ethics* 54, no. 2 (2004): 129–47.

Polzer, Jeffrey T. "Making Diverse Teams Click." *Harvard Business Review*, July/August 2008. https://hbr.org/2008/07/making-diverse-teams-click.

"PwC's Talent Exchange: Find Exciting Opportunities with PwC." PwC Talent Exchange. Accessed March 27, 2020. https://talentexchange.pwc.com.

Quiñones, Adam. "Bridging the Gap Between Old and New Schools of Construction." Construction Executive, June 14, 2019. www.constructionexec.com/article/bridging-the-gap-between-old-and-new-schools-of-construction.

Ramovš, Ksenija. "Medgeneracijsko sožitje in solidarnost (Intergenerational Cohesion and Solidarity)." In *Staranje v Sloveniji* (*Ageing in Slovenia*), edited by J. Ramovš, 63–97. Ljubljana: Inštitut Antona Trstenjaka, 2013.

"Re:Work—Guide: Understand Team Effectiveness." Google. Accessed March 27, 2020. https://rework.withgoogle.com/guides/understanding-team-effectiveness/steps/foster-psychological-safety.

Reece, Andrew, Gabriella Kellerman, and Alexi Robichaux. "Meaning and Purpose at Work." BetterUp, 2017. https://get.betterup.co/rs/600-WTC-654/images/betterup-meaning-purpose-at-work.pdf.

"The Rising Cost of College." *College Choice*. Accessed March 25, 2020. www.collegechoice.net/the-rising-cost-of-college.

Robison, Jennifer. "Millennials Worry about the Environment—Should Your Company?" Gallup, May 29, 2020. www.gallup.com/workplace/257786/millennials-worry-environment-company.aspx.

Rockwood, Kate. "Hiring in the Age of Ageism." SHRM, August 16, 2019. www.shrm.org/hr-today/news/hr-magazine/0218/pages/hiring-in-the-age-of-ageism.aspx.

Rogelberg, Steven G., Janet L. Barnes-Farrell, and Charles A. Lowe. "The Stepladder Technique: An Alternative Group Structure Facilitating Effective Group Decision Making." *Journal of Applied Psychology* 77, no. 5 (1992): 730.

Rubin, Joni. Interview with authors. April 23, 2019.

Sammer, Joanne. "Unlimited Paid Time Off: A Good or Bad Idea?" SHRM, August 16, 2019. www.shrm.org/resourcesandtools/hr-topics/benefits/pages/unlimited-pto.aspx.

Samuel, Lawrence. "Young People Are Just Smarter." *Psychology Today*, October 2, 2017. www.psychologytoday.com/us/blog/boomers-30/201710/young-people-are-just-smarter.

Schein, Edgar H. "Defining Organizational Culture." *Classics of Organization Theory* 3, no. 1 (1985): 490–502.

———. *Organizational Culture*. Cambridge, MA: MIT, 1988. https://dspace.mit.edu/bitstream/handle/1721.1/2224/SWP-2088-24854366.pdf?sequenc.

Seemiller, C., and M. Grace. *Generation Z Goes to College Study*. San Francisco: Jossey-Bass, 2016.

Sherbin, Laura. "Diversity Doesn't Stick Without Inclusion." *Harvard Business Review*, February 1, 2017. https://hbr.org/2017/02/diversity-doesnt-stick-without-inclusion.

Silverman, Rachel Emma. "Young Boss May Make Older Workers Less Productive." *Wall Street Journal*, December 20, 2016. www.wsj.com/articles/young-boss-may-make-older-workers-less-productive-1482246384.

Sinek, Simon. "Why Good Leaders Make You Feel Safe." Filmed March 2014, TED video, 11:47. www.ted.com/talks/simon_sinek_why_good_leaders_make_you_feel_safe?language=en.

Snape, Ed, and Tom Redman. "Too Old or Too Young? The Impact of Perceived Age Discrimination." *Human Resource Management Journal* 13, no. 1 (2003): 78–89.

Snelling, Sherri. "A New Era: Companies Supporting Caregivers." *Forbes*, April 14, 2015. www.forbes.com/sites/nextavenue/2015/04/14/a-new-era-companies-supporting-caregivers/#72f17937b136.

Sonsev, Veronika. "Patagonia's Focus on Its Brand Purpose Is Great for Business." *Forbes*, November 27, 2019. www.forbes.com/sites/veronikasonsev/2019/11/27/patagonias-focus-on-its-brand-purpose-is-great-for-business/#1d13fea054cb.

"South Africa's Born Free Generation." *BJP Online*, June 7, 2019. https://1854.studio/communities/south-africas-born-free-generation.

Spector, Nicole. "'OK Boomer' Is Dividing Generations. What Does It Mean?" *NBC News*, November 6, 2019. www.nbcnews.com/better/lifestyle/ok-boomer-diving-generation-what-does-it-mean-ncna1077261#anchor-Boomerhasbecomeacatchallphraseforsomeoneolderwhoisclosemindedandresistanttochange.

Spisak, Brian R., Allen E. Grabo, Richard D. Arvey, and Mark van Vugt. "The Age of Exploration and Exploitation: Younger-Looking Leaders Endorsed for Change, and Older-Looking Leaders Endorsed for Stability." *Leadership Quarterly* 25, no. 5 (2014): 805–16.

Staley, Oliver. "How the Average Age of CEOs and CFOs Has Changed since 2012." *Quartz*, September 11, 2017. https://qz.com/1074326/how-the-average-age-of-ceos-and-cfos-has-changed-since-2012.

Standage, Tom. *The Victorian Internet: The Remarkable Story of the Telegraph and the Nineteenth Century's On-Line Pioneers*. New York: Bloomsbury, 2009.

The State of Independence in America. MBO Partners, 2019. www.mbopartners.com/wp-content/uploads/2019/02/State_of_Independence_2018.pdf.

Strauss, William, and Neil Howe. *Generations: The History of America's Future, 1584 to 2069*. New York: William Morrow, 1991.

Stress in America™: The Impact of Discrimination. American Psychological Association, 2016. www.apa.org/news/press/releases/stress/2015/impact-of-discrimination.pdf.

Suderman, Peter. "Tyler Cowen Thinks Coronavirus Could Be This Generation's World War II." *Reason*, March 18, 2020. https://reason.com/2020/03/18/tyler-cowen-thinks-coronavirus-could-be-this-generations-world-war-ii.

Sugarman, Jim. "Jim Sugarman's LinkedIn Profile." LinkedIn. Accessed October 17, 2020. www.linkedin.com/in/jimsugarman4gennow.

"Supporting Flexible Work: 6 Tips for Executives." *FlexJobs Employer Blog*, September 13, 2016. www.flexjobs.com/employer-blog/supporting-flexible-work-tips-for-executives.

Tate, Ryan. "Google Couldn't Kill 20 Percent Time Even if It Wanted To." *Wired*, June 3, 2017. www.wired.com/2013/08/20-percent-time-will-never-die.

"Tate Appoints Youth Engagement Trustee." Tate Modern, March 11, 2019. www.tate.org.uk/press/press-releases/tate-appoints-youth-engagement-trustee.

Taylor, Bill. "To Build a Strong Culture, Create Rules That Are Unique to Your Company." *Harvard Business Review*, December 16, 2019. https://hbr.org/2019/12/to-build-a-strong-culture-create-rules-that-are-unique-to-your-company.

———. "Why Zappos Pays New Employees to Quit—and You Should Too." *Harvard Business Review*, February 21, 2018. https://hbr.org/2008/05/why-zappos-pays-new-employees.

Thiel Institute. "The Thiel Fellowship." Accessed March 27, 2020. https://thielfellowship.org.

"Third Annual 'Future Workforce Report' Sheds Light on How Younger Generations Are Reshaping the Future of Work." Upwork, March 5, 2019. www.upwork.com/press/2019/03/05/third-annual-future-workforce-report.

Thomas, David A., and Robin J. Ely. "Making Differences Matter: A New Paradigm for Managing Diversity." *Harvard Business Review*, April 29, 2016. https://hbr.org/1996/09/making-differences-matter-a-new-paradigm-for-managing-diversity.

Tippett, Elizabeth C. "Why Saying 'OK, Boomer' at Work Can Be Age Discrimination." *CBS News*, November 21, 2019. www.cbsnews.com/news/why-saying-ok-boomer-at-work-can-be-age-discrimination.

Toffler, Alvin. "Riding the Third Wave." *The Rotarian*, July 1980.

Trawinski, Lori. *Disrupting Aging in the Workplace: Profiles in Intergenerational Diversity Leadership*. AARP Public Policy Institute, 2017. www.aarp.org/content/dam/aarp/ppi/2017/08/disrupt-aging-in-the-workforce.pdf.

Tsui, Anne S., Katherine R. Xin, and Terri D. Egan. "Relational Demography: The Missing Link in Vertical Dyad Linkage." In *Diversity in Work Teams: Research Paradigms for a Changing Workplace*, edited by S. E. Jackson and M. N. Ruderman, 97–129. Washington, DC: American Psychological Association, 1995. https://doi.org/10.1037/10189-004.

Twenge, Jean M. *Generation Me: Why Today's Young Americans Are More Confident, Assertive, Entitled—and More Miserable Than Ever Before*. New York: Free Press, 2006.

———. *iGen: Why Today's Super-Connected Kids Are Growing Up Less Rebellious, More Tolerant, Less Happy—and Completely Unprepared for Adulthood—and What That Means for the Rest of Us*. New York: Simon and Schuster, 2017.

———. "A Review of the Empirical Evidence on Generational Differences in Work Attitudes." *Journal of Business and Psychology* 25, no. 2 (2010): 201–10.

U.S. Bureau of Labor Statistics. "Employer Costs for Employee Compensation." Accessed March 27, 2020. www.bls.gov/opub/btn/volume-2/paid-leave-in-private-industry-over-the-past-20-years.htm.

———. "Labor Force Statistics from the Current Population Survey." Accessed March 27, 2020. www.bls.gov/cps/cpsaat18b.htm.

U.S. Census Bureau. "Older People Projected to Outnumber Children for First Time in U.S. History." 2018. www.census.gov/newsroom/press-releases/2018/cb18-41-population-projections.htmlV.

"Uhuru Generation: Over 3 Million Will Retire into Poverty." *The East African*, May 24, 2009. www.theeastafrican.co.ke/news/2558-602434-view-printVersion-3082pxz/index.html.

United Nations, Department of Economic and Social Affairs, Population Division. *World Population Prospects 2019*. United Nations, 2019. https://population.un.org/wpp.

Urick, Michael J., Elaine C. Hollensbe, Suzanne S. Masterson, and Sean T. Lyons. "Understanding and Managing Intergenerational Conflict: An Examination of Influences and Strategies." *Work, Aging and Retirement* 3, no. 2 (2016): 166–85.

"The US GE Permissive Approach to Paid Time-Off Is Peace-of-Mind for My Family, My Team and Me: GE Careers." GE. Accessed March 27, 2020. www.ge.com/careers/culture/the-us-ge-permissive-approach-to-paid-time-off-is-peace-of-mind-for-my-family-my-team-and-me.

"US Outdoor Clothing Brand Patagonia Wins UN Champions of the Earth Award." UNEP—UN Environment Programme. Accessed March 27, 2020. www.unenvironment.org/news-and-stories/press-release/us-outdoor-clothing-brand-patagonia-wins-un-champions-earth-award.

Valovick, Holly. "CEOs & Mandatory Retirement Age." Quick Leonard Kieffer, July 2, 2018. www.qlksearch.com/blog/ceo-mandatory-retirement-age.

Van Dam, Andrew. "Baby Boomers Upend the Workforce One Last Time." *Washington Post*, March 1, 2019. www.washingtonpost.com/us-policy/2019/03/01/baby-boomers-parting-gift-workforce-one-last-mess.

Varoquiers, Carrie. "Five Ways We're Building Opportunity Onramps in the Workday Community." *Workday Blog*, December 27, 2018. https://blog.workday.com/en-us/2018/five-ways-were-building-opportunity-onramps-in-the-workday-community.html.

W. Edwards Deming Institute. Accessed October 23, 2020. https://deming.org/quotes/10083.

Wade-Benzoni, Kimberly A. "A Golden Rule over Time: Reciprocity in Intergenerational Allocation Decisions." *Academy of Management Journal* 45, no. 5 (2002): 1011–28.

Warrick, D. D. "What Leaders Need to Know about Organizational Culture." *Business Horizons* 60, no. 3 (2017): 395–404.

"We're on a Mission to Change the Dirt World. Ready to Join?" BuildWitt. Accessed October 25, 2020. https://buildwitt.com/careers.

Weeks, Kelly. "Generational Differences in Definitions of Meaningful Work: A Mixed Methods Study." *Journal of Business Ethics* 156, no. 4 (2019): 1045–61.

Wegge, Jürgen, F. Jungmann, S. Liebermann, M. Shemla, B. C. Ries, S. Diestel, and K. H. Schmidt. "What Makes Age Diverse Teams Effective? Results from a Six-Year Research Program." *Work* 41, supplement 1 (2012): 5145–51.

Weier, Mary Hayes. "Generation Workday: A Look at Workday's Future Leaders." *Workday Blog*, October 18, 2019. https://blog.workday.com/en-us/2015/generation-workday-a-look-at-workdays-future-leaders.html.

Welbourne, Theresa M., Skylar Rolf, and Steven Schlachter. "Employee Resource Groups: An Introduction, Review and Research Agenda." *Academy of Management Proceedings* 2015, no. 1 (August 2015).

"What Is Wrong with Young People Today?—A View from the Past." *Proto-Knowledge* (blog). https://proto-knowledge.blogspot.com/2010/11/what-is-wrong-with-young-people-today.html.

"What We Stand for as People and as a Company." BuildWitt. Accessed October 25, 2020. https://buildwitt.com/about-us.

"Why Diversity and Inclusion Matter: Quick Take." Catalyst, June 4, 2020. www.catalyst.org/research/why-diversity-and-inclusion-matter.

"Why Top Companies Are Ditching the 9-to-5 for Flexible Working Arrangements." Upwork, August 16, 2019. www.upwork.com/hiring/enterprise/top-companies-ditching-9-5-flexible-working-arrangements.

"The Whys and Hows of Generations Research." Pew Research Center for the People and the Press, December 31, 2019. www.people-press.org/2015/09/03/the-whys-and-hows-of-generations-research.

Williams, Alex. "Actually, Gen X Did Sell Out, Invent All Things Millennial, and Cause Everything Else That's Great and Awful." *New York Times*, May 14, 2019. www.nytimes.com/2019/05/14/style/gen-x-millenials.html.

Williams, Michele. "Being Trusted: How Team Generational Age Diversity Promotes and Undermines Trust in Cross-Boundary Relationships." *Journal of Organizational Behavior* 37, no. 3 (September 1, 2015): 346–73.

Witt, Aaron. "Aaron's Travels: A Journey with Anxiety." BuildWitt, June 7, 2019. https://buildwitt.com/aaron-talks-anxiety.

Witt, Aaron, and Dan Briscoe. Interview with authors. February 24, 2020.

Woodhouse, Brent. Interview with authors. May 24, 2019.

Yarow, Jay. "Tim Cook Is Giving Apple Employees Two-Week Breaks to Work on Special Projects." *Business Insider*i, November 12, 2012. www.businessinsider.com/apple-tries-20-time-2012-11.

Young, Julianna. "7 Zappos Amenities That Boost Employee Happiness." Zappos, June 12, 2019. www.zappos.com/about/stories/employee-happiness-amenities.

Zacher, Hannes, Kathrin Rosing, Thomas Henning, and Michael Frese. "Establishing the Next Generation at Work: Leader Generativity as a Moderator of the Relationships between Leader Age, Leader-Member Exchange, and Leadership Success." *Psychology and Aging* 26, no. 1 (2011): 241–52.

"Zappos 10 Core Values." Zappos Insights. Accessed October 17, 2020. www.zapposinsights.com/about/core-values?utm_campaign=newsroom&utm_medium=about-us&utm_source=what-we-live-by&utm_content=our-core-values.

Zemke, Ron, Claire Raines, and Bob Filipczak. *Generations at Work: Managing the Clash of Boomers, Gen Xers, and Gen Yers in the Workplace*. New York: Amacom, 2013.

Zenger, Jack, and Joseph Folkman. "What Younger Managers Should Know about How They Are Perceived." *Harvard Business Review*, September 29, 2015. https://hbr.org/2015/09/what-younger-managers-should-know-about-how-theyre-perceived.

Index

About the Authors

Megan Gerhardt, PhD, is a professor of management, director of leadership development, and Robert D. Johnson Co-Director of the Isaac and Oxley Center for Business Leadership at the Farmer School of Business at Miami University. She is also the founder of the Gerhardt Group, LLC, a leadership consulting practice.

Megan has published widely on individual differences, motivation, leadership, and generational differences in the workplace, and her work on Gentelligence has been featured on Forbes.com, NBCNews.com, the *Washington Post*, the *Chicago Tribune*, *Inc. Magazine*, the *San Francisco Chronicle*, *MarketWatch*, *Business Insider*, and the *Houston Chronicle*, among others. In 2017, her TEDx talk "Why I Love Millennials . . . and You Should, Too" was released, kicking off the Gentelligence movement.

Josephine Nachemson-Ekwall is an associate director of financial crime prevention policy at UBS, focusing on implementation and adherence to policies, local requirements, and global standards. Josephine's work in leadership development focuses on strengths-based development, individual coaching, and the importance of personal mission and values in driving one's life and career. She most recently gave a presentation at the Clifton Strengths Summit on "Why Strengths Work" and published an article on generational conflict and tension in December 2019.

Brandon Fogel is a senior consultant at Ernst & Young LLC in the People Advisory Services practice, which specializes in organizational change and people management. Brandon's work in leadership development focuses on strengths-based development, effective teaming strategies, and the value of goal setting.